The New Art
of
BREEDING BETTER DOGS

by Kyle Onstott
revised by Philip Onstott

BOOK HOUSE
New York

Howell Book House
Macmillan Publishing Company
866 Third Avenue, New York, NY 10022
Collier Macmillan Canada, Inc.

Library of Congress Catalog Card Number 62-1538
Printed in U.S.A.   ISBN 0-87605-400-9

Macmillan books are available at special discounts for bulk purchases
for sales promotions, premiums, fund-raising, or educational use.
For details, contact:

> Special Sales Director
> Macmillan Publishing Company
> 866 Third Avenue
> New York, NY 10022

20 19 18

Printed in the United States of America

To
DROSOPHILA MELANOGASTER
may its tribe increase

"Life is not for science; but science is for life."

HERBERT SPENCER

Foreword to the Second Edition
by
Kyle Onstott

The first edition of this book was written and completed in manuscript about 1938, but it was not published until 1946. The reason for the delay was lack of confidence on the part of the publishers to whom it was submitted, not in the worth and validity of the book itself, but in the dog breeding public's ability to understand its contents and such public's willingness to lay out the money to buy such a book. I was discouraged of the unlikelihood of ever finding someone who would undertake its publication until the manuscript came to the casual attention of the late Milo Denlinger. He had previously published many books about dogs, was acquainted with many dog persons, and did not doubt the ability of the breeders of dogs to read and to comprehend simple English prose. And so he accepted the hazards and brought out this book. If I remember correctly, there were only five thousand copies in the first printing, but that first printing was soon exhausted and the book went back to press for a much larger printing. This in turn was sold, and twice more the book was reprinted, always in greater numbers. There have been at least four printings of it to date, but no revision.

The various printings as they occurred were called new editions, which they were not in fact, since there was no alteration in the text of any of them from the 1946 edition.

When the book was about to go out of print, I was asked to revise the text and incorporate in it as I saw fit such of the findings in genetics as had transpired, as they pertain to practical breeding of dogs, since its first publication. This I was reluctant to undertake since it meant extensive research in a field in which I am no longer vitally engaged. I accordingly, with the publisher's consent, passed the chore along to Professor Philip Onstott, my son. To him fresh research was unnecessary since he must be conversant with genetics which he incorporates in his lectures in anthropology, of which he is an instructor.

This, then, is really a new edition, with the old material refurbished and brought up to date. Much of the matter in the former edition is permitted to stand unchanged and many additions that are made to it are minor but all are believed helpful. I am amazed to find that so many of the statements made in the original book are still valid, and that so few applicable and practical findings have been made.

In writing it, I had taken a great deal of pains to keep the style simple and to make its facts comprehensible by readers who might be unfamiliar with the science of genetics. This I cautioned my son to continue in his revision and this I believe he has done. Indeed, he has reconstructed many of my original sentences and simplified them to relieve them of what he calls my "Teutonic" style.

Genetics, at its simplest, is not a simple subject, and I had no concept of the temerity I was displaying when I first undertook to set forth in simple and readily understandable phraseology, its practical fundamentals for the dog breeding public. How well I succeeded is evinced, at least to me, by the small number—not more than half a dozen—of objections that have come to me about readers' difficulty in understanding the facts set forth, and those few from the obtuse or the lazy who could hardly expect to understand an article in a newspaper.

On the other hand, the book was very favorably received, and reviews of it in the press—especially in the kennel press— were so flattering as to be embarrassing. One reviewer called it a "minor miracle." Literally hundreds of persons whom I have encountered at dog shows have assured me that they have applied to their breeding of dogs the counsel I enunciated in the book and all of them asserted that they attained success in doing so. One man whom I had never seen went to best in show with a Standard Poodle, which he assured me was my handiwork since the mating which produced the dog was made according to principles set forth in this book. I hope at least that the book has made some contribution to the betterment of dogs.

But dogs have been improving generation by generation for a very long time. Dogs that were thought marvels of excellence twenty-five years ago would be fortunate to be awarded third in a good class of four or more today. Breeders as a lot are more intelligent, and better informed than they formerly were. They have laid aside their empirical rules of thumb and their guesswork; they are employing such genetic science as they can learn about. Not only are dogs better than they were, but so are horses, cattle, and even human youth. I do not seek to claim that this book brought about the improvement that has come about in our dogs, for that improvement was begun long ago and was gathering momentum at the time this book was first published. I like to believe, however, that this book has made its contribution, large or small, to the betterment of dogs. I am convinced of it.

If the book had done no more than state the premise that dog breeders were laying a mosaic of discrete genes rather than blending blood, it would have served its purpose. That fact and its implications are indeed the theme of the book, the very heart and substance of it. If the book induces its readers to adopt that concept and put it to practice, the purpose of the book is served and its author is much pleased.

KYLE ONSTOTT
Sacramento, California

Reviser's Foreword to the Second Edition
by
Philip Onstott

When my father asked me to undertake the revision of the *Art of Breeding Better Dogs,* I accepted the task with a light heart and an easy conscience. After almost two years of intermittent work, I was the more deceived.

Genetics, whether of the dog or of *Homo sapiens,* is never a simple subject that can be simply explained. Not only is genetics a science the determining units of which—the genes—are intangible even to the most powerful microscopes, it is not a science of individual cases. The laws of genetics rest upon statistical probabilities. Herein lies a trap for the novice breeder of dogs who, armed with a little genetic knowledge, sets forth to breed *a* dog that will go best in show at Westminster, paws down. The likelihood of this being accomplished in a single breeding, even from a sire and dam of undeniable excellence, is of the same order as the total numbers in a Mexican lottery. It is true that in the lottery somebody wins, but we are stressing the probability, not the win. The purpose of this book is to "rig" the lottery so that the probability of winning is increased. Not guaranteed, mind you, but only increased. Many breedings may be required before the numbers (the genes) in the lottery will drop and continue to drop into the desirable genetic slots. The reader of this book who plans to execute in a selective breeding program the principles herein set forth will be spared many disappointments, many anxieties, and many uncertainties if he but remembers that genetics is a statistical science. To win, he must calculate the odds and learn how they can be reduced to work in his favor. There is no quick way, there is no easy way, there is no better way for the breeder who wishes to produce fine dogs consistently.

My father writes the unvarnished truth when he notes in his foreword that I sought to recast his "Teutonic" sentences. All things are relative, even that which is "simple phraseology." The problem of trying to explain something simply, particularly complex phenomena, is one that I have had to face for ten years as an instructor in anthropology. It is sad, but true, that far too many students upon entering college have scarcely more than a nodding familiarity with the English language. When confronted with the intricate terminology of genetics, they seem to fall into a verbal stupor and render themselves impervious to linguistic rescue. Diagrams help, but not much. Ultimately, the concepts of genetics, the Mendelian laws, must be expressed in words. Symbols other than words are mere substitutes. One picture may be worth ten thousand words but those words have to be forthcoming if we hope to communicate whatever values the picture might contain. And so, the revision of this book meant simplifying much which already seemed simple. Also, I dare say that my revision will seem to lack simplicity for the reader venturing for the first time onto the thorny pathways of genetics. If this be so, the fault is entirely mine.

I would like to express my appreciation to my wife, Ramelle, for the drawings and diagrams and for her amazing patience in keeping me at the typewriter. Further, I would acknowledge the assistance of my two small daughters without whose unstinted interruptions I could have finished in half the time.

PHILIP ONSTOTT
Sacramento, California

TABLE OF CONTENTS

Kyle Onstott (left) with Ch. Sprucewood's Chocki

Introduction

The breeding of domestic animals is one of the most fascinating of human activities and of all the domestic animals, the breeding to type of purebred dogs is perhaps most satisfying. There are several reasons why this should be true, the first and best of which is that of all the animals the dog is recognized to have been the first brought under domestication and its attachment to man and man's attachment to the dog are closer bonds than exist between man and any of the other animal species. Man has utilized the dog and made him part of his work and his play. However, human dependence upon the dog is for much more than mere utility. A man rightly looks to his dog for an unalterable and inalienable loyalty such as he can hope from no other creature of his own or any other genus and species. The very dependence of the dog upon the master, which has made the homeless dog an object of proverbial pity, endears them mutually to one another. Man and dog fulfill a reciprocal emotional need.

One may allege that a man's wife is a wanton, his son a sot, his mother a narcotics addict, he himself a thief, and the man's resentment may not be great. If, though, one hints that his dog is a cripple or a coward, one engenders an eternal enmity. Though men do not love their dogs with the abject, unutterable, and unquestioning devotion with which the dogs love their masters, the love of a dog is one of the finest affects of which the human spirit is capable.

It is not the affection alone between man and dog that makes the members of *Canis domesticus* so adequate a medium for the breeder's art. The wide diversity of canine breeds enables the breeder to choose for his purposes a variety congenial to himself with respect to size, appearance, function, and temperament. The tiny Chihuahua, the tremendous Irish Wolfhound, the Mexican Hairless, the shaggy Old English Sheepdog, the sledge dog of the Eskimo, the racing Whippet, the perky Pomeranian, and the dignified Bloodhound, all are equally dogs, and he would be difficult to please who could not find among the recognized breeds one that fulfilled his concept of the kind of dog he would like to keep.

Moreover, the dog matures rapidly and reproduces itself with great rapidity. The breeder can advance a generation in his breeding of dogs every year. Of the human species a generation requires a minimum of sixteen years and in actual fact is generally reckoned as being twenty-five years. A horse must be at least three years old before he is used for breeding and is seldom used so young. Hamsters, because of their greater and more rapid fecundity, might serve even better than dogs if one's urge to breed animals was purely experimental. Vinegar flies, of which one can obtain a new generation of a hundred flies from a single breeding pair in some ten days, are in that respect even better than either dogs or hamsters. But who could take pride in a perfect hamster or a fine vinegar fly?

Hamsters and vinegar flies have taught us much that we know of the science of breeding animals and much of the contents of this book is due directly or indirectly to experiments made with them. While they are not to be scorned, they are hardly the species of which any large number of people would undertake the breeding as a matter of pleasure and self-expression.

Not only do dogs reproduce themselves at an early age, but bitches ordinarily produce numerous puppies at each pregnancy, the number varying from one to ten or twelve, according to the breed, the individual bitch and the fortuitous circumstances of the pregnancy. This writer has had whelped in his own kennel as many as fifteen puppies in a single litter and there are many well authenticated cases of litters numbering twenty or more puppies. This multiplicity of puppies at a pregnancy serves a double purpose: it gives the breeder a numerous choice for his future breeding operations and leaves him puppies to be sold.

The cost of establishing and maintaining a kennel of dogs need not be great if discretion is used and many breeders who have only one or two bitches, not so much to save the cost of kennels for them as for the mere pleasure of their companionship, keep them in their own living quarters as a part of the family. A large kennel requires labor to care for it, but a breeder who has only a few dogs will derive pleasure and recreation from the care he devotes to them.

A breeding kennel of purebred dogs should at least pay its own way if conducted without undue extravagance. The sale of stock and of breeding services of the male dogs of popular breeds are in many cases quite profitable. There are single dogs that yield their owners comfortable livelihoods. The Pointer Fishel's Frank is declared to have earned more than fifty thousand dollars for his stud services in his career, and an owner of a comparatively small kennel in Texas declared that in one year of the depression, 1934, he was taking in an average of one thousand dollars a month for breeding fees in addition to his stock sales.

Despite that there may be profit in the breeding of dogs, it is not for pure financial gain that it is here suggested that the avocation be undertaken. The successful breeder of dogs breeds dogs not for the money to be made, but for the love of dogs, their improvement, and the pride he derives from the ownership and breedership. Undertaken merely for the money to be made from it, the breeding of dogs either will fail of that unworthy purpose or will degenerate into merely turning out great numbers of dogs without regard to their merits or the betterment of their breed. That is not breeding dogs at all. Breeding dogs is not an industry but is a hobby. It should surely pay its way, and if it be enough of a hobby and intelligently ridden it should yield its profits.

15

The possession of a good dog—especially if one has bred it oneself—is a ticket of admission to the inner shrine. At a dog show, millionaire or ditch digger, preacher or racketeer, socialite or scrub-woman, all meet on the level of equality of interest in dogs.

There is one drawback in dog breeding about which a note of warning must be given and that is the tendency to permit it to run away with one and to keep more dogs than one needs. Dogs, if healthy, are prolific breeders and from a single bitch and her daughters and granddaughters one may soon have a kennel (at least a collection of miscellaneous dogs) of such numbers that it is an unwieldly burden.

One must resolve to dispose of all dogs which do not promise to be useful for the breeding operations of the kennel or do not fit into the proposed breeding program. It is not vast hordes of dogs which make a kennel successful, but rather the excellence of the few. In the large kennel of whatever breed, the most excellent progeny will have come from a limited parental stock. Great numbers of dogs in a kennel are usually indicative of the owner's failure or lack of courage to clean out the culls that are mere parasites upon his good stock and his food bill.

In the past there have been two kinds of books written which have been directed in part or in the main to the practical breeder of domestic livestock. In one kind of book there is usually a single chapter on breeding, although there are a number of books in this category in which a good deal of space is devoted to the breeding and maintenance of dogs. For the most part in "the space devoted to breeding" the information is either impractical or partly true, which makes it completely untrue. The theories advanced were scientifically superseded long before the books were written; the principles espoused are off-hand observations from a limited number of cases; the hoary superstitions and old mid-wives' tales that fill the pages have hampered the breeding of animals since man first domesticated them.

Such barnacled volumes of misinformation are worse than

useless. Even those books which do contain some true statements and useful knowledge are so contaminated with phony science and seventeenth and eighteenth century surmises that it is impossible to separate the grain of truth from the chaff of falsehood.

While the other kinds of books are true and useful, they are written by scientists and their practical truths are not infrequently obscured in a welter of technical verbiage from which few dog breeders would care to bring them to light. The long, painstaking researches of the great geneticists from Gregor Mendel through Hugo De Vries to Thomas Hunt Morgan have practical connotations which, when properly applied, will enable the breeders of animals to approximate more nearly to the perfection of their hearts' desires.

To paraphrase Solomon, go to the vinegar fly, thou breeder; consider her chromosomes and be wise.

Even though it may seem like a far cry from the breeding of vinegar flies to the breeding of Great Danes, the fundamental principles that apply to one apply to all. Hummingbirds or elephants, the laws of biological inheritance are equally valid.

It is the purpose of this book to restate these laws. To sift out of the available information only such of it as may be applied to the breeding of dogs, to strip it of its technical jargon, to show how the discoveries of the workers in pure science may be used by the practical breeder of animals, that is the task before us. It is impossible to reduce this information to words of one syllable. However, we do feel that it is possible to state it so that it may be understood rather easily by readers with only an elementary knowledge of biology. Even though it cannot be concentrated, predigested and sugar-coated, it can be at least cooked and seasoned for palatability to the practical breeder of dogs.

Of the statements made herein, none of them is at variance with the truths which the workers in the great science of genetics have discovered and which they accept themselves. From the whole of genetic truth we have abstracted only those parts

17

which are of direct application to the breeding of dogs.

While it is necessary to include in our cast of characters such performers as the garden pea and the vinegar fly, they are merely incidental. They exist as instruments of research to lead to our true hero, the purebred domestic dog. It is not that we are uninterested in other species but, rather, that they serve us herein only so far as research with them has contributed to the knowledge which enables us to breed better dogs.

Some of the chapters of this book may appear at first consideration to be of no practical worth, mere description of scientific phenomena which have nothing to do with the union of two animals to produce a third and better one. Many readers will want a short cut to the "end" without any curiosity about the "means." However, it is only in the light of the "means" that the "end" can be read.

There is no denying that good dogs have been produced by breeders ignorant of the laws and principles of heredity. We would submit, however, that the recent rapid progress in the breeding of good dogs is due in large part to the ever-growing acquaintance of breeders with fundamental laws and principles of genetics. And we would further maintain that many more good dogs can be bred by substituting scientific biological procedures than by the rule-of-thumb practices which determine the breeding of dogs in far too many kennels today.

The misconceptions and mistaken theories which determine the breeding programs of so many dog breeders are not so harmless as they seem. Not only do they hamper the breeder in his application of genetic laws, but they constitute countless hours of wasted effort. The superstition that causes one to refuse to sit thirteen at a table may not only prevent one from enjoying the meal but may also force one to go without one's dinner. In brief, it is just as necessary to remove the false theories as it is to know, to accept, and to apply the reliable and valid knowledge of genetics.

The dog breeders whom one meets are, as a lot, people of intelligence who profess a deep interest in what is for many of them a paramount hobby. Yet it is appalling to find so large a number among them who know so little about even the most simple of scientific principles of reproduction. They have been so interested in the trees of their own kennel that they have failed to see the vast forest of biology.

For the sake of argument and because we are not here concerned with the subject, let us concede that it may be very well for wild dogs to breed by instinctive selection of mates. But in the breeding of domestic dogs, to obtain the best progeny it is necessary to choose the breeding stock with discriminating knowledge and to mate the individual bitch with the available dog most suitable for her.

The purpose of this book is to provide the breeder of dogs with the knowledge that will show him how those choices may best be made.

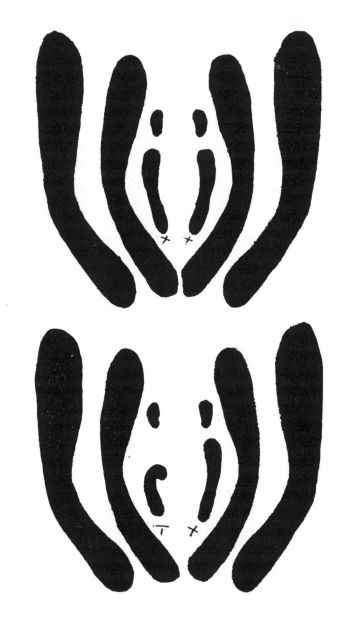

The eight Chromosomes of the Diploid set of the Male of the Vinegar Fly (*Drosophila melanogaster*). Note that there is in the Male but one X Chromosome and one Y.

The eight Chromosomes of the Diploid set of the Female of the Vinegar Fly (*Drosophila melanogaster*). Note that in the Female there are two X Chromosomes and no Y.

20

CHAPTER I

The Breeding of Dogs as a Creative Art

The impulse to create which is so urgent an attribute of the human spirit can and does find its release in the breeding of dogs. In his ability to ordain the existence of a new organism and to order what it shall be like, the breeder realizes a power that is but little short of godlike.

Bringing together the germ plasm of two dogs from which to mold a third to his own liking, he becomes a veritable sculptor in living flesh. Any critical verdict about his creature as a work of art must rest upon whether or not the breeder has employed the right materials in the right manner best to approximate the breeder's ideal dog of any specific breed.

For a fine dog may well be a work of art. However, if the dog be merely the result of the unplanned, chance union of the parental * gametes, the words *art* and *artistry* can hardly be applied to its production. The person who passes as breeder of such a one is not a breeder at all but merely the possessor of the dam at the time of her copulation with the sire.

It is futile to deny that good dogs do so arise. Indeed, it was not until recent years that enough was known of the reproductive processes to permit of more than merely the mating of the best available male to the best available female and trusting to luck (and *her* excellence was considered as of only minor moment). Much credit is due to the practical breeders of those earlier years who did, indeed, choose their breeding stock

* A glossary of technical terms is to be found on pages 249-258.

carefully and mate the best to the best and who utilized to the extent of their ability such empiric knowledge of the breeding as was available. All of the older breeds of domestic livestock were so developed.

That such procedure failed so often is easier to comprehend than that it succeeded at all. Even of those who best utilized the limited knowledge which was available, indeed, especially of those, it is safe to assert that the mantle of success fell only upon the shoulders of the fortunate. With the knowledge now available, improvement of the various breeds might have gone ahead at a much faster pace.

The earlier successful breeders had their ideals. They knew what they wanted. And many of their ideals were more practical and serviceable than some that we now entertain. They also had the materials with which to realize their ideals, but they did not know how to use them.

To employ inbreeding required courage in the face of the prejudices against it and in the face of the presumed hazards of such a procedure. But it was only by inbreeding that the varieties could be developed and stabilized. We know now wherein lie the dangers of inbreeding and how we may achieve its benefits without the risks of its incorrect employment.

The older breeders accepted as valid a host of taboos and hocus-pocus beliefs that we now know to be mere superstitions, although many present day producers (we shall not call them breeders) of livestock continue to subscribe to them. Little was known of veterinary science, and distemper could wipe out a whole kennel in a few days.

We have yet many worlds to conquer in practical genetics, but enough is known to enable us to proceed with our breeding operations with a confidence impossible even fifty years ago. The vast improvement and greater uniformity of the various breeds of dogs is an earnest that the breeders are utilizing their new knowledge.

What a breeder seeks to produce, the ideal he formulates, is self-expression. His choice of a breed with which he works is a reflection of his personality. The emphasis he places upon soundness, or head, or coats, in the choice of his breeding stock, declares his own nature. He who would achieve beautiful arbitrary markings and color at the cost of honest structure is a different kind of person from him who prefers a correctly made dog.

And it is in this self-expression, this fulfillment of the creative urge, that lies the joy of breeding dogs. The mere possession of a dog may be achieved by purchase, gift, or theft, and much pride, pleasure, and companionship may result from such possession. However, the thrill of achievement, the emotional satisfaction of the impulse to create, cannot be achieved by the mere possession of a dog, no matter how excellent a one, that somebody else has bred. That joy is the breeder's.

Just as the painter of a great picture, selling it to some parvenu, retains the emotional effect that arises from self-expression, so the breeder of a good dog, who sells his masterpiece to a mere dog show mug-hunter, does not along with the dog sell the satisfaction and joy of having bred him.

Insofar as the breeder formulates an ideal in his own mind of what he wishes to produce, and insofar as he bends his efforts as a breeder to the realization of that ideal, just insofar is he a creative artist. His medium of expression is the living protoplasm of the animals with which he chooses to work.

This is, of course, not to say that all ideals are valid ones or that the embodiments of them are all 'successful. There are good painters and bad painters and there are good breeders of dogs and bad breeders of dogs. Even a good painter turns out some mediocre or bad pictures and breeders of good dogs will sometimes produce some indifferent ones. But, in the mental conception of a worthy end, there is the pleasure of the effort and, in the approximation of the product to the breeder's ideal, there is a spiritual fillip which only the creative artist can feel.

To assert that the breeding of fine dogs is an art does not imply that it is not also a science. Art and science are by no means mutually exclusive. In this art, as in all others, science is its handmaid. Science is the means employed to attain the conceived ideal, whereas the breeder's art lies in the conception of the ideal and in the skillful employment of the means to attain it.

Another chapter of this book, entitled "Know What You Want," is devoted to the formulation of the ideal. The chapters immediately ensuing are given to a discussion of the science of reproduction and the latter chapters of the book to the application of that scientific knowledge to the art of breeding fine dogs.

The purpose of our emphasis upon the creatively artistic aspect of dog breeding is not an apology for an activity which requires no apology. It is not an effort to dignify and ennoble an endeavor which is as dignified and noble, and only as dignified and noble, as the man or woman who engages in it. That purpose is rather to imbue the breeder and the would-be breeder with that spirit of serious aspiration which motivates the artist, whatever his medium. It causes one to forget that "Art is long and time is fleeting," and to remember only that "Beauty is its own excuse for being."

Fine dogs of whatever breed are things of beauty. The consistent production of them through the intelligent employment of the laws of heredity to perpetuate the desirable in the ancestral germ plasms and to eliminate the undesirable is artistry of a high order. And it is as an art, with a full awareness of it as such, and only so, that the breeding of dogs should be seriously undertaken.

CHAPTER II

The Mechanics of Reproduction

It might seem that what occurs when two unisexual mammals copulate is too well known to require restatement in a book for adults, especially for adults who are actual or potential breeders of dogs or other domestic livestock. The outward aspects of the sexual act are fairly well known and, even if they were not known, would be of but little consequence. But there is an incomprehensible lack of information on the part of the public about the fundamental reproductive processes: the basic and functional sex cells, their origin, their structure, how they unite and how the new organism develops. Even that part of the public whose particular business it is to utilize such knowledge in the breeding of animals is all too often deficient in such information.

Mere egotism, the circumstance that we are ourselves unisexual mammals, curiosity about how our own species reproduces itself, would seem to be a stimulus which should prompt us as humans to want to know the fundamental facts about the sexual mechanism. But for a very large part of the population mere curiosity has not been great enough to justify the intellectual effort.

Many lower organisms reproduce themselves without resort to sex. In others, somewhat higher in the biological scale, both sexes exist in one organism. While the evolution of the reproductive process is an interesting theme, its consideration is not essential to our subject and would prolong this text beyond practicable limits. We must confine our discussion of the subject to the reproductive processes of the dog. Any mention of other species is made only insofar as it is analogous to or illuminative of the breeding of dogs.

The canine species, of which the domestic dog (*Canis familiaris*) is a part, is a placental mammal. Like all such higher mammals it is divided into two sexes: females (bitches) and males (dogs). The term *dog* may be correctly applied to a member of either sex. The primary differences between the two sexes lie in their reproductive apparatus and the part each plays in the reproductive process.

Both dogs and bitches are normally equipped with glands of reproduction, known as gonads, from which issue the cells which unite to form the new organism. The two gonads of the female are known as the ovaries and in them the ova (singular, ovum), or eggs, have their origin. The gonads of the male dog are known as the testes (singular, testis), or testicles, and produce the spermatozoa (singular, spermatozoön), or sperm cells, which unite with the ova, thereby fertilizing them. The spermatozoa carry in themselves the determining contribution of the male to the new organism. The ova and spermatozoa are known collectively as gametes.

The gonads serve other purposes than merely to develop and discharge the reproductive cells. They are also ductless glands of internal secretion and their hormones have much to do with the character and appearance of their host. The *corpus luteum* function of the ovaries and its effect upon the development of the embryo are discussed later in this chapter.

The resultant sex of the new organism is determined at the very moment of the fusion of the sperm and the ovum. The mechanics of this phenomenon, which is *conception*, will be treated in the chapter "Determination of Sex." It is sufficient here to say that it is true.

From the fusion of the parental gametes, from the single fertilized egg, will develop the entire organism destined to be a newborn puppy. By the division and proliferation of the cells there will come into being bones, muscles, and tissues, to form that complex animal, a dog. By the fourth week of embryonic development some cells are specialized and set aside, ultimately to act as reproductive cells to enable the dog to reproduce its kind. These basic reproductive cells form but a small fraction of one percent of the dog. As such, they serve the individual in no way. They play no direct part in his metabolism or body chemistry. The dog is merely their host and carrier. They are the stuff of future generations. The other cells of the body nourish and care for them, but they contribute nothing in return. Their duty is to the species, not at all to the individual animal.

In the male the reproductive material is housed in the testes and develops into spermatozoa; in the female it is in the ovaries and develops into ova. New life in the higher animals arises only from the union of a spermatozoön and an ovum.

The ovaries are the organs which house the germ plasm of the female and which produce the egg or ovum. In addition to the reproductive cells the ovaries also contain the interstitial cells which have other functions not primarily concerned with the reproductive process. The female is born with all of the ova (in an undeveloped and unripened state) that she will ever produce. Each ovum lies in a *Graafian follicle,* a tiny spherical vesicle which nourishes the developing egg. In the sexually mature bitch the ova in various stages of growth are scattered about in the ovary. The *Graafian follicle* is originally a simple layer of cells, but as the ovum ripens the follicle thickens and becomes more complex in structure.

When the ovum is fully ripe the Graafian follicle bursts, discharging the ovum. The empty follicle now becomes the *corpus luteum,* "yellow body," ready to regulate several of the processes of pregnancy. In effect, the *corpus luteum* is a gland of internal secretion, producing hormones to counteract other hormones which would bring about menstruation and expel the foetus prematurely. The hormones of the *corpus luteum* also stimulate the milk production in the mammary glands. (It

27

is from the presence of these special milk-producing glands that the entire biological class derives its name *MAMMALIA*.) The *corpus luteum*, by the exhaustion of its hormones, determines the time of birth of the new organism.

Having burst from their follicles, the ripe ova pass into the oviducts, or Fallopian tubes, which lead, one from each of the two ovaries, to the uterus. The ovarian end of the oviduct is larger than the tube itself and partly surrounds the ovary. In the dog, but not in man, the ends of the oviducts surround the ovaries with a membrane in such a fashion that it is impossible for the ova to escape into the bitch's abdominal cavity where they might possibly be fertilized by the persistent sperm. In this respect, at least, the dog is more complexly evolved than Man, for in *Homo sapiens* the female lacks such an enclosing membrane and an extra-uterine pregnancy is possible.

It is in the Fallopian tube that the ripe ova normally encounter the sperm cells and are fertilized, provided of course that the bitch has been mated, that the sperm mass is sufficiently large, and that the sperm are motile and functional. Of the many millions of sperm released by the male at a single copulation, only a small percentage reach the oviduct and, even of them, only as many can be utilized as there are ova to be fertilized. The rest of them will die as a result of chemical changes brought on by the fertilization.

The ripe and unfertilized ova will survive in the oviducts for some seventy-two hours awaiting their fusion with the sperm. If fertilization does not occur, the ova die and are discharged from the body in the next menstrual flow. Once fertilized the growing mass moves from the oviduct into the uterus where it attaches itself to the wall. The fertilized ovum will then continue its proliferation to form all of the new organism.

The vagina is the canal which connects the uterus with the external orifice of the female genitalia in the vulva, the small, muscular organ visible between the rear legs of the bitch. Into this canal the semen is ejaculated by the male dog and passes upward through the cervix and the uterus into the oviduct to seek and fertilize the ova. It is through this canal that the resultant puppies are born into this breathing world.

That the urethra, the urinary outlet from the bladder, empties itself at the exterior end of the vaginal canal, is not a matter for extended comment.

The uterus, or womb, is situated in the ventral posterior part of the abdominal cavity. When the bitch is not pregnant, or "in whelp," the uterus is small, only some three inches long in the larger varieties of dogs, and proportionately smaller in smaller breeds. The uterus has two "horns," or branches, the end of each of which connects with one of the oviducts. As pregnancy progresses, the uterus stretches and enlarges to accommodate the developing embryos. When the pregnancy terminates and the embryos are expelled, the uterus will contract to its smaller, non-pregnant size.

Only the briefest mention need be made of the clitoris in the bitch since this small organ plays no part in the reproductive process. Located just above the vaginal opening, the clitoris is the counterpart in the female of the male penis. In the human female its stimulation will ordinarily induce orgasm, though in the dog its purpose is not so clear-cut. There is very little evidence relating to the orgasm in lower forms.

It should also be noted that the virgin bitch has no *hymen* or maidenhead.

In the male dog the testes, or testicles, are normally two in number. Roughly egg-shaped, they hang suspended from the body between the hind legs in a sack of skin, the scrotum. (Cryptorchidism, the retention of the testicles in the abdominal cavity, will be dealt with in the chapter, "Sterility, Impotence, and Cryptorchidism.") It is in the testicles that the spermatozoa are developed from the basic sex cells.

A testicle is fundamentally a structured mass of tubular tissue, the lining of which is constantly throwing off new cells. Some of these new cells will become functional spermatozoa while others will produce only additional sperm-forming cells.

Basically, each testicle is actually two glands: one for the

29

production of functional sperm; the other a male endocrine gland manufacturing needed hormones which are only incidentally a part of the reproductive process. A single, normal testicle in a healthy dog will produce enough useable sperm to repopulate the entire canine world and the fact that each normal dog has two such organs is merely nature's "margin for safety."

Within the testicle is the *epididymis*, another tube, very small, many feet long, but tightly coiled. The ripe spermatozoa enter the epididymis and remain there until required, when they are forced out by muscular contraction into the *vas deferens*. The *vas deferens*, another spermatic duct, carries the sperm to the base of the penis where they are bathed and further activated by secretions from the prostate and other glands. So bathed and mixed, the sperm are now a single component in the seminal fluid or semen (seed). In the dog no seminal vesicles are present and the sperm are discharged directly from the *vas deferens* into the urethral canal of the penis and from there into the vaginal canal of the bitch. Also absent in the dog are Cowper's glands, the secretion from which in so many animals dilutes the seminal fluid.

The absence of the seminal vesicles and of Cowper's glands makes it necessary for the dog to have prolonged copulation to enable it to discharge its full complement of semen. Instead of a gush of semen from the seminal vesicles, as occurs in organisms equipped with such reservoirs, the orgasm of the dog must be a slow trickle which may require from several minutes up to half an hour or longer.

The characteristic method of coitus in the dog is made both possible and necessary by the peculiar structure of the penis and by the grasping muscles (*Sphincter cunni*) of the bitch's vagina. The penis consists of two erectile parts, in the anterior of which there is a bone. The posterior portion, the *corpus cavernosum*, is much larger and, grasped spasmodically by the bitch's vaginal sphincter, it facilitates the prolonged copulation, during which the male dog may and usually does dismount from the female and stand on all-fours with her, posterior to posterior. Until erection begins to subside, it is impossible for the mating animals to separate one from the other, and forcible separation is liable to injure one or both.

The single spermatozoön is a minute, rounded head, which contains the all-important nucleus of the cell, and a long, whip-lash tail by means of which the spermatozoön propels itself in its search for the waiting ovum. Since the over-all length of the spermatozoön is only one five-hundredths of an inch, the lashing tail is "long" only in relation to the extremely small head.

In the head of the spermatozoön is the nucleus of the cell, and in that nucleus is the entire hereditary potential which the male and his ancestors can contribute to the new organism. It has been estimated that a male dog can release between 300 million and 600 million spermatozoa in a single orgasm, each one of which is theoretically capable of fertilizing an ovum. So large a number of sperm seems to imply that nature is over-generous in the production of male procreative material. However, it has been recently learned that there is a significant correlation between sperm-mass and fertilization. When the sperm-mass falls below 150 million the likelihood of fertilization occurring is reduced by almost seventy-five percent. The larger sperm-mass is necessary to the proper acid-alkaline balance of the bitch's genitalia, for if the bitch's uterus or oviducts are too acid or too alkaline the sperm are immobilized and die before they can reach the ova. The size of the sperm-mass acting as a chemical reagent is quite independent of the fact that even in the smaller mass the sperm might be motile and thoroughly functional, i.e., capable of fertilizing the ova. The use of artificial insemination will be discussed later in this book.

The onset of menstruation usually occurs for the first time in the bitch somewhere between her eighth and tenth month of age. There is a fairly wide range of variation with respect to the menarche (the *first* menstrual period). Menarche tends to vary inversely with the size of the breed, being at an earlier age in the smaller breeds. Even within a single breed there is considerable variation of the time of menarche since the phenomenon is contingent upon adequate or inadequate nutrition, upon environmental factors, and also upon a hereditary element which hastens or retards it with respect to the norm for the given breed.

Menstruation is a cleaning of the walls of the uterus in its preparation to receive the fertilized eggs. Hormones originating in the anterior portion of the pituitary gland, the Graafian follicle, and the corpus luteum initiate the process. The first indication of menstruation is a swelling of the vulva, which may be noticeable at any time from a few hours to a few days before the onset of menstruation proper and the discharge of the bloody menstrual fluid. This discharge normally continues some eight to ten days, although its duration may be much shorter, seldom longer than that.

Various psychic phenomena, or none, may occur during menstruation. Some bitches seek seclusion, some take to wandering and prowling, some are erratic of appetite.

It is after the cessation of the menstrual flow that the bitch's mating instinct asserts itself. Normally, it is only during the week to ten days, more or less, following menstruation that the bitch is "in heat" and will permit copulation with the dog. Some bitches, especially old and experienced ones, will accept the male before the end of the menstrual flow, whereas, others, usually virgin or young bitches, although menstruation has stopped and the bitches are physiologically ready for breeding, will not accept the dog at all and if they are to be mated they must be held and forced to submit to copulation.

As in most mammalian species, sexual maturity in either sex of the dog is usually attained before complete physical maturity. It is a debatable question as to whether a bitch should be bred at her first heat or before full physical maturity. The answer must depend somewhat on the breed under consideration, somewhat upon the type of the bitch in relation to her breed, and somewhat upon her approximation to physical maturity. It is argued by many breeders that bitches of such breeds as Bulldogs, French Bulldogs, and Boston Terriers, which as breeds are given to difficulties of parturition, should undergo their first pregnancy while the bones of the pelvis are yet flexible, to the end that they may have less difficulty in the whelping of their young, not only in the first but also in subsequent pregnancies.

It is recognized that maternity fills out and matures the higher animals and many bitches of certain breeds may be better specimens of their breeds because of maternal experience. A bitch that lacks skeletal substance, or is too much cut up in the region of the loin, may be improved in either or both those respects by maternity. On the other hand, a bitch of a breed required to have a racy outline may be harmed in her type by being bred and it is better to await the end of the exhibition career of such a one before a matronly figure is permitted to mar her type.

Neither the humane nor the wise breeder will be likely to subject to pregnancy a bitch which falls far short of physical maturity and which requires all her nourishment for the development of her own body without diverting any of it to the development of a litter of puppies and to the suckling of them. However, if the bitch is reasonably healthy and mature, eats well and assimilates her food, to await her full maturity before breeding is probably a waste of time. Genetically, there is absolutely no difference in the viability of the progeny of young bitches and the progeny of older ones. It is a biological law that the developing embryo is parasitic upon the mother and that if there is a problem of insufficient nutrition, the one to suffer will be the mother rather than the embryo.

Some breeders, especially German breeders of German Shepherd dogs, are insistent that bitches should not be bred until full and complete maturity—not before the second, better not before the third, menstruation. In the case of a bitch with an abnormally long back or loin, or one with a tendency to a sway of the spine, or where the food supply is inadequate as it concerns quantity, quality, or balance, this delay is certainly justified; but the using of such a bitch for breeding, or any bitch not properly nourished, at any time is a very dubious experiment. There is, however, much unnecessary loss of time in the awaiting of full physical maturity of normal and well developed dogs before utilizing them for breeding. (The early use of the male dog for breeding will be discussed in Chapter XIV, "Things That Are Not True.")

It is all but needless to say that it is necessary to keep bitches confined during their period of heat, and, indeed, it were best during the entire menstrual and rutting period, unless one choose to take the very probable risk of their being mated promiscuously to such dogs as they may encounter while running at large.

Modesty is not the usual attribute of a bitch in heat and she will use all her ingenuity to escape to find a mate and will usually give her favors to whatever dog or dogs may come her way. The odor of the urine of the bitch in menstruation, or in heat, is an advertisement to dogs of the neighborhood of her condition and it is better not to exercise her where her excretions may serve to attract all and sundry of the neighborhood dogs.

It is possible, and by no means unusual, for a bitch to be bred to two or more dogs during one breeding season, in which case it is frequently impossible to know which is the sire of her litter. Indeed, it is possible that a part of the ova may be fertilized by sperm from one dog and another part of the ova by sperm from another dog. This interesting and not generally recognized phenomenon can occur only when the breedings with the two or more dogs occur without too great an interval between them. The progeny from such matings are not true siblings but are only half-brothers, half-sisters, although it is seldom possible to recognize which puppies are the progeny of which sire.

In cases such as that just mentioned, if the bitch has been bred to only two dogs, both known to be purebred animals of her own variety, some stud books, by special dispensation, will admit the registrations of the progeny with "alternate sires," especially if the dam and both the sires are of such merit as individuals and for their germ plasms that their progeny is believed to contribute to the improvement of the variety. All of the members of the litter may be sired by one of the dogs, part by one and part by the other, but none can be sired by both. However, for the stud book record, since the actual sire of any puppy is not known, the names of the possible sires must be stated.

Misalliances and such accidents as the ones described are due to a carelessness on the part of the keeper of the bitch, and great care should be used to avoid them.

The bitch does not normally encourage the sexual attentions of the dog between breeding seasons, although coitus when she is not in heat may and sometimes does occur. It is usually a painful experience for the bitch and, since there are no ripe ova, pregnancy does not result. A few bitches are always in heat, probably due to a pathological condition, attracting and accepting the sexual attention of the dog at all times. They are seldom fertile and are nuisances as pets and useless for a breeding kennel.

Occasionally a bitch will menstruate and come into heat at an abnormally short time after her previous normal period of heat. At such "false heats," as they are called, it is believed that there are no ripened ova in the tubes and if she is mated no pregnancy results.

In the normal condition, the fertilization of the ova hastens the subsidence of the heat, which usually lasts but a few days after a successful mating. That, however, is not always true. Whether bred or not, the bitch will gradually go out of heat. This usually requires some eight to ten days during which she attracts the sexual interest of the dog but responds to it at first reluctantly and later not at all.

The favorable time to breed the bitch is as soon after the subsidence of the menstrual discharge as she will readily and willingly accept the breeding service of the dog. This is merely taking time by the forelock. There is no reason to believe, despite old theories to the contrary, that the time of conception determines or influences the sex of the progeny. Early deposited sperm live several days in the uterus and oviducts of the bitch to await the ripening of the ova, just as the ova will live several days awaiting the arrival of the sperm. Early breeding leaves time for other efforts if either the dog or the bitch refuses the advances of the other; and, if the copulation is only doubtfully complete or is in any way unsatisfactory, it permits of a second breeding.

That the parties to the copulation should hang together, as the effect of the grasping of the *corpus cavernosum* by the *sphincter cunni,* is not an absolute requisite for fertilization. However, if the mated dogs fail so to hang together, there is reason to doubt the success of the mating. The duration of the hanging together is no criterion of the efficiency of the breeding service, very brief copulations yielding as good results as prolonged ones.

While it is only the primary sexual organs, their products and functions, that are here discussed, sight must not be lost of the influence of sex upon the whole organism. Just as surgical removal of the gonads (castration) will affect the whole character, behavior, metabolism, and even the appearance of an animal, just as pregnancy stimulates the enlargement of the mammary glands, just as menstruation may effect psychic changes in the female, so all sex manifestations have their repercussions throughout the whole dog. Knowledge of the structures and purposes of the endocrine glands and their products, the hormones, is of relatively recent date in biology. Even today, such knowledge is far from complete. It seems highly probable that the procreative instinct is brought into play by the hormones of the endocrine glands; and, again through them, the organism is affected by that instinct and by whether or not it is indulged.

Sex and the sexual apparatus cannot be considered as something apart, a mere adjunct to the animal. Sex is a part of the very warp and woof (!) of the dog's being.

We have seen in this chapter how the sperm, bearing the

ancestral material from the male dog, is proliferated in the testes, is stored in the epididymis, expelled from there into and through the *vas deferens,* is bathed and activated by the secretions from the prostate gland, and is ejaculated into the vagina of the bitch. We have seen how, propelled by its lashing tail, it makes the long journey through the uterus into the oviducts to meet and fertilize the ripe ova deposited there from the ovaries. Of the fertilization and the gestation which follows it we shall learn in the ensuing chapter.

CHAPTER III

The Pre-Natal Life of the Dog

In the former chapter we left the ripe ova in the oviducts, or Fallopian tubes, of the bitch awaiting fertilization by the spermatozoa from the male dog. If the spermatozoa fail to ascend into the oviduct within a few days of the deposit of the ova, they lose their vigor and perish. (In the original edition of this book it is written that the sperm "pine and die of loneliness." A "pining" sperm would be a sight to see. P.O.) Let us assume, however, that the bitch has been mated to a dog of vigorous fertility and that we are ready to note what occurs.

The process of fertilization has been observed under the microscope and even photographed as it occurs between the gametes of lower forms of life. There is sufficient evidence that the process is the same in the higher animals to justify our assumption of what occurs at this stage in our friend, the dog.

We are not sure at the present level of knowledge what it is that once the sperm are deposited in the vagina attracts them to the ova. Whatever the attraction—a chemical field or an electrical field or both—one of the sperm will eventually reach the outer membrane of an ovum. At the touch of the sperm, a tiny bump rises on the ovum at the point of juncture and the sperm is seemingly sucked into the egg. Its journey is far from over, however, since it has yet to make its way through an inner membrane, across the area of cytoplasm, and through the nuclear membrane. It had been previously thought that the tail of the sperm, having served its function of propelling the sperm to the ovum, dropped off when the sperm-head penetrated the outer membrane. Quite recent evidence indicates that the tail does NOT drop off but, rather, remains intact to the point of nuclear penetration. We must bear in mind that the sperm must penetrate *three membranes,* as well as making its way across a relatively vast expanse of cytoplasm.

As soon as the sperm has penetrated the outer membrane an immediate chemical reaction takes place which hardens the outer membrane so that no further penetration of additional sperm is possible. Also, the sperm within the membrane cannot withdraw. When each ripe ovum in the tube has been penetrated by a single sperm, the remaining male gametes, being superfluous, perish. ("Superfluous" may be the wrong word since it is entirely possible that the remaining sperm act as nutriment for the developing embryo or serve to maintain a vital PH balance.)

Within the minute head of the sperm is the cell nucleus and within that tiny compass is compressed all of the sire's contribution to the development of the new organism.

Within the female ovum is a tiny, dark spot—the nucleus— which contains the hereditary contribution to the new organism from the dam and her ancestors. When the head of the sperm fuses with the nucleus of the ovum, fertilization has then, and *only then,* taken place. If the sperm should die between the outer and the inner membranes or between the inner membrane and the nuclear membrane, that ovum will not be fertilized.

The fusion of the two nuclei produces a single nucleus and from this nucleus will develop the dog that is, if not to see the light, for puppies are born with closed eyes, at least to breathe the air and conjure up our admiration and delight and wonder some nine weeks later.

In the dog each of the nuclei which unite to form the new nucleus contains the haploid number of chromosomes (39), which is just half of the diploid number (78). In fact every cell in the body of the dog contains the diploid number, except only the functional gametes after their meiotic reduction. The intensely interesting drama of the chromosomes and their genes is too involved for discussion at this point and will require a complete chapter in itself. Suffice it to say here that the new cell, formed by the union of the nuclei from the male and female cells, contains the full diploid number of chromosomes. This reference to the chromosomes should not be permitted to confuse the reader and may well be ignored until its significance is made clear.

The new cell formed by the union of the male and female gametes is technically known as a *zygote* (Greek, "yoked"). In mammals the zygote is also known in its early stages as an embryo and in its late stages as a foetus.

It may be useful to think of cells as the fundamental units of living matter, the bricks from which all living structures are built. Most individual cells are microscopically small, although there are many cells large enough to be visible to the naked eye and some are of considerable size, *e.g.*, the yolk of a newly laid bird egg is a single cell.

We shall not here go into the details of cell structure, more than to say that the cell is made up of its nucleus, or central body, and its surrounding material known as the cytoplasm. All animal or vegetable growth is the result of the splitting and proliferation of cells. (See diagram on page 70.)

The nucleus of the zygote or fertilized ovum, now a single cell, begins to halve and separate, its parts drawing toward opposite poles. The spherical cytoplasm grows ovoid in shape, half of the original nucleus in each end of it. An indentation creeps around the equator of the cytoplasm and grows deeper. The two parts later are connected by a mere isthmus of cytoplasm and the isthmus finally disappears, making two cells of what has previously been one. Each of these new cells has its nucleus and its cytoplasm. These new cells are called daughter cells and each one of them has the full number, the diploid count, of chromosomes as had the original zygote, the chromosomes having split longitudinally to supply each daughter cell with its full complement. This miracle of the splitting of the cell is technically known as *mitosis* (see *glossary*) or cleavage.

Each of the daughter cells in its turn divides into two more cells in the same manner. They, now four, in their turn divide into eight, the eight into sixteen, and the organism develops more and more rapidly by the division of cells by geometric progression. There are soon hundreds, thousands, millions, billions of cells in a higher organism such as a dog.

As soon as the ovum is fertilized, the new zygote normally begins to move gradually down the oviduct toward its ultimate destination in the uterus. The progress is slow and the journey may require several days. Meanwhile, the cell division continues, but it is yet a slow process and the new organism is yet minute. The tiny yolk substance of the ovum forms the bulk of its nourishment and cleavage cannot proceed very far without food.

Occasionally an embryo settles down to develop in the oviduct and does not pass on toward the uterus. Such a condition, known as a tubal pregnancy, is abnormal, very rare, and equally dangerous to the mother. The tubal pregnancy must be surgically removed else the developing foetus will cause a rupture.

Normally, the developing organism reaches the uterus, but it is yet only a tiny mass of a few hundred cells. But the cells not only have continued to proliferate, they have begun to structure themselves in a preliminary but definite pattern to form the new organism. This process of the beginning of structure is the same for all higher animals from jellyfish to man. The similarity of this basic beginning reveals the essential unity of all life.

There is a potential design hidden in the chromosomes of the germ plasm which decrees the pattern the segmenting cells shall assume. A kind of chromosomatic blueprint in the zygote lays down a plan which determines that the developing organism, of which the parental gametes were from dogs, shall take the pattern of a dog. If the parental gametes were from giraffes, the pattern would be that of a giraffe; if a parrot, the pattern would be that of a parrot. And the blueprint not only describes a dog but also describes what kind of dog, Dachshund or Greyhound, Pekingese or Saint Bernard, and not only the breed but also the type within the breed. All the attributes, good or bad, desirable or hateful, which it is possible for the organism ever to possess, are innate in this unfolding design.

If this small mass of cells should die at such an inter-uterine stage, it is needless to say that the design would never be executed, and if the design were of a Collie it will never herd sheep, if a Pointer it will never hunt birds. And even if it lives, environmental influences may knock the design into a cocked hat. However excellent the design, insufficient or incorrect nourishment may produce rickets, or an amputated leg may make a cripple of the organism. But that would be no fault of the design.

The new puppy is a-forming. The other fertilized ova also have begun their segmentation and proliferation and have also descended into the uterus, each of the embryos developing after the design laid down in its zygotic chromosomes.

To follow this design, development by development, involves the use of a lot of technical nomenclature which would confuse more than it would clarify the subject for most readers. Suffice it to say that the cell mass is no longer apparently amorphous but has begun to grow into a puppy.

The walls of the small uterus are tough and thick. Menstruation has cleaned it out. Its lining has been broken up, washed away, and replaced by fresh and young tissue in anticipation of the embryos which have now arrived.

Arrived in the uterus, our embryo fastens itself to the prepared wall to spend a couple of months while it grows into a puppy and builds itself in accordance with the design and specifications set forth in its chromosomes. Warm and snug as it is in this dark chamber, which has been all house-cleaned and relined for its reception, yet it has nothing to eat. The tinier yolk in the tiny ovum has been consumed. The original zygotic cell has segmented into hundreds of cells, each complete with its nucleus and cytoplasm. Now if the cell mass is to continue to grow it must have nourishment from some source.

The embryo is a hollow mass of cells. Settling down in the uterus, it embeds itself into the uterine lining, eating its way into the walls and destroying some of the uterine cells. It digs in and is surrounded on all sides by the maternal tissue and laved with the maternal blood, which provides it with the nourishment of which it was in need. Now, with a food supply, the little parasite, for such it is, can grow and can continue its segmentation and development of its pattern. It should be understood that at no time does the blood of the mother mingle with the blood of the embryo, the two systems being completely separate throughout the entire pre-natal period. As we shall see, however, the nourishment for the embryo is filtered from the blood of the mother just as waste material from the embryo is filtered back to the blood of the mother.

None of the organs of the future puppy are yet detectable. The first noticeable growth is not of the puppy itself but rather of the elaborate membranes to enwrap the embryo and the ducts to feed it.

Indeed, the group of cells which implants itself in the uterus is not, properly speaking, the puppy itself but is one of these covering membranes, the *chorion,* within which the embryonic body is later to appear. During the early development, the embryo consists of three hollow vesicles, one inside the other.

On the wall which separates these two inner chambers appears a minute disk, and across it is a shallow groove, the so-called primitive streak. This is the first appearance of the puppy itself. The other part of the development so far detectable has been only of the apparatus for his growth and nurture. This disk, the new puppy, proliferates and develops very rapidly. In nine short weeks it is to be a dog, squeaking and whining and crawling about in search of its mother's teats.

The embryo is immersed in a solution called the *amniotic fluid,* which is contained in a membrane known as the *amnion.*

43

This liquid absorbs jars or blows which the maternal organism may receive and saves the developing embryo from discomfort. The amniotic fluid is germicidal and its bath prevents bacterial infection of the embryo. Later it is to prove of similar service to the membranes of the bitch while she whelps her brood.

Outside the amnion is another membrane known as the *chorion*. And over all is a layer of maternal tissue. So we see that our precious pup is triply housed and antiseptically bathed.

In the center of the ventral surface of the embryo is a small orifice known as the *umbilicus* (later to be known as the navel). From it a tube grows out which develops into the umbilical cord. At birth this cord appears attached to the belly of the puppy. The umbilical cord connects with and grows into a disk of tissue called the *placenta,* which is in intimate contact with the walls of the uterus. The placenta is the essential organ of nutrition, excretion, and respiration for the embryo. From the placenta by means of the umbilical cord, food and oxygen are filtered from the bloodstream of the mother to the foetus and waste products in gaseous form are eliminated to the placenta and thence back to the bloodstream of the mother.

The umbilical cord houses two arteries and a single large vein. The cord has no nerves and so the only communication between the mother and the foetus is by way of that complex filtration plant, the placenta. It is not possible for any nervous stimulus, favorable or unfavorable, to be transmitted to the offspring. Naturally, any factors which affect the nutrition of the mother will in turn have an affect upon the nutrition of the foetus.

Thus we see that the growing organism is as well protected as is naturally possible. Bathed with an antiseptic solution, swaddled in protecting membranes, kept at an even, warm temperature, fed through a tube to its belly, the foetus lives "a life of Riley"—nothing to do for nine weeks but to grow and grow and grow.

And grow it does. It seems as it develops that things have gone amiss, that the design being realized is most anything but a dog: first, a fish, then an amphibian, then a reptile, then a prim-

44

itive mammal. All of the seemingly false starts can now be evaluated in the proper perspective. The embryo has re-enacted in nine brief weeks the entire evolutionary development of its race. A billion years of evolutionary history have been compressed unbelievably into nine weeks.

It would serve no purpose to follow in detail the various stages in the development of the foetus. But it is worthy of note that, since the placenta serves in lieu of lungs, intestines, and kidneys combined, the development of those organs can be postponed. But the puppy does need a heart very early and it is the first of the major organs to develop, begins to function in the worm-like embryo and keeps up its incessant beating until the dog, worn out with age, lies down and gives up the ghost. (Note: it should not be thought that the embryonic heart when it first appears is structurally complete. The first heart has only two chambers, as does that of the fish. The complete four-chambered mammalian heart, like the mammalian kidney, develops in the closing week of the dog's pre-natal life.)

Nature is zealous that the species shall not die. Very early in the development of the embryo some cells are set aside from the proliferation with which the puppy can reproduce his kind, if all goes well and if he can find a mate. These reproductive cells, the germ plasm, exist for one sole purpose, that the race may not die. Bathed and fed and cared for by the other, so called somatic, cells, they take no part in the growth or activity of the organism but lie in patient waiting until instinct prompts the adult animal to mate with another of the opposite sex, at which time they supply the material for the gametes which are to contribute to the new generation.

The chromosomes of the basic reproductive cells, *i.e.*, before they split to become functional reproductive cells, are of the full number (the diploid count). The chromosomes are, in fact, exactly like those in all of the other cells of the body, as we shall see in Chapter V, "The Chromosomes and Their Genes."

It would be impossible, even if desirable, to state the size of the embryo at the various stages of its development since it must needs vary as the various breeds of dogs vary in their size.

Growth is rapid. The segmentation of the cells becomes less rapid as the foetus develops, and even yet less rapid in the growth of the puppy after birth and up until maturity, when it is only adequate for replacement of tissue and not at all for growth. However, despite the retarded rate of segmentation, as the organism becomes larger and larger there are so many more cells to proliferate that the rate of total growth gathers momentum.

As the foetuses grow, the uterus grows and stretches, stuffed like a two horned sausage.

Externally, while some change in the mammary glands may be noticed earlier, no enlargement of the mother's abdomen is apparent before the fifth week after she is bred, and more frequently it is the sixth week before one can be reasonably certain that she is in whelp, i.e., pregnant. Sometimes there is doubt of her pregnancy up until the very time she whelps her puppies, but it is usually apparent by the sixth or seventh week from the enlargement of her abdomen that she is entertaining guests within. In the doubtful cases, listening on a stethoscope would reveal the heartbeat of living foetuses even when the dam's abdominal enlargement failed to betray their presence.

Hence, little can be guessed from the external appearance of the mother about the number of puppies she is about to litter.

On the other hand, sometimes, but rarely, a bitch may give every external indication of being pregnant, with enlarged abdomen and developed breasts, even with a flow of milk, and yet may prove not to be in whelp. She may even make a bed for her litter. At the end of nine weeks from her menstrual season, the enlargement of belly of such a one recedes. She may accept and suckle puppies from another bitch, but in her own case it is a matter of hope deferred.

All during the pregnancy, and even before, the *corpus luteum,* the follicle in which the ovum had grown and ripened, a benevolent little busy-body and master of ceremonies, has been sticking its figurative nose into the internal economy of the mother. Once assumed to be merely an envelope to enclose the ovum, it is now known to function as a gland of internal secretion, *i.e.,* an endocrine gland, sending its hormones through the blood stream on all kinds of imperious errands.

The hormones from the *corpus luteum* stimulate the development of the mammary glands, the secretion of milk in them, and are believed to affect markedly the general metabolism of the pregnant bitch.

The active life of any *corpus luteum* is limited and by the end of nine weeks the hormones from it have lost their authority—their work has been accomplished. No longer do they inhibit the whisperings to the uterus of the hormones from the pituitary gland that the star boarders will never pay their bills and had best be thrown out on their heads. *Corpus luteum* had constantly counseled the uterus to be patient, to give them time.

Aware that its counsel of patience to the uterus will not be heeded for long, the *corpus luteum* takes steps to soften the junction of the two halves of the pelvis to make easier the exit of the foetuses, when the uterus shall finally give them notice to go. And some secretion from the ovaries, either one from the *corpus luteum* or from the female interstitial gland, activates the mother to prepare a bed for the impending birth. At the end of nine weeks, the *corpus luteum* ceases to function, the uterus heeds the advice of the pituitary gland, and both literally and figuratively clamps down upon her no longer welcome guests.

If the hormone from the pituitary is not strong enough to force the uterus to expel the matured foetuses, it is often necessary for the veterinary obstetrician to strengthen the action by injection into the blood stream of the mother of a pituitary extract to produce greater uterine contractions.

The bitch, left to herself, has prepared a bed by digging a hole in some sheltered ground. Most dog breeders aid their bitches by furnishing them with a suitable whelping place, which should be warm and dry, secluded from possible disturbance by dogs or people. When the bitch is about to whelp

47

she may be nervous and restless for a day or two with premonitions of her ordeal.

After the bitch has whelped her litter, her uterus, which had grown and stretched to accommodate them, gradually shrinks until it is again of the size it was before the pregnancy.

The period of gestation, the duration of normal pregnancy, in the dog is generally reckoned at sixty-three days. While that is by no means the maximum, it is in actual fact somewhat longer than the average pregnancy. Puppies whelped at any time after the fifty-seventh day cannot be considered as seriously premature. It is without any intention to discredit tales of thriving puppies born on the fifty-third day that we offer the caution that misalliances are not unheard-of in dog breeding and keepers are not always as careful of their records as might be wished. It is that, also, which makes hazardous the acceptance of statistics about the matter and the categorical statement of any normal gestation period.

Late births, sometimes as late as the seventy-fourth day, may be due to the ripening of the ova several days after copulation, although the possibility of an unrecognized and unrecorded breeding is not to be overlooked in such cases.

The presence of milk in the breasts is not a sure sign of approaching parturition, nor is its absence indicative that the bitch's time is not yet, to use a Biblical phrase. Milk is to be found in the breasts of some bitches several days before they whelp, and in some it does not appear until hours after all the puppies are born. Indeed, milk sometimes appears in the breasts of bitches some nine weeks after their menstrual period even if they have not been pregnant at all.

The bitch usually gives birth to her young without great difficulty and without manifestation of excessive pain. When labor is normal, the less human obstetrical assistance offered her, except praise, sympathy, and encouragement from a beloved master, the better off she and her puppies will be. She will usually refuse food for several hours before the onset of labor, which may last from three to twelve hours, or even longer, before the appearance of the first puppy. The pains of labor often make a bitch restless. She goes off into a dark, secluded place, or scratches at her bed, rearranging it. She may whimper or moan in a plea for sympathy. She is likely to squat in a urinating position.

Most puppies are littered between midnight and morning, although some bitches are much more leisurely in their whelping and twenty-four hours between the delivery of the first and last pup is by no means unheard-of.

In the passage of the foetus through the *os uteri*, the foetal membrane is burst and the amniotic fluid is released to flood the vaginal passage, lubricating it and sterilizing its mucosa. The bitch makes a muscular contraction and the puppy is born. He is wrapped in foetal membranes which the bitch normally removes from him with teeth and tongue. Following the puppy and attached to him by means of the umbilical cord is the placenta which the bitch will eat, severing the cord with her teeth.

Many breeders choose to sever the cord themselves, lest the bitch bite it too short, and for bitches with badly undershot or uneven mouths, this assistance may be quite essential to the life of the puppy. If this is done, the cord should be tightly bound with a sterile thread some three or four inches from the puppy's belly and severed with sterile scissors. The remaining portion will dry and sluff off in the course of a few days. Hemorrhage may result from cutting it too short or from the bitch's biting it too short.

Whether or not the bitch be permitted to sever the cord, she should in any event be allowed to eat the afterbirth. Some persons are nauseated at this normal habit of the bitch but the eating of the placenta is known to stimulate the secretion of milk, and it should not be interfered with. (The human female is not at all loath to take and is, indeed, given placental extract, in an unrecognizable form, of course.)

The bitch licks the puppy dry and her massage of it compresses the small ribs and the puppy breathes and grunts. If

49

the membrane is not quickly removed from its head after its advent into the air, it smothers and dies.

Thrust headlong into a big world, it is forced to breathe for itself and to forage for its food. Instinctively, it makes toward the teats of its mother's breasts and, its quarters braced against the floor of the nest, treading, straining, sucking, it obtains the exercise as well as the nourishment which enables it to grow. The breeding process is finished: the miracle of reproduction has been wrought. Two gametes have fused to form a zygote which proliferated into an embryo, later to be known as a foetus. Forced from the mother's uterus into this breathing world, that foetus is now become a dog.

In the zygote was all that this organism could ever be. In the puppy is all that the dog may become. Only the optimum of environment will permit this newborn dog to realize all the possibilities of maturity inherent in him. However good a puppy it may be, subject it to an unfavorable environment and it will fail to be the mature dog for which we hope.

Food, housing, exercise, grooming, and training—all those are the problem of the keeper, not of the breeder, although keeper and breeder are frequently, even usually, one and the same person. The litter safely launched in the world, the breeder's task is done, be it well or be it ill, until the puppies are mature and another generation must find its mates. Again the keeper must retire and the breeder once more assumes command.

The pregnancy just described may be taken as the normal one. Any one or several of many abnormalities may occur to cause the breeder much concern and possibly to nullify all his efforts. Well kept dogs are, as a lot, normal in their reproductive processes but they vary somewhat, one from another, and accidents do occur.

We have seen that tubal pregnancy sometimes occurs and requires surgery to prevent the death of the bitch. Another hazard is the death of the embryo at any of its stages, due to any one of many causes including malnutrition, poisoning, or a blow to the bitch. Abortion may, of course, occur at any stage of the pregnancy and is usually the result of excessive and unusual activity or excitement of the bitch or to some accident to her.

Most bitches deliver their puppies without excessive difficulty for themselves or for their keepers, but there are obstetrical circumstances which must be watched for. Labor pains and uterine contractions may be too weak to dislodge the foetuses. The pelvis may be too contracted and narrow to permit of the passage of the foetuses. Scar tissues or tumors may obstruct the vaginal passage. One or more of the foetuses may be abnormally big, a monstrosity. One or more foetuses may enter the vagina breech first or in some other abnormal presentation. Or even, though rarely, there may be a torsion of one of the horns of the uterus.

Any of these abnormalities demands the services of an expert obstetrical veterinarian, and it is a wise dog breeder who, in advance of his emergency, decides what man he is to call. It is desirable to choose a veterinarian in whom one can have utter confidence and to accept his advice and decisions unconditionally.

Sometimes Caesarian section is indicated, and in the hands of a clever and experienced veterinary surgeon it is not a difficult or very hazardous operation. It is certainly an interesting one to watch. If it is in all ways successful, the bitch may be in her bed suckling her puppies in less than an hour from the time she goes on the table. The operation does not necessarily interfere with subsequent use of the bitch for breeding. It is resorted to most frequently in small breeds with large heads, such as Bulldogs, French Bulldogs, and Boston Terriers.

Amateur obstetrics in complicated cases often results in much trouble, the loss of the litter, infection of the bitch and her possible death. Bitches do not in most cases require professional assistance in parturition but amateur bungling cannot take its place when it is needed.

Puppies are blind at birth, at least their eyes are not to open for some eight to twelve days. It is a wise and experienced breeder, indeed, who can sort a litter of puppies for their comparative excellence at the time of their birth, and even a wiser breeder who reaches the conclusion that such evaluation so early is almost, if not entirely, impossible.

It is true that some serious deformities and malformations can be detected and the defective puppy can be destroyed as not worth the rearing. Among these undesirable attributes which should be eliminated are hare-lips, cleft palates, the absence of an essential member such as a leg or foot, short tails on long tailed breeds, or long tails on naturally short tailed breeds. It is better to get rid of such defectives, which are few among judiciously bred dogs, and to devote all of one's energy to the rearing of the sound and promising rather than dissipate care upon the unfit.

However, it may be well to give warning that the comparative sizes at birth of the members of a litter provide no final criterion of their comparative sizes at maturity. The smallest puppy in the litter may develop into the largest dog. Hence it is unwise to base eliminations upon size alone.

Color and markings at birth are subject to some change with growth. Many a litter of Dalmatians has been destroyed at birth by ignorant breeders because the puppies were completely white, as they always are in that breed, the black spots appearing later. Colored patterns are likely to enlarge, white to decrease. Nose bands, face blazes, white collars, will grow narrower in proportion to the colored pattern as the puppy matures. Small spots of white on toes or chest may entirely close up and disappear. Breeds of a black and tan pattern, such as Airedale Terriers, Manchester Terriers, and Doberman Pinschers, are born with a much larger proportion of black and much smaller proportion of tan than they are to possess later on. Yorkshire Terriers are almost black and tan at birth, their true color developing later. And so, caution must be used not to bucket a newborn puppy which is only apparently, and not really unrepresentative of the breed of its parents.

Happily, there is no law to restrain the destruction of the newborn, unfit dog.

These considerations belong not strictly to a discussion of pre-natal life. But the new-whelped litter is the end and reason for pregnancy. Only he who has squatted by a stream rocking a gold pan and found among the black sands in its bottom tiny nuggets presaging checks from the mint, knows a kindred thrill to that of the dog breeder who handles and examines a newborn litter from his favorite bitch. What visions of triumphs in the show ring, ribbons, and silver cups, and championships these grunting whelps evoke! The sire expertly chosen to complement the dam in pedigree and type, the bitch conditioned and nourished and coddled to give these potential paragons the optimum of environment those nine, warm weeks within her womb; here in their nest, squirming and nuzzling, are the dog breeder's achievement. So far as pertains to this particular litter, his work as a breeder is at an end. What he will do with these newborn puppies as keeper, rearer, and exhibitor is outside our province and beyond the scope of this book.

CHAPTER IV

Genetics—What It Is

The year 1866 brought the announcement of a scientific discovery comparable in its import and implications to Copernicus' theory of the sun as the center of our universe, to Newton's law of gravity, and to Darwin's theory of biological evolution. Indeed, it is perhaps due to the concern of the world of biology with the then new Darwinian doctrine that this other, at least equally great and far reaching revelation, was so neglected as to be forgotten. That revelation is known today as the science of genetics embodying the *laws of Mendelian inheritance.* These laws provide the fundamental truths behind all we know about the manner in which animal and plant parents, by means of heredity, transmit to their progeny their own traits and characters and those of their ancestors.

Gregor Johann Mendel was abbot of a monastery at Brünn, in what is now Czechoslovakia. For eight patient, long years he had experimented in the crossing of distinct varieties of garden peas. Publishing the results of his research in an obscure botanical journal, he died disappointed that the world of science had taken no cognizance of what he had so laboriously learned. As Columbus did not know that he had found a new half of the world, it is to be doubted that Mendel was aware of the tremendous significance of the phenomena which he revealed. If he had known how much they meant to the practical welfare of mankind, he would surely have forced his truths upon the reluctant world with as much energy as he had used to discover

54

them. But Mendel was a plodding scientist, not a propagandist. Perhaps he did know; perhaps it was his little joke.

Like seeds of some giant sequoia, the Mendelian laws lay dormant from the time of their publication until 1900 when two Germans, Correns and Tschermak, and a Dutchman, the great Hugo de Vries, working separately and independently of each other, rediscovered them. Researchers turned up Mendel's original publication in the *Proceedings of the Natural History Society of Brünn*, which of course gave to the abbot scientific priority and to the world Mendelism.

To some readers it may seem a far cry from the breeding of peas in a monastery garden in Brünn to the breeding of pure-bred dogs in America. The bearing of the discoveries made in those plants upon the breeding of animals is, however, direct, and the discoveries Mendel made are just as applicable to the germ plasms of our dogs as to that of the peas in our garden.

Mendel's peas may seem, too, rather dry. But seasoned with a realization of their far reaching implications, and well masticated to facilitate their digestion, they are excellent mental nourishment for anyone who wishes to breed good dogs. Now let us look briefly at the regularities discovered by Mendel.

Mendel's first great contribution was to discover that the individual was not the basic unit of inheritance, but, rather, that each individual is composed of a number of characters which may be inherited separately. These "characters" are known as "unit characters." Mendel based his experiments on unit characters which, unbeknown to him, were to provide the key to the riddle of heredity which had puzzled mankind for centuries.

Unit characters are traits which normally appear as unmodified entities or do not appear at all and, within the given variety, they are found in contrasting pairs. The garden peas with which Mendel experimented provided contrasting pairs of unit characters: they were either tall or short and their seeds were either smooth or wrinkled. From his researches, Mendel deduced two basic kinds of inheritance. His method was so simple that anyone through controlled matings of plants or animals can repeat his experiments and reach the same conclusions.

First, let us take as our unit character blossom color and we will cross a pure purple-flowered plant with a pure white-flowered plant. (The word "pure" refers to the fact that both the purple and the white plants had been separately bred for some six or seven generations and had produced respectively only purple and white plants.) Mendel dutifully noted that the progeny of this purple-white cross were ALL PURPLE, *i.e.,* all of the plants of the First Filial (the F_1) generation resembled only the purple parent. Now let us take the next step and breed these F_1 plants to each other (the pea is particularly good for this demonstration because it is self-fertilizing). In the Second Filial (F_2) generation we do not get all purple or all white but, rather, 3 purples to 1 white, a ratio of three to one. In fact, the F_1 purples will continue to produce the 3-1 ratio as long as they are self-pollinated, *i.e.,* bred to themselves. You and I might have been content to call off the experiment at this point, but not Mendel. The abbot was an excellent scientist and he knew well that all probability factors had to be tested. He therefore proceeded to the flowers of the F_2 generation.

Now let us look at the results. We note that in the F_2 generation there are three purple flowers and one white. We assume that we have only two kinds of flowers, purple and white. However, what we really have with respect to heredity is *three* kinds of flowers. (1) The white flowers when bred to themselves produce ONLY white flowers; (2) of the three purple flowers, one of them when bred to itself will produce ONLY purple flowers; (3) the two remaining purple flowers will produce purple and white flowers in the 3-1 ratio. Genetically, the flowers of the F_2 are ¼ pure purple, ½ hybrid purple, and ¼ pure white. ("Hybrids" are forms resulting from the mating of parents showing contrasted unit characters. In our illustration all of the F_1 purples are hybrids.) Because in the F_1 hybrids no white flowers appeared, Mendel called white *recessive* in contrast to the *dominant* purple color.

56

Mendel theorized that traits like flower color are passed on as units in the sex cells. One unit can be purple *or* it can be white but *never* a mixture of the two. From pure purples only purple units are transmitted; from pure whites only white units are passed on; but from the hybrids, purple and white units in equal numbers are transmitted.

The reader may clarify for himself the concepts involved here by performing the following experiment: take 100 white marbles and 100 black marbles; put them into a bag and mix them thoroughly. The resultant mixture may be considered as analogous to the F_1 generation, *i.e.*, the mixture of the germ plasm of the purebred parents with respect to the single trait of color.

Blindfold a child and ask him to withdraw marbles from the mixed lot, two at a time. While two hundred marbles is too small a number to give exact mathematical probability, the reader can see that the probability factor is that the child will select 25 pairs of marbles of which both are white, 50 pairs of which one marble is black and one is white, and 25 pairs of which both marbles are black.

If we consider the white marbles as the recessives and the colored marbles as the dominants, we will see that in the F_2 generation of marbles we have the Mendelian ratio of 25% pure recessive white pairs, 50% hybrid black and white pairs, and 25% pure dominant black pairs. By now the reader should be able to calculate what results would obtain from crossing a pure white with a hybrid purple and from crossing a hybrid purple with a pure purple. (If not, you should review the material to date.)

We said previously that there were two basic kinds of inheritance. Let us proceed to the second type. We will state it and then give Mendel's First Law of Inheritance.

Let us begin this experiment by breeding pure white Four O'Clocks *(Mirabilis jalapa)* with pure red Four O'Clocks. Purity has been established by breeding whites to whites and reds to reds for enough generations to make sure that no other type appears. Instead of getting all whites or all reds in the F_1, as we might have expected, we get ALL PINKS. The genetic transmission has produced in the F_1 a blend of the original parental colors. Before jumping to any hasty and ill-conceived conclusions, let us breed these F_1 pinks to themselves. In the F_2 we get ¼ red, ½ pink, and ¼ white. Note carefully that both of the original parent colors reappeared in the F_2. Several puzzling factors now become apparent: (1) the F_1 pinks were hybrids carrying in their germ plasm as discrete units the red and white parental traits; (2) the "blended" effect of the F_1 color did NOT involve a blending of the unit traits in the germ plasm for if the units had blended in the germ plasm the F_2 would have yielded only PINKS, no REDS or WHITES would have appeared. It therefore becomes obvious that the color PINK is only *in the blossom* and that there is no blending of the unit characters themselves.

Perhaps one more step will bring in proper focus the form of genetic transmission. If the REDS of the F_2 are bred to each other they will produce only REDS. If the WHITES of the F_2 are self-pollinated, they will produce only WHITES. If the PINKS of the F_2 are "selfed," they will produce RED, PINK, and WHITE in the ¼ RED, ½ PINK, ¼ WHITE ratio. If the whites and reds of the F_2 are bred together, they will produce pinks and you can start the whole thing all over again.

It is most important for the reader to understand that the unit characters remain discrete entities and that the blended effect is only in the blossom.

We must also note that the genetic ratios for the F_2 in both of our experiments are fundamentally the same. The purple and white flowers in the F_2 had a blossom color ratio of 3-1, but we saw that their genetic ratio was ¼ pure purple, ½ hybrid purple, and ¼ pure white. In the second experiment the pinks of the F_1 when self-pollinated, produced the same genetic ratio: ¼ pure red, ½ hybrid pink, and ¼ pure white. What appears to be a second type of inheritance is actually a conformation to the same fundamental genetic laws.

Likewise, the roan color in shorthorn cattle is the hybrid

dominant manifestation of the cross of the pure dominant red with the recessive white. The blue Andalusian chicken is the hybrid dominant manifestation of the cross of the white chicken and the black chicken of that breed.

And there are innumerable other instances that could be cited of opposing unit characters in both animals and plants: simplex-blue eyes and brown human eyes, albinism and pigmentation in all species, red eyes and white eyes in the vinegar fly *(Drosophila),* the normal mouse and the waltzing mouse. Such pairs of opposing factors are known as alleles or allelomorphs.

Organisms which are alike in their body characteristics, without respect to their germinal character, are said to be of the same *phenotype.* Organisms of the same genetic makeup, without respect to their body characteristics, are of the same *genotype.* Thus, all of our pure recessive white flowers have both the same phenotype and the same genotype. All of the purple flowers are of the same phenotype but the hybrid purples have a different genotype from the pure purples.

The First Law of Mendel, known as the "Law of Segregation," is as follows:

That some attributes of living organisms are due to factors (dominant and/or recessive) in the gametes from which the organisms developed; that these factors do not blend but are individual and indivisible entities; that two parents with any factor as pure dominants in the gametes from both will produce in their immediate progeny pure dominants only, as pertains to that factor; that two parents with any factor as recessive in the gametes from both will produce in their immediate progeny only recessives as pertains to that factor; that in the crossing of parents, one pure dominant as pertains to the given factor, the other recessive for that factor, all of the immediate progeny will be hybrid-dominant for that factor; that two hybrid-dominant parents will produce progeny in the approximate ratio (large numbers of progeny to be considered): 25% recessive, 50% hybrid-dominant, and 25% pure dominant.

In the statement of this law, the phrase "some attributes of living organisms" is deliberate because Mendel, when he promulgated the law, was unaware that it might apply to all attributes of all living matter. Indeed, it is impossible to make such a categorical assertion even at this time, but it is the opinion of most workers in genetics that, with the possible unexplained transmission of leaf color in a few plants and a very few other similar phenomena, every attribute that flesh is heir to is, in all likelihood, the result of Mendelian inheritance. Whether a cat is to be black or white, whether a horse is to be fast or slow, whether a man is to be musical or unmusical, short or tall, blond or brunette, whether a dog shall have a long tail or a short tail, whether a dog shall bay on the trail or keep silent; all, everything that any living organism is or can become, is believed, by those who best should know, to be inherited in the Mendelian manner.

Mendel made further experiments with peas, considering at least seven sets of allelic factors. He found tallness of plant dominant over recessive dwarfness; unripe, green seed pods dominant over yellow seed pods; inflation of pods between seeds dominant over recessive constriction of pods; flowers borne along stem axis dominant over recessive flowers bunched at the top of the plant; colored seed skins dominant over recessive, white seed skins; yellow cotyledons dominant over recessive, white cotyledons; and smooth seed dominant over recessive, wrinkled seed.

It is fortunate that Mendel's experiments were made with a plant in which he was able to distinguish so many simple alleles dependent upon a single factor for their phenotypic traits. Had he chosen to work with organisms more complex in the genetic requirements for each phenotype, he might never have arrived at his conclusions. Indeed, it is possible, even likely, that other workers before Mendel, who had experimented with the breeding of other organisms with equal zeal and equal acuity of observation, might have discovered his laws but that the genetic transmission of their experimental material was so involved as to obscure the facts. This we shall see in the discussion of "Neo-Mendelism" in Chapter VI.

Now, obviously, there is more than one pair of unit characters going into the hereditary makeup of plants. Mendel knew this and he knew, too, that eventually he would have to solve the problem of following two unit characters at a time, of how they are transmitted, and of how they behave relative to each other. By solving this problem, Mendel arrived at his Second Law, the Law of Independent Assortment.

We will illustrate the law with one of Mendel's own experiments. In working with his peas Mendel crossed a plant that was pure strain for "tallness" and for "yellow seed" with a plant that was pure strain for "dwarfness" and for "green seed." Two unit characters were involved here, the allelic structure being: tall with dwarf, and yellow seed with green seed. Every plant in the F_1 generation was tall and had yellow seeds. Now look at the diagram at the bottom and note that every plant in the F_1 is a *double hybrid, i.e.,* it contains in its germ plasm the unit characters TALL, Dwarf/YELLOW SEED, Green Seed, with TALL-YELLOW SEED manifesting as dominant in the phenotype. (Recessive traits are shown in lower case letters.) Remember, also, that only *two* traits are involved, *size* (TALL-dwarf) and *color* (YELLOW SEED-green seed) and that each trait has a single contrasting pair of unit characters.

Let us proceed to self-fertilize these double hybrids of the F_1 generation and observe the results. The F_2 generation yielded *four* distinct plants in phenotype: (1) TALL/YELLOW SEED; (2) TALL/green seed; (3) dwarf/YELLOW SEED; (4) dwarf/green seed. These four phenotypes were in the ratio of 9:3:3:1, respectively.

Now bear with us and we'll do the whole thing once more, slowly, and this time with pictures.

	Unit Characters
1) The Parental Cross:	TALL/YELLOW SEED x dwarf/green seed
2) The F_1 Generation:	(all plants) TALL/YELLOW SEED *and* dwarf/green seed

61

3) The F_1 Generation self-
   fertilized:

    TALL: dwarf/YELLOW SEED:
   green seed x TALL: dwarf/YEL-
   LOW SEED: green seed

4) In the F_2 all possible combinations appear by pure chance.
   The possible combinations being:

    a) TALL/YELLOW SEED   9   Note: This is an in-
    b) TALL/green seed   3   variant ratio when
    c) dwarf/YELLOW SEED *Ratio* 3   pure strain double
    d) dwarf/green seed   1   hybrids are bred to-
                            16 gether.

The following diagrammatic table will show how the genotypes of the 16 plants are distributed, each square representing
an individual plant.

DOMINANTS   *RECESSIVES*
T-TALL Y-YELLOW SEED   d-dwarf   g-green seed

TTYY	TTYg	TdYY	TdYg
TTYg	TTgg	TdYg	Tdgg
TdYY	TdYg	ddYY	ddYg
TdYg	Tdgg	ddYg	ddgg

Thus we can see that each plant has received one factor (unit
character) for each set of alleles from each parent. (It is important to recognize that allelic unit factors cannot be passed on together. For example, TALL and dwarf cannot be transmitted
as a single combination, nor can YELLOW SEED and green
seed.) The presence of a single dominant unit factor determines
the manifestation of that dominant trait of the allelic unit in
the phenotype. When dealing with pure strain dominants and
recessives, as we are here, recessive unit factors must be in

62

"double doses," *i.e.,* one derived from each parent, to manifest in the phenotype. Where the unit factors in the genotype are a contrasting pair, *i.e.,* one dominant and one recessive, the recessive trait remains buried in the genotype and the dominant trait manifests in the phenotype. That buried recessive, however, is not discarded from the genotype pattern for it stays there and in the next mating if it pairs with another recessive of the same kind that recessive trait will now appear in the phenotype.

When two sets of alleles are involved in a cross, it is called a *dihybrid cross* and the plants of the F_1 generation are called *dihybrids*. When three allelic sets (three unit characters) are involved, the plants of the F_1 generation are *trihybrids*. When more than three sets of alleles are involved, the resultant generations are *polyhybrids*.

As we have seen, a dihybrid cross in the F_2 generation produces 4 possible phenotypes in the approximate ratio of 9:3:3:1, and it produces 9 genotypes, of which only one is recessive for both factors, and one pure dominant for both factors. The remaining 7 are hybrid dominant for one factor or for both.

A trihybrid cross produces 8 phenotypes with 27 possible genotypes, the ratio of the phenotypes being 27:9:9:9:3:3:3:1. The possible genotypic patterns in the trihybrid cross could be illustrated in a diagram of 64 squares, as is the dihybrid cross in the 16 squares of the diagram on page 62.

Recapitulating, the Second Law of Mendel, or the Law of Independent Assortment, is: ". . . when double hybrids are bred together all possible combinations occur in the offspring by pure chance." We shall subsequently see that this Second Law of Mendel is not categorically valid. However, before we can understand why it is not absolutely valid, we need to discuss the chromosomes and their genes, which we shall do in the next chapter.

If all of these figures, squares, and ratios have seemed tedious, we excuse ourselves by saying that they are the very flesh of the skeleton of Mendelism. They *must* be understood before we can turn our attention to matters of more far-reaching and practical consequence.

The importance of "independent assortment" is set forth by Dunn and Dobzhansky in *Heredity, Race, and Society:*

"This independence in inheritance of separate traits of plants, animals and men was an entirely new idea which Mendel was the first to recognize and to prove. It has many important and interesting consequences. For example when Mendel crossed *two* varieties of peas, one with yellow round and one with green wrinkled seeds, he obtained four varieties in the second generation. The two new ones had yellow wrinkled and green round seeds respectively. Thus new varieties can be obtained by crossing, and the number of kinds from which the farmer or gardener may choose can be greatly increased. This is of great importance in practical agriculture. Suppose that you have two varieties of a crop or vegetable plant, and that each variety possesses an advantageous trait which the other does not have. For example, one variety may yield well but may not have sufficient resistance to frost, while the other is frost resistant but produces unsatisfactory yields. It is obviously desirable to have a combination of good yield and frost resistance in the same plants. If yield and resistance are chiefly influenced by two pairs of independent genes, then according to Mendel's second law, this may often be accomplished by crossing the two varieties, and selecting in the second generation of hybrids the plants which possess the desired combination of traits. Plants in which the undesirable qualities of the initial varieties are combined will also appear among the hybrids, making a careful examination of individual plants and their progenies essential. Many of the best varieties of cultivated plants have been arrived at by combining through appropriate crosses the desirable traits which were present separately in several older varieties."

Even though Dunn and Dobzhansky have used plants to illustrate the importance of independent assortment, their paragraph is equally applicable to animals.

For long ages it was assumed that the germ plasm of the

parents blended to form a new generation as if one mixed water and wine, and that the child would manifest attributes somewhere intermediate between the analogous attributes of the parental pair. It seemed like common sense but, like much else that we have accepted as common sense, upon investigation it turned out not to be true. It is one of the "Things That Are Not True," discussed in Chapter XIV, of that title.

Rather than being like the mixing of wine and water, the breeding of plants and animals is like mixing together black and white beads which can again be segregated at will.

That, indeed, is Mendelism—the fact that parental germ plasms do not blend irrevocably together like wine and water but rather that the factors lie side by side, complete entities, unblending and indivisible in the germ plasm, like different colored beads in a box.

This is Mendelism, Mendelism as it was set forth by the Abbot of Brünn in 1865, forgotten until 1900, rediscovered and promulgated at the beginning of this century. However, Gregor Mendel saw the truth but through the glass darkly.

Using the two Mendelian laws as a point of departure, the twentieth century workers in the science of genetics, no less patient, no less careful, no less wise, have gone far. Every year new genetic truths are revealed, startling in their implications. So much is known now that, if adequately applied, man would be so able to hasten and direct organic evolution that it could move in a decade as far as it has previously moved in a millennium, and, moreover, could be forced to move in the desired direction. Man, through selective breeding, can make of his plants, his animals, and his descendants whatever he may wish them to be.

What Mendel saw so darkly, the modern geneticist sees clearly, ever more clearly. The new knowledge which has grown from the roots of Mendel's discoveries is called *Neo-Mendelism,* which will be discussed in Chapter VI of that name.

CHAPTER V

The Chromosomes and Their Genes

We have seen in the chapter on Mendelism that the various traits of plants and animals are carried as unit characters from one generation to another. We know that the determining factors are carried in the gametes (the sperm and the ovum) which unite to form the zygote of the new organism. But what are these determining factors and how are they carried in the gametes to register themselves in the new organism?

We have also seen that each of the billions of cells in the dog's body is made up essentially of transparently clear cytoplasm in which is embodied a tiny gray nucleus. That the cell structure is somewhat more complicated than merely a point of nucleus within the cytoplasm, need not concern us here. It is within the nucleus that we shall find the material which contains the determining factors of the germ plasm.

The nucleus of each cell is a minute, clear, gray mass which contains one or more nucleoli slowly stirring around. As the cell prepares for its division, the nucleoli vanish and are replaced by grayish granules (called chromatin), which in turn draw out into a tangle of fine threads of various length, which writhe and wiggle uneasily. At length these threads slow down their activity. They grow shorter and stubbier as tiny rods of various lengths.

These rods are our *chromosomes*. The word is derived from the Greek *chroma* (color), and *soma* (body). This name is due to the fact that the tiny rods take a deep stain which facilitates their microscopic observation.

The number of these chromosomes in each body cell is constant in each organism and tends to be constant throughout each species. Indeed, some workers consider that the number of chromosomes in each body cell is the final determinant of species, for which word there is no hard and fast definition. (The last statement is not meant to imply that there is a different chromosome count for every single species, but, rather, that the count should be constant *within* the particular species.)

The reproductive cells before their reduction division contain the same constant number of chromosomes as do the body cells. After reduction division (meiosis), which is to be described somewhat later in this chapter, the chromosome number in the reproductive cells is but half the number in the body cells, and is now called the *haploid* number.

In Man, the number before reduction division, called the *diploid* number, is 48; in the mouse it is 40; in *Drosophila*, the vinegar fly, it is 8; and in the dog it is 78.

In each of the body cells the chromosomes occur in pairs, like the animals in Noah's Ark. The number of the pairs is one-half the total number of chromosomes in any body cell and in the reproductive cells before reduction division. The shape and length of the various pairs may be different but as they are seen under the microscope there is no apparent difference in the members of any single pair, with the exception of the one pair which is known as the sex chromosomes, the so-called X and Y chromosomes, which carry the factor which determines sex, together with other factors.

The sex chromosomes are discussed more fully in Chapter VIII, "The Determination of Sex."

One member of each pair of the chromosomes is derived from each parent, the haploid number (39 in the dog) of chromosomes being in the nucleus of the sperm and the haploid number in the nucleus of the ovum. These unite to provide the full diploid number (78 in the dog) of chromosomes in the zygote.

Now, let us proceed to the process of cell division. There are two kinds of cell division, *mitosis* and *meiosis*. We will consider mitosis first. (The reader is urged to consult the diagrams on pages 70 through 74, as we move through this process, phase by phase.)

In Phase I we see the cell at rest, noting its basic structure.

PHASE I

There is a cell membrane within which is a large area of cytoplasm. Within the cytoplasm we make out the nuclear membrane enclosing the nucleus, which in this phase is merely a relatively small mass of undifferentiated protoplasm. At the top of the cell is a small, star-shaped body, the centrosome. The cell is at rest and the process of mitosis has not yet begun.

PHASE II

The only significant change in this phase is that the undifferentiated protoplasm within the nucleus looks like a tightly coiled mass of thread-like material, the chromatin. The centrosome remains unchanged.

PHASE III

The nuclear membrane has dissolved away and the chromatin has broken up into a definite number of rods or segments. (Four in our diagram.) These rods are the chromosomes. The centrosome has split into two parts, taking their places at the opposite ends of the diameter of the cell and radiating fine fibers toward the chromosomes. The bodies and their fibers are called the *asters*. It is believed that the fibers act to pull the chromosomes apart, though the evidence is far from clear on the point. Note especially that the chromosomes are lined up linearly in the cell.

PHASE IV

The cell splits down the middle, forming two new daughter cells, each of which is exactly like the original parent cell. The chromosomes have split longitudinally, from end to end. The chromosomes are of the same length but of half the volume.

PHASE V

The chromosomes in the new daughter cells regroup themselves in the approximate center of the cell; the nuclear membrane reforms around them; they revert to chromatin and then to undifferentiated protoplasm. The process of mitosis is completed. The daughter cells are then ready to undertake another mitotic division which will be precisely like the one that brought them into being.

Mitosis is a process of cell division in which two new daughter cells are formed from the original parent cell. These daughter cells are exactly like the parent cell and each contains precisely the same number of chromosomes as the parent cell. It is important to remember that in mitosis there is neither an increase nor a decrease in the chromosome number between the daughter cells and the parent cell.

Each of the new cells contain one half of each chromosome which was in the parent cell. These halves function as complete chromosomes in the daughter cells, and when they in turn divide to form four new cells, their chromosomes split themselves lengthwise again, a half of each going into each new cell. Thus we see that the number of chromosomes is constant in all of the somatic, or body, cells.

It is, however, the reproductive cells in which we are particularly interested, and the behavior of the somatic cells is only pertinent insofar as it pertains to them. The chromosomes of the reproductive cells carry within them the factors which determine what the progeny of the organism shall be like, and the animal breeder should know in what manner those factors are conveyed from parent to offspring.

The behavior of the reproductive cells in their division is much like that of the somatic cells, but the reproductive cells undergo reduction division. This process is different in the reproductive cells of the male from those cells of the female.

It should be obvious that if the sperm and ovum should each contribute the full diploid number of chromosomes to the zygote cell of the new organism, each succeeding generation

Phase I - Mitosis

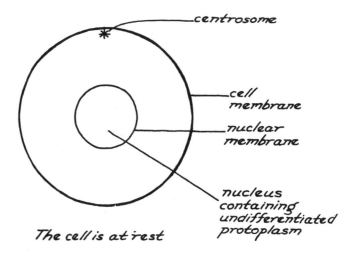

centrosome

cell membrane

nuclear membrane

nucleus containing undifferentiated protoplasm

The cell is at rest

Phase II - Mitosis

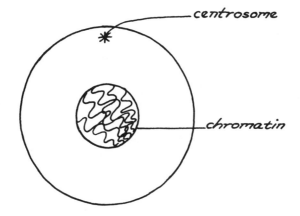

centrosome

chromatin

Phase III – Mitosis

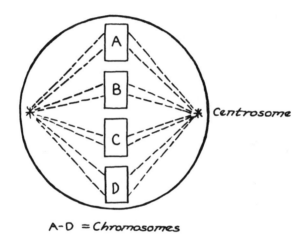

A-D = Chromosomes

Phase Ⅳ - Mitosis

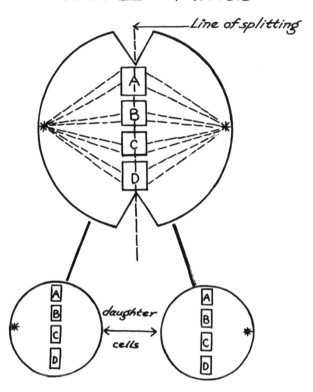

Line of splitting

A
B
C
D

daughter
cells

A
B
C
D

A
B
C
D

73

Phase Ⅴ-Mitosis

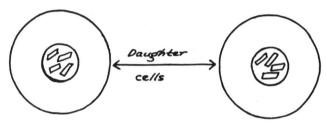

Daughter
cells

Each will become a parent cell
and the process of mitosis will continue

would contain in its cells twice the number of chromosomes of the cells of its parents. With such a doubling of the chromosome count for each new generation, it would not require many generations until all cells contained literally thousands of chromosomes. That, of course, does not happen.

Let us deal first with meiosis (reduction division) as it occurs in the male. We will show it first in diagrammatic form and then discuss it. The reader is asked to compare this process with the diagrams of mitosis.

In meiosis Phases I and II are essentially the same as they are in mitosis. The first noticeable change can be detected in Phase III.

PHASE III

The nuclear membrane has dissolved away and the chromatin has broken up into the same number of chromosomes as in mitosis. Now, however, the chromosomes do NOT line up linearly in the cell, but, rather, in pairs. Technically, in this formation the chromosomes face each other in homologous pairs, *i.e.,* pair A and A_1 are alike in structure; pair B and B_1 are alike in structure but are different from A and A_1. In the dog, then, there would be 39 pairs of homologous chromosomes, no two pairs being exactly alike. [Homologous—homo (like) + logos (structure or body)] The action of the centrosome is like that in mitosis.

PHASE IV

The cell splits down the middle, forming two new cells, each of which contains only half the original number of chromosomes in the parent cell. *This* is reduction division. The new cells, not yet functional sperm, contain the haploid count of chromosomes.

PHASE V

The two new cells, after going back to Phase I, divide again, but this time the division is a mitotic one so that there is no further reduction of the chromosome count. The four new cells now develop tails and are functional sperm, *i.e.,* they are capable of fertilizing the ovum. They are ready to go; ready to be used.

Phase III-Meiosis
Reduction Division

$\left(\begin{array}{l}\textit{Phases I and II are}\\ \textit{the same as those in}\\ \textit{mitosis.}\end{array}\right)$

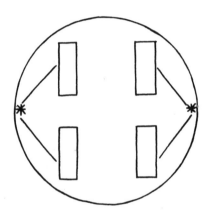

Phase Ⅳ-Meiosis

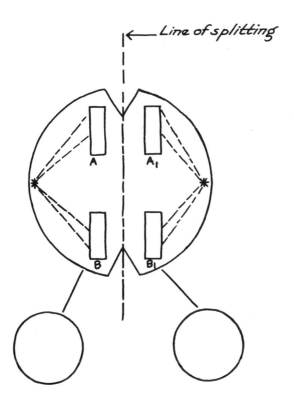

Line of splitting

77

Phase V - Meiosis
⚲⟶ (Male)

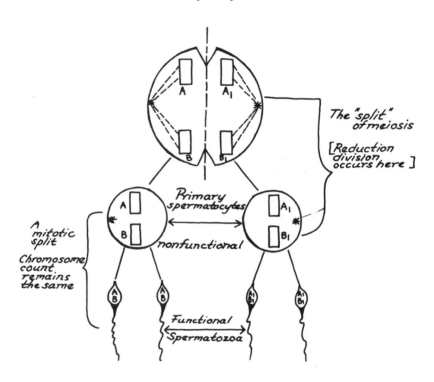

The "split" of meiosis

[Reduction division occurs here]

Primary spermatocytes

nonfunctional

A mitotic split

Chromosome count remains the same

Functional Spermatozoa

Phase Ⅴ-Meiosis
♀ (Female)

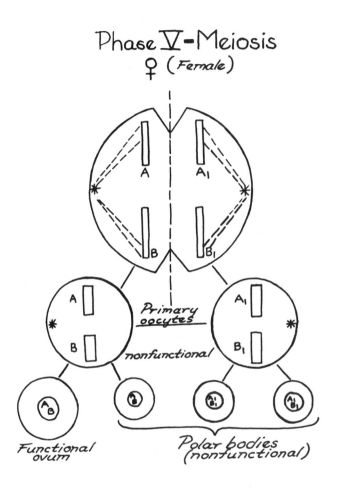

Primary oocytes

nonfunctional

Functional
ovum

Polar bodies
(nonfunctional)

In the male, then, meiosis is a process of cell division in which ultimately four functional sperm are formed, each one of which contains only half the original number of chromosomes in the basic sex cell.

In the female the process of meiosis is the same through Phases I, II, III, and IV as it is in the male. In Phase V, however, a distinct change occurs.

PHASE V

The two new cells return to Phase I and then divide again *mitotically*. Four new cells are formed but only ONE of them is a large functional ovum. The other three are relatively small, non-functional *polar bodies*. In both the ovum and in each of the polar bodies there is the haploid count of chromosomes.

Thus we see that in the female meiosis is a process of cell division in which ultimately one functional ovum and three non-functional polar bodies are formed, each one of which contains only half the original number of chromosomes in the basic sex cell.

Two very important factors must be remembered about meiosis. They are: (1) during meiosis the chromosomes line up in *homologous* pairs and (2) meiosis is called "reduction division" because when the cell makes its first division the chromosome count is reduced by one-half. (The second splitting of the sex cell, because it is by mitosis, does NOT increase or decrease the chromosome count.

Let us consider the process of making functional sex cells, spermatozoa and ova, in some detail.

In the formation of spermatozoa, the basic reproductive cells divide and redivide, as in ordinary mitosis, until there are vast numbers of them. Each of these new cells that is to mature undergoes a period of growth in which it not only enlarges but in which the material of its nucleus is much changed. After this period of growth the cell is called a *primary spermatocyte,* and it is non-functional, *i.e.,* it cannot yet fertilize an ovum.

The chromosomes of these primary spermatocytes gather on the equatorial plane of the spindles as we have seen in the division of the body cells. However, to form sperm they pair off, two and two, each chromosome derived from the organism's paternal parent lining up alongside the homologous one from the maternal parent.

This process of the pairing of the chromosomes preparatory to reduction division is known as *synapsis*. When the chromosomes have all located their partners, they do not split lengthwise as in mitosis but one member of each pair moves to each pole to form the new cell. In the cells thus formed there are but half the diploid number of chromosomes to be found in a somatic cell, and the reduced number is haploid. Dogs and men are diploid; gametes, functional sex cells, are haploid.

After reduction division, to each cell has gone, in all likelihood, some members of the set of chromosomes derived from the male parent and some members derived from the female parent. It seems to be a merely fortuitous matter, which member of each pair shall go to which pole. It would be remotely possible that all the chromosomes from the sire would go to one pole, all from the dam to the other pole; but the mathematical probability of such a division would be the same as the probability of shuffling a deck with the number of cards of the diploid number of the chromosomes, an equal number of red cards and of black cards, and finding all the cards of either color on top of the pack, all of the other color on the bottom of the pack. Thus, it is all but impossible.

If it should occur, however, the resultant sperm would be related to but a single parent and could transmit to its zygote none of the traits derived from the other parent of the organism in which it arose, and the progeny arising from it in a genetic sense would be quite unrelated to one of its grandparents.

Each of these secondary spermatocytes, as the cells after the reduction division are called, soon divides by the splitting of the chromosomes, as in ordinary mitosis, into two spermatids, each of which sluffs off the largest part of its cytoplasm, grows

81

a long tail, and becomes a spermatozoön, ready to be discharged into the female and to fertilize an ovum.

It will observed that the two haploid sets of chromosomes of the two secondary spermatocytes derived from any primary spermatocyte must be very different in their content, since those sets are made by the separation of members of homologous pairs rather than by the splitting of the chromosomes of the parent cell.

On the other hand, the two spermatids which result from the splitting of a secondary spermatocyte are exactly alike, for each chromosome in the parent cell has split lengthwise to produce two.

Thus, from each primary spermatocyte comes four spermatozoa, of which there are two pairs which are entirely different, one pair from another, but of which the members of any pair are exactly alike.

Of the billions of spermatozoa proliferated in a single male organism in a normal lifetime, of the millions ejaculated at a single sexual orgasm, of the many thousands in a drop of the seminal fluid, only an almost infinitesimally small number are destined to encounter and fertilize ova; the others are destined to extinction. If a male dog begot two litters of ten puppies each, every week over a period of ten years, he would produce only 14,000 immediate offspring. Such a record has perhaps never been made by any dog, but at a normal single breeding a dog would expel from himself all the sperm necessary and would leave to die disused many, many millions more.

The likelihood that the two like sperm derived from any primary spermatocyte will both succeed in fertilizing ova is so remote that the probability could be expressed only in astronomical figures; but, if they should, the resulting progeny would derive from its male parent a heredity as identical as that of identical twins, produced by the fertilization of a single ovum by a single sperm. The heredity of such progeny derived from the female parent need, however, be no more alike than that of mere fraternal twins, or of two members of a litter. Indeed, fraternal twins are only litter siblings. (The word "siblings," which is not to be found in older dictionaries, denotes the children of the same parents, whether male or/and female. Derived etymologically from the Anglo-Saxon "sib," it is a convenient word and is coming into more frequent usage.)

In the female the basic sex cells, as they develop, undergo a period of enlargement after which they are called *primary oöcytes,* a term analogous in the female to the primary spermatocytes in the male. The chromosomes of the primary oöcyte pair come together in synapsis, as in the male, one set moving to each pole of the spindle. After that, however, instead of the cell dividing into two cells of equal size, there is a most unequal division. The cell throws off a tiny part of itself which contains a haploid set of chromosomes, but very little cytoplasm. This smaller cell is called the *first polar body.* These two cells, one so much larger than the other, are analogous in the female to the secondary spermatocytes in the male.

The larger cell again subdivides by discharging another cell much smaller than itself, the chromatin content of which results from the splitting of the chromosomes lengthwise, as in ordinary mitosis as we have observed in the splitting of the primary spermatocytes to form the spermatids. This smaller cell is known as the *second polar body;* the larger one is now the female pronucleus and will soon become a ripe ovum, ready for fertilization by the sperm.

The first polar body, like its larger sister, will again subdivide by the splitting of its chromosomes lengthwise, but the resultant cells and the second polar body cannot be fertilized. Recent evidence indicates that the polar bodies serve as an extra food supply in the event that the ovum is fertilized. However, the polar bodies with the ovum preserve the analogy of the division in the male of the original germ-cell into four cells.

Size in the sperm is a hinderance rather than a help and the spermatozoa sluff off a large part of their cytoplasm in their development—strip for action, as it were. They have no need for any large amount of food material since the nuclear head, with

83

its closely compressed content of chromosomes, is its sole contribution to the zygote. The ovum, on the other hand, must supply most of the material for the development of the embryo while it finds its way through the oviduct into the uterus and there digs in and establishes relations with the maternal organism which will ensure it nourishment for its growth. By stingily throwing off the polar bodies so much smaller than itself, instead of halving and re-halving as does the male germ-cell, the oöcyte conserves its cytoplasm for the development of the early stages of the embryo. Some conception of the comparative size of the gametes is conveyed by the estimation that in man the egg, despite its minuteness, is some 85,000 times the volume of the sperm.

We now recognize the chromosomes as tiny, elongated capsules in which are enclosed the stuff of heredity, and we know that they have a constant number for the species and that each of the body cells has the same number. We have seen how that number as it appears in the basic reproductive cell is cut in half to the end that each gamete may contribute the haploid number to form the diploid number of paired chromosomes in the zygote.

But what is inside these capsules which we call chromosomes? The answer is, the *genes*. And what are the genes? We cannot be absolutely sure. Nobody has ever yet isolated a gene, taken it apart and looked at it. The word gene (Latin for "birth" or "breeding") is used to designate that part of the content of the chromosome which is responsible for any Mendelian factor. For practical purposes, the genes and the Mendelian factors which they convey are one and the same things. Practically, the terms are interchangeable. Technically, the gene is the *unit carrier of heredity*.

While nobody will yet say definitely that he has seen a gene, Painter, of the University of Texas, and Bridges, an associate of Morgan at the California Institute of Technology, have seen and made microphotographs of minute bands along the chromo-

84

somes of the large cells of the salivary glands of *Drosophila*. These bands, they believe, may be the genes.

While it is not known exactly how a gene is chemically constituted, it is known that genes lie in a systematized' order along the length of the chromosome, like beads on a string. In any homologous pair of chromosomes in a given species, the gene for any specific factor exists in the same part of one member of the pair as the gene for the same factor or its allelomorph exists in the other member of the same pair. (For the distinction between *alleles* and *allelomorph,* the reader is referred to the glossary.)

> In the above pair of homologous chromosomes, genes A and A_1 are alleles; genes B and B_1 are alleles, genes C and C_1 are alleles. Thus we note that the chromosomes are homologous not only in their external structure but in the gene structures as well.

In each haploid set of chromosomes, the gene for any given factor or its allelomorph is to be found in the same chromosome; and, not only the same chromosome, but in the same position in relation to the other genes along the length of the chromosome, just as in the spine the first lumbar vertebra has a constant position between the twelfth or last dorsal and the second lumbar vertebra. So a given gene or its allelomorph has a given normal position in the arrangement of the genes along the chromosome. Abnormalities in the behavior.of the chromosomes do occur, and they are likely to cause either the death of the zygote or the malformation of the organism which derives from it. For the most part, however, the chromosomes can be depended upon to keep their regimented place.

The work of Thomas Hunt Morgan with *Drosophila* has contributed more to the knowledge of chromosomes and their behavior than has that of any other single worker, winning for him the Nobel Prize in Medicine in 1933.

Morgan was able to formulate a map, not yet and perhaps never to be complete, showing the arrangement of several hundred of the various genes along the various chromosomes of his beloved vinegar flies. Morgan's map was made before Painter and Bridges had observed the bands on the chromosomes which are believed to be the genes. This accomplishment is staggering in its seemingly insuperable difficulties. That Morgan has been able to declare that any recognized gene, let us say the gene for red eyes or its allelomorphic gene for white eyes, lies in a given chromosome and in a definite position in relation to the other given recognized genes in that chromosome, is due to the comparatively small number (diploid, eight; haploid, four) of the chromosomes in the *Drosophila* cell, to the rapidity with which it reproduces itself, with a new generation every ten days, and to the small size of the flies, which enables one worker to maintain vast numbers of them. Even then, but for the phenomenon of "crossing-over," the exchange of places of two or more genes in one chromosome with the same gene or its allelomorph in the other member of the chromosome pair, this mapping would have been impossible.

We return here briefly to the consideration that the Second Mendelian Law, that the sets of alleles behave independently one of the others, is not categorically true. The phenomenon that saves the Second Law from at least partial invalidation is "crossing-over."

Mendel was not aware of the chromosomes and their genes. He found that the sets of factors behaved in a certain fashion in the garden peas, but he did not know the physical mechanism of such behavior. He observed the phenomena without being able to understand their causation.

The factors with which he worked are in the garden pea each dependent upon a single set of allelic genes. And the sets of alleles in the garden pea are to be found in different pairs of chromosomes. It was only the genetic simplicity of the garden pea, as pertains to the sets of factors with which he experimented, that enabled Mendel to reach his conclusions. When he later worked with hawkweed and other plants he was baffled by the failure of what he thought to be simple factors to behave as they had done in peas. We know now that his bafflement was due to the circumstance that some of the characteristics of a plant which he thought depended upon a single factor, in reality depended upon two or more factors, *i.e.*, two or more allelic pairs of genes.

We may amend the Second Mendelian Law to say that the sets of genes within any pair of chromosomes behave independently of the sets of genes within any other pair of chromosomes. While it is indeed true that the genes are the unit carriers of heredity, they are located within specific chromosomes and it is the chromosomes that behave independently.

This tendency of particular genes to remain together within a particular chromosome and to be passed on together is called *linkage*. If Mendel had been aware of the phenomenon of linkage, he would not, perhaps, have promulgated the Second Law precisely as he did. If the factors for smooth seed and for tall growth in the garden pea had been in one chromosome, instead of in separate chromosomes as they are, Mendel would not have been able (barring the possibility of "crossing-over") to breed tall peas with wrinkled seed nor dwarf peas with smooth seed, and could not have declared the independent assortment of the genes.

We have said that there is a "tendency" for given genes to stay in their own chromosomatic backyard. Adherence to such tendency is the normal behavior. But the violation of that tendency does take place, and it is this observance of behavior that saves the Second Mendelian Law.

When the chromosomes pair off for reduction from the diploid to the haploid number, one or more genes of one chromosome may exchange places with the homologous genes of the other member of the pair of chromosomes. (See diagram on p. 76.) It appears that in synapsis, the members of a pair of chromosomes sometimes become entangled one with the other, and one or both ends of both break off and exchange positions, joining on to the correct place in the opposite member of the pair. This occurs at either end of the chromosomes and the

87

fragment may be of a single gene or any number of genes. If it occurs at both ends of the same pair in one synapsis, it is as if a segment from the middles were exchanged. This phenomenon is known as "crossing-over."

It is as if, in dancing a Virginia reel, a part of the pairs of partners at the end of a line should exchange lines, each making the exchange with his own partner. This might occur at both ends of the line, leaving one or more pairs of partners in the same line as before.

From the observations of thousands of individual *Drosophila*, it was possible to determine which genes tended to linkage within which chromosome. Having located the genes in their respective chromosomes, and recognizing that "crossing-over" occurs at each end of the chromosome, it is reasoned that the gene which is observed to be most frequently out of its normal place is the end gene of its chromosome, that the gene from the same chromosome which shifts with the second degree of frequency is the second from the end; and so the map of the four haploid chromosomes of *Drosophila* was drawn.

With such a map and an assortment of *Drosophila* of known ancestry, it is possible to produce at will flies with any recognized assortment of traits.

To make such a map of the chromosomes of the dog by such a method would involve a thousand years of time and the maintenance of a kennel as large as the harem of Solomon. The large number of chromosomes involved, the length of time required for each new generation, and the great amount of space, food, and care necessary for so large a number of dogs would place the undertaking quite beyond the boundary of the practicable. Indeed, the possession of such a map, finished and complete, with an adequate assortment of dogs, would reduce the breeding of dogs from a creative art to an exact science, even to a mere assembly of traits like the putting together of standardized parts of a machine. The breeding of dogs would be just about as interesting then as erecting pre-fabricated houses. And the results would be as stereotyped.

Not only do the genes "cross-over" from time to time, but occasionally chromosomes break up into permanent segments, or one chromosome may affix itself to the end of another, or a part break off of one and join another. Such behavior is rare and abnormal and is of little practical interest to us. A zygote formed of the union of such a gametic cell with a normal one, if it survives at all, would probably produce an abnormal organism fit only for destruction. However, it is possible for a variety with new and desirable variations so to arise. The breeder of dogs may, however, well ignore such a possibility. It is recognized that change of the genetic contents of a cell may be effected by X-radiation, by excessively high heat, or by certain chemicals, such as colchicine; but until further research yields controlled effects such changes can be of no value in the betterment of the higher animals.

There is no danger that we shall ever learn enough of the mechanics of the heredity of the dog, however, to sink in the prosaic certainty of a standardized product the fascination which attaches to dog breeding. An absolute rule-of-thumb procedure would destroy at once the art and the pleasure. However, in our yet benighted ignorance of the subject, lighted only faintly by the morning star of Mendelism and the nascent dawn of recent work in genetics, any new knowledge which may guide us along the way to better dogs cannot be ignored. Substitute exact knowledge as far as we are able for the haphazard of trial and error, we yet have left enough of uncertainty, and will have for centuries to come, to give zest to the breeder's art.

The value to the dog breeder of the knowledge of the chromosomes and genes is that it brings to him a realization that when he brings together two dogs of opposite sex for the purpose of producing a litter of puppies, he is not merely mating female to male, bitch to dog, egg to sperm, or even chromosome to chromosome, but rather he is pairing two hosts of genes. What the puppy shall look like, how he shall behave, how he shall thrive in a given environment, and even how long he shall live depend upon the genes which find their way to the zygote.

We thus see that the age-old idea of the mingling in the progeny of the blood of the two parents is a fallacy. The individual is a mosaic of the hereditary factors of the two ancestral lines, rather than a blend of the parental bloods which in their turns had been blended from the bloods of their ancestors.

From such a mosaic, the creative breeder can choose the genetic stones he wishes for the design of the ensuing generation, whereas, if we were dealing with blended blood it would be impossible to segregate the desired part from the undesired part of the contents. We are dealing, to use a figure of speech, with platters full of hard boiled eggs rather than of scrambled eggs, and it is much easier to sort out and discard the rotten eggs from the hard boiled units than to unscramble the eggs and get rid of the unfit parts of such a mass.

To change our figure again, the chromosomes and their genes as they appear in the zygote are a full set of plans and specifications for the organism. Therein every detail is laid down and described minutely. If environment, as the executive builder from those chromosomatic and genetic plans, fails of its execution, it is no fault of the breeder-architect who made the blueprints.

The chromosomes and their genes have been likened in heredity to the molecules and atoms in chemistry; and if it were possible to analyze an organism's genetic content in the same manner in which matter's atomic content can be analyzed, we should be able to produce in our dogs whatever traits we chose.

Without the map of the genes within the chromosomes, which we shall perhaps never achieve for so complex an organism as the dog, we shall not be able to breed exactly the kind of dogs we wish every time we try. But the chromosomes and genes are the material elements of Mendelism and understanding of them leads to profound implications which have their practical application in the breeding of dogs. These "Implications of Mendelism" will form the subject matter for Chapter VII.

Many facts about the chromosomes and genes of only theoretic interest to the breeder have, for lack of space and for their impracticability of application to the subject in hand, been omitted here. The subject must needs be intriguing to anybody enough interested in the breeding of dogs to attempt the comprehension of the apparent miracles here described, and even the host of facts and theories as they pertain to other organisms than the dog are worthy of the dog man's interest. The brief bibliography attached to the volume will make possible to such readers as may be curious the exploration of the byways of the biology of reproduction.

Indeed, to many readers it may seem a far cry from garden peas to Great Danes, or from vinegar flies to Fox Terriers. However, garden peas and vinegar flies have served as tiny candles (to glimmer only dimly, it is true) in the darkness where the dog breeder has been working. That early breeders achieved our beautiful varieties of dogs with the scant knowledge at their command is a credit to their patience and persistence. With our present and increasing knowledge, if the dog fancy will utilize it, we can improve those varieties with a celerity and certainty undreamed of by the enthusiasts who founded them and brought them as far as they have come. A sound knowledge of the materials of heredity, of the genes and chromosomes and their behavior will save us from a vast number of false starts and a vast amount of wasted effort. If it does nothing else, it will prune a lot of dead wood, delete a host of old-wives' tales and superstitions from previously entertained theories of breeding. It shows us why these "Things That Are Not True," as we call them in Chapter XIV, cannot be true, and enables us, in disregarding them, to divert the efforts otherwise spent upon them into the channels of constructive breeding.

Upon the person who wishes simply to produce some puppies eligible to registration, for the purpose of sale or of the gratification of some vanity in winning a few cups and ribbons, the mysteries of genetics are wasted. Why should one bother about so small a thing as a gene? Nobody knows what a gene is anyway. His bitch has won a ribbon and he is going to mate her to the latest and most fashionable champion and trust to luck. May he have his luck, with our blessing! Such a person is not a dog breeder in our sense that the breeding of dogs is a creative art.

The true breeder of dogs is one interested in the betterment of dogs for dogs' own sake; interested, not in producing a single chance specimen of some degree of excellence, but rather in the improvement of the whole breed as much by conserving the good in the germ plasms of the strain as by eliminating the bad; interested not in a single generation, but in the breed's whole future. To such a person (certainly in the long run and probably in the beginning) will come more of monetary profit and of consistent show-ring success than the chance trifler with dogs can ever attain.

And no consideration can be of greater value to the serious breeder of dogs than the realization that his dogs and bitches, from a genetic standpoint, are merely bundles of genes neatly wrapped up in chromosomes. It is his business to deal those decks, of which the chromosomes are the cards and the genes are the pips on the cards. If he can mark and stack those cards in his little game with old Dame Nature, who has herself often enough taken unfair advantage of the breeder's ignorance, it but evens the score. Hitherto he has mixed the drinks of blood and blood, permitting the old lady to shuffle the cards of chromosomes and genes. Try as he may to cheat her, she will out-cheat him and win often enough.

CHAPTER VI

Neo-Mendelism

When Gregor Mendel in 1866 published his laws that revolutionized the science of genetics, he was unaware that all the physical attributes an organism is heir to are transmissible from generation to generation in consonance with those laws. The great mass of evidence accumulated since the rediscovery of Mendelism in 1900 all points to the conclusion that every trait of every part of every organism is the result of the presence of the gene for some Mendelian factor or its allelomorph. The single possible exception so far observed is in the color of certain plants, the leaves of which are green, white, or mottled. This condition seems to be produced by certain so-called "plastids" in the cytoplasm of the cell and to depend only in part, if at all, on the chromosomes. This single exception need not confuse the breeder of dogs or turn him from the full acceptance of Mendelism. The testimony of the whole faculty of authoritative geneticists is for the universality of the Mendelian laws.

Mendel's garden peas fortunately had characters, manifestations of which were dependent upon single pairs of allelic genes, and the genes for these various sets of characters were in different chromosomes of the haploid set. Else he might never have reached his conclusions. We have seen in the previous chapter that only "crossing-over" saves from invalidation the Second Law as it pertains to such genes as may be found in any single pair of chromosomes.

The discovery of the chromosomes and genes and their behavior was made long after the death of Mendel, who was unaware of the material entities which carried his factors from one generation to another. His experiments with hawkweed and other plants were in their results baffling to the point of discouragement. What he thought were individual factors refused to split out in the same ratios as in peas.

We now know that most traits which appear to our observation as single attributes in the phenotype of an organism depend genetically upon two or more sets of genes, which sets may be in separate pairs of chromosomes. What seems a single factor is in reality a complex of factors, and the phenotypic attribute may appear only with the dominance of both or all, the recessiveness of both or all, or the dominance of one or some and the recessiveness of one or some of the members of that complex. We now know that Mendel was dealing with two or more sets of alleles in hawkweed when he believed he was dealing with a single set.

Then the presence or absence of what seems to us a single unit attribute is in reality the result of dihybrid or polyhybrid factors.

This complicates the Mendelian situation seriously. In fact, Mendel himself could not figure it out. How easy it would be for the dog breeder if there were a single set of genes which determined whether the head in his variety should be good or bad, another set which declared for or against correct fronts, another pair for correct and incorrect coat, and so through the organism. Might we not go further and wish for a single set of genes which would determine whether the whole dog should be good or bad? Of course, such a conception is preposterous.

We might wish that we could breed together Pekingese and Great Danes and be able in the second filial generation (F_2) to sort out the respective varieties in as pure a form as if the mating had never been made. To say that it is impossible is not categorically true, for once in a number of experiments, to be expressed only in some weird astronomical figure, such a phenomenon might occur. But in the next million years no dog breeder should expect to see it.

It is worthy of repetition that the breeder of dogs is dealing not with whole single organisms but with thousands of sets of reciprocal, allelic genes. Which members of any of those thousands of sets is in a dog's chromosomes may determine what he shall look like and what he may transmit to his progeny.

Whether a dog's eye shall have pigment or not, whether he shall have yellow or brown eyes, or china or wall eyes, may be due to the presence or absence of a single gene for each eye. But how deep that pigmentation may be probably depends upon which of several genes, which make for intensification of pigmentation, may be present or absent. Thus, the right member of each of several pairs of genes is probably required to produce the darkest eye color.

In fact many traits are the result of gene complexes, *i.e.*, two or more allelic pairs. Eye color appears to be the result of one major allelic pair, the "determiners," and at least three minor allelic pairs, the "modifiers."

Indeed, eye pigmentation in the dog may behave as does skin color in crosses between Negroes and whites. In that cross, there are known to be at least two sets of factors involved, the dominant genes of either of which produces dark color. When both genes for color are doubly dominant in the zygote, we have the darkest color of the pure Negro. Mulatto parents (by mulatto is meant the first cross between purebred Negro and purebred white) may then produce progeny of any of nine intensities of skin color, ranging from the darkest color of the pure Negro to the lightness of the white parents of the mulattoes. Such extreme extractives are genetically pure and will breed as true for pigmentation of skin as if there had been no introduction of the genes from the opposite race in the matings. That does not, of course, imply that such a person, purebred for skin pigmentation, would not have other attributes of the opposite race. That would be as weird as to expect

95

to sort out in the F_2 generation purebred Pekingese from the Pekingese-Great Dane cross.

In *Drosophila* alone there are at least fifty genes recognized to affect the different eye colors.

Moreover, the manifestation of an attribute in the phenotype may be due to the dominance or recessiveness of any one of several sets of genes. An instance is that there are three recognized varieties of chickens in which whiteness is due to entirely different genes.

Modifiers, which are separate genes whose results are superimposed upon specific other genes, may only intensify the effect of the primary genes (the determiners) for a given trait, or they may alter the trait completely. Such modifiers are quite inert except in the presence of the primary determiners.

There are also "supplementary factors" such as those influencing the shape of combs of fowls. To the primary genes which determine that a fowl shall have a single comb may be added either of two other genes, one of which determines that the comb shall be a rose comb, the other that it shall be a pea comb. When both the supplementary factors are present along with the factor for single comb, the fowl develops a walnut comb. Until the purity of the dominance of all of the genes for both supplementary factors is fixed through selective breeding, fowls with walnut combs are prone to produce in their progeny any of the four kinds of comb we have mentioned.

Another Mendelian surprise was the discovery of two true breeding white varieties of sweet pea which when crossed resulted in colored progeny. This phenomenon is due to the fact that color is dependent upon the dominance of *two* genes. If either is absent, white flowers result, and each of the two true breeding white varieties has within its chromosomes one of those dominants, but only one. When they are crossed, each of them contributes a dominant gene and color results.

An analogous, almost a parallel, phenomenon to the appearance of colored sweet peas from the hybridization of the two white varieties is the production of rabbits with agouti coloration from the crossing of the white Beveran rabbit with the white Polish (albino) rabbit. Each of these two varieties of white rabbits carries in the homozygous dominant form genes, both of which are necessary for the expression of agoutism, but the set of genes dominant in the white Beveran is recessive in the Polish, and vice-versa. When the two varieties are crossed, the resulting zygote is hybrid-dominant for both genes and agoutism is expressed in the phenotype.

It is as if self-colored Pekingese should result from the cross of an albino Peke with a dark-eyed, white Pekingese. The results of such an experiment should be enlightening.

Indeed, the elaborate analysis of the Mendelian factors which determine the expression of colors, markings, and coats of rabbits is amazing in its revelations. At least twenty-six pairs of genes were found which in various combinations determine the length, color, and markings of coat. (Both its complexity and length preclude its publication here, but an excellent presentation of the results is to be found in *The Mechanism of Creative Evolution* by C. C. Hurst.)

Similar extensive experiments have been made to determine the exact behavior of the Mendelian factors as they affect the expression of various lengths, textures, shape, color, and markings of the coat and skin color of the dog. This will be discussed in Chapter VII.

There are also "lethal" factors, such as the one which prevents the embryonic development of a mouse pure dominant for yellow coat color. Yellow mice never breed true for that color, which cannot be fixed. Two yellow parents, no matter how many generations of yellow in their ancestry, produce gray progeny in the approximate ratio of one gray to two yellows. The solution of the problem is that the double dose of yellow (one from each gamete), necessary for homozygous dominance of the factor, causes the death of the resultant zygote. The zygote tolerates one gene for yellow color, which produces hybrid dominance, but homozygous dominance, *i.e.*, two such genes, will result in its death.

Whether there are lethals in the dog is not yet recognized. Morgan and his associates have found some forty lethals in *Drosophila*. It certainly seems reasonable to assume that in the more complex organism of the dog there are probably many lethals or semi-lethals. If such lethals exist in the dog, they need not be discouraging since they do not preclude our producing what we want except in its pure, homozygous, breeding form. It is even more likely that the lethals do not affect those traits for which selection is made in the officially recognized breeds of dogs. Most lethal or semi-lethal traits are deleterious to the organism.

The influence of the sex hormones from the gonads of the male animal upon some Mendelian traits is most interesting, as, for example, the matter of horned and hornless sheep. Both sexes of Dorset sheep have horns; of Suffolk sheep, both sexes are hornless. In the progeny of the first cross of the Dorset with Suffolk sheep, the males only are horned, the females hornless. In the F_2 generation, which results from breeding a horned, crossbred ram to a hornless, crossbred ewe, 75% of the males and 25% of the females are horned, the other 25% of the males and 75% of the females are hornless.

By way of explanation, it requires both genes of the pair in the zygote to produce a horned female, whereas a single gene of the pair, reinforced by the male hormone, will produce horns in the hybrid dominant male. The horned females and hornless males are respectively recessives and pure dominants. Of the horned males in the F_2 generation, $33\frac{1}{3}\%$ (*i.e.*, 25% of the entire generation, horned and hornless) are pure dominants, $66\frac{2}{3}\%$ are hybrid dominants. So of the hornless females in the F_2 generation, one-third are pure recessives and two-thirds are hybrid dominant. Thus they segregate into the expected Mendelian ratio for a single pair of factors.

In the various breeds of purebred dogs, except for somewhat greater average size in the males, and for a general masculinity of character, expression, and type in the male as opposed to femininity in the female, there are no recognized secondary sex characters. And so, such Mendelian manifestations as horns and absence of horns in sheep, baldness and haired scalp in man, beards and beardlessness, need not be sought and do not require to be avoided. The standards of the recognized breeds of dogs are the same for male and female, except that in a few of them allowance is made for difference in that well-nigh indefinable thing called sex-character.

Indeed, many of the phenomena here cited, at first consideration, have nothing to do with dogs. Since, however, the dog is an expression of a constellation of Mendelian factors, the breeding of dogs is the combination and recombination of such factors. It, therefore, is worth our while to consider the behavior of the genes in their Mendelian segregation somewhat more elaborately than merely to describe Mendelism in its simplicity as Mendel knew it.

To go into the details of what has been learned about Mendelian expression by the many workers in the science of genetics since the rediscovery of Mendel's laws would require a library of volumes of this size. These few references to the complexity of the behavior of the genes will demonstrate in part that many phenomena of inheritance, which upon superficial examination seem not to be Mendelian at all, upon careful analysis are seen to observe the Mendelian laws as categorically as Mendel's own garden peas did.

Especially must we take cognizance that a trait may appear to manifest itself as a single entity, though it may be in fact due to a complex of allelic genes. For the simplification of our task of breeding dogs, we might desire that a single gene should determine what we chose to denote as a single trait. Indeed, the great value of Mendelism in its entirety is that it brings us an understanding of the fact that most of the traits of our dogs which we look upon as units are genetically analyzable into groups of factors, all of which must, willy-nilly, be taken into account in our efforts toward the improvement of any breed of dogs.

The intelligent breeding of dogs is not all beer and skittles.

Good results are sometimes obtained by ignorant breeders through luck, persistent trial and error, main force and awkwardness; but a fickle fortune is liable to withhold her largesse from such a one at any time. The knowledge of the immutable laws is the safest guide for the breeder of animals. That the laws are somewhat complex in their application adds at once to the difficulty of breeding toward a definite ideal and to our delight when we approach that ideal. Good dogs would be good friends of men though they were easy to come by, but the difficulties and complexities of breeding them add to the joy of achieving them. Mendelism is the law which governs heredity and the breeder can violate it only at the price of his strain.

Mendel no more than found the end of the yarn in the vast tangled skein of heredity. It has remained for the twentieth century geneticists to straighten the snarls, loose the knots, and bring order from the confusion of that interminable complexity. Every new yard which is untangled and added to the orderly wound ball of knowledge, every new discovery in the genetic realm, tends to confirm the now accepted belief that the whole skein of heredity is of but a single thread and that the Mendelian factors determine every aspect of every organism. In Mendelism lies the whole secret of the breeding of better dogs. How the knowledge of the Mendelian laws may serve us to that end is discussed in the ensuing chapter, "The Implications of Mendelism."

CHAPTER VII

The Implications of Mendelism

Even if one does not discredit the Mendelian findings of heredity, even if one accepts them and assumes their truth, how may the knowledge be applied, how may it guide a practical breeder to the production of better dogs?

The theory of the chromosomes and genes, the Mendelian laws, the results of the twentieth century work that has been based upon those laws; none of these require further proof. They are not the imaginary figments of a cult, not mere hypotheses to explain the mysteries of life, not esoteric superstitions. They are scientific facts, fully accepted by every biologist worthy of the name everywhere, Soviet geneticists to the contrary notwithstanding.

They fit together almost too neatly, these facts, like the pieces of a jigsaw puzzle. They are so pat and so orderly that they are difficult to credit.

We have been accustomed to think of heredity as something fortuitous in its behavior. "Like begets like," we believed. "Like father, like son," we said, except that no son is exactly like any father—or mother either—for that matter. When like failed to beget like, it seemed that something was wrong. But what was wrong we did not know. Empirically, we bred together male and female most nearly approaching as individuals the ideal we desired in the progeny, and then trusted to luck.

In the face of a thousand observations of progeny which is much unlike its parents, we are still prone to parrot "like begets like." We see an agouti rabbit from two white parents; we see a smooth Fox Terrier in a litter of wire Fox Terriers of which we know the pedigree and that the parents and grandparents and great grandparents have been rough for generations. We are disgusted to find a "splash" in a litter of Boston Terriers of well marked ancestry; and yet we insist that "like begets like." We shrug our shoulders and mutter, "reversion, atavism —a throw back," without knowing what we mean.

And what is this reversion, this atavism? What is this "throw back"? Mendelism gives us our answer, as we shall see.

That early breeder who first uttered the dictum that "like begets like" was simply talking because he thought he had to say something. He observed that animals sometimes looked much like one of the parents, often looked somewhat like both the parents, and blurted out the false law. Perhaps because it sounded well, because the words had a nice epigrammatic finality, or, perhaps, because if it were only true it would solve all of our breeding problems, we accepted as law this glib aphorism of wishful thinking as if it had been engraved on tablets of stone and brought down to us from Sinai. Generations of breeders of animals have uncritically parroted "like begets like." "Like father, like son."

But does like beget like?

As the statement has been made and acted upon through the years since its acceptance by breeders, it is one of those half truths which are more harmful than good, outright, honest lies which can be nailed and stricken from the record. That like organisms always produce like progeny is simply not true. To modify the statement and say that like organisms *tend* to produce similar progeny takes from the maxim all of its finality and certitude, leaving us nothing for practical use.

The early promulgators of the "like begets like" idea knew nothing of Mendelism and less of the genes. The "like begets like" idea is much older than the modern science of genetics. What was meant is that animals look like their parents and grandparents. They do, sometimes, *resemble* them.

102

When the "like begets like" theory, however, is applied to the genes, it becomes true. Like organisms do not of necessity beget like organisms. Like dogs do not beget like dogs. *Like genes do produce like genes. And like complexes of genes find like expression in the organism,* be that organism a garden pea, a vinegar fly, or a *Homo sapiens*—a *Homo sapiens* insapient enough, in the face of ocular evidence that like often begets difference, to continue to cry that like begets like.

Mendelism proves that the breeder is matching and balancing genes, not merely mating dogs and bitches. It reduces the operation to its smallest factors. Using those gene factors as stones, the breeder builds the mosaic of the new organism.

Fortunately, or unfortunately, in any single mating he must choose and utilize two animals only as the carriers of the genes he wants. He cannot choose genes for one kind of head from one dog, genes for a given kind of tail from another, genes for correct front from a third, and genes for a particular kind of coat from a fourth. He must, perforce, select two dogs for mates whose germ plasms he believes to include the genes he chooses to perpetuate. If he wishes to introduce genes from another dog, he is compelled to wait for another generation.

And yet, utilizing the genes from a single pair of dogs, he is considering those genes as derived from all their line of ancestry. Mendelism throws another spotlight on the significance of the pedigree. The pedigree becomes to us a guide as to what genes may lurk hidden and unexpressed in these dogs whose genes we are about to unite.

When an attribute not present in either parent appears in the progeny we call it a "throw back," or atavism or reversion, recognizing perhaps that it is a "throw back" to some ancestor identified in the pedigree. But have we stopped to consider what atavism is? Except for Mendelism, it has no explanation. Have we not been given to the fatalistic acceptance of the phenomenon as some trick of a joke-loving Providence? It is no such thing. It is rather the working of immutable law. The genes which determine its expression lay hidden in the parents and, when those genes are brought together in the right combination, the atavistic attribute finds its expression in the progeny.

It may be that it is a mere recessive trait which has lurked hidden in hybrid dominance in the parents. We know that, except for sex-linked traits, it requires a pair of recessive genes for the expression of a recessive factor. Each of the hybrid dominant parents contributes one recessive gene of the pair, and the recessive trait in the phenotype results: a wall eye from dark-eyed parents, or a smooth coat from wire-haired parents. Such an attribute may lie buried for fifty generations and finally come to the surface of expression in the phenotype. Mendelism shows us how and why. The longer the recessive gene is buried, the less the likelihood of its appearance. We know that this is true because it is impossible for a recessive trait to manifest itself in the phenotype of an organism of which even one parent is a pure dominant for the set of genes of which the recessive trait under consideration is one of the alleles. If both parents are hybrid dominants for the particular set of genes, then there is a three-to-one chance for the appearance of the trait if it be a dominant, a 25-75 chance if it be a recessive.

We shall see in Chapter X, "Inbreeding, Line Breeding, and Outbreeding," how consanguineous breeding serves as a sieve in which to catch such recessives. They may slip through our sieve in combination with dominants, but when two genes for a recessive factor come together they will not go through the mesh and the breeder can nab them and do with them as he sees fit. If the genes are undesirable, he can then gradually cast them out of his stock until he has animals which are pure dominants for those factors, in which case their recessive expression will never occur again. Or, if the traits are desirable, he can hold onto them and perpetuate them with almost absolute certainty.

These so-called atavisms, on the other hand, may not be recessives. They may be hybrid dominants between two sets of factors, of which one dominant gene from each member is requisite for the expression of the atavistic trait. Recall the

104

origin of the agouti rabbit from the crossing of two distinct and different varieties, the white Polish albino and the white Beveran with dark eyes.

Such a trait, however desirable it may be, will fail to breed entirely true when mated to its like, for it will tend to split out the parental types in approximately 50% of its immediate offspring. The parental types, though, when crossed will continue to produce the trait under consideration.

And even if undesirable in itself, such an atavistic animal need not be a complete loss for breeding. If it has some other traits which one wishes to conserve, a cross with the desired parental type should in 50% of the progeny get rid of the undesirable atavism forever and may add the other traits which it is wished to conserve.

But in any event, Mendelism takes the fatalism out of breeding. "As ye sow, so also shall ye reap," remains as true as ever and even more apparent. But we must remember that we are sowing genes, not whole dogs. It is, however, very easy to sow unawares some genes we do not want to reap, hidden and buried underneath others which we do wish to reproduce. An intelligent analysis of the pedigrees of our animals reveals the source of such buried genes and we can make up our minds whether we shall utilize an animal for his genetic virtues or discard him for the faults that we know to be a part of his heritage.

Mendelism enables us to evaluate an animal not for what he is but for what he will produce. It explains why of two litter brothers, equally good looking, one may be a potent force for the betterment of his breed and the other may be utterly worthless to improve his line.

This is not, of course, usually the case, for the desirable animal is usually the one which produces desirable progeny. The genotype expresses itself very largely in the phenotype, and the experienced breeder can hazard an at least partially valid opinion about what kind of progeny an animal should produce merely from an examination of the animal.

If this were not true, the whole scheme of artificial selection would be invalid and our fine breeds of domestic livestock could never have been developed and improved by that empiric method. Merely by weeding out the worst and breeding from the best, nineteenth century breeders, and earlier ones, endowed our century with all of our true breeding varieties. There is no gainsaying that the method, however crude and empiric it may be, accomplishes the end in view. Indeed, the general run of present day breeders continues to employ that method, and if all could be induced to employ it consistently, if all could be deterred from breeding from the undesirable, the improvement of the breeds would gather an increased momentum. But Mendelism gives us the clue to a better method.

More artificial selection of phenotypes was all the technique which the breeders had, all that most contemporary breeders employ. Mendelism enables us to select the genotype. Why should we rub two sticks together to obtain fire (although there is no doubt that such friction will produce fire) when we have matches and cigarette lighters? Why waste the time and effort which might be devoted to getting warm?

These earlier breeders did not, and most current breeders do not, recognize the difference between genotype and phenotype. That the genotype to a large degree determines the phenotype is all that has made possible the progress that has been made. But how much of the best germ plasm has been lost because its carriers were not typical specimens of their breeds, and how much bad germ plasm has been perpetuated because its carriers have satisfied a breeder's eye, we shall never be able to estimate. It is only because good animals carry more good germ plasm than do bad animals that progress has been possible.

That one can no more determine from looking at it what kind of progeny an organism will produce than one can determine by looking at a frog how far he will jump, is illustrated by the well known work of East and Jones with Indian corn. This work has gone far and will go further to revolutionize and increase the acreage yield and the quality of that crop.

East and Jones chose two fine strains of corn. For twelve generations they forced these strains to self-fertilization, keeping the two strains separate. This will be recognized as the closest sort of inbreeding. All sorts or undesirable recessive traits appeared and were eliminated. The strains were permitted to degenerate as they would, except for the elimination of these undesirable recessives. At the end of the twelve generations, when degeneration seemed to have ceased and no further recessives appeared, the two inbred lines were hybridized. Immediately, in the first hybrid generation arose corn which was surprisingly superior, not only to the degenerated, inbred parents but to either of the two excellent strains with which the experiment was begun.

This superior hybrid corn is not yet a true breeding variety, being but hybrid dominant as to most of its sets of genes. It is only the first cross of the two degenerate strains which results in the superior corn and generations of self-fertilization and careful artificial selection will be required to so eliminate the reversion to the degenerate ancestry and produce a true breeding variety.

The experiment with corn is cited here only to show that the genetic possibilities of the organism cannot be accurately surmised from the phenotype. No intelligent, practical farmer would have planted the seed from those degenerate ears of corn in expectation of a bumper crop. The fine corn to be derived from the degenerated strains could no more have been guessed from their appearance, without consideration of their ancestry, than could agouti coloration have been expected in the progeny of the two varieties of white rabbits. So with a dog—the phenotype may not reveal the genotype.

It should be needless to say that the reader is not to accept the mention of that experiment as an encouragement to dispense with artificial selection or to include degenerate or atypical dogs in his breeding program. However, a good dog is not to be discarded because of a single fault without consideration of whether it is one that is likely to reproduce itself. And no

107

matter how excellent a dog may be, if it fails consistently to produce desirable progeny when discriminately mated, it should be discarded for breeding and in its place substituted even a poor dog provided that it produces better puppies.

One can be guided by three considerations in choosing a dog or bitch for breeding. First, is what is the dog like itself, how nearly it approaches the breeder's ideal of that breed and how far and in what manner it falls short of that ideal. Second, its ancestry must be considered, its pedigree analyzed to ascertain what excellencies and what faults it may have derived from which of its parents and grandparents. Third, and perhaps most important of all, one should ascertain what kind of puppies it produces when adequately mated. This last is not always possible with a young dog, and especially with a young bitch, and it is often necessary to make one's own tests of the animal's ability to transmit the typical virtues of its variety.

However, the observation of a very few litters from a dog or bitch, with a consideration of the mate and of the mate's pedigree, will reveal with what consistency it tends to produce good progeny. And dogs do tend to produce progeny with an approximation to a given excellence of type with much greater consistency than is usually believed.

Mendelism explains that consistency. If, for a given set of genes, a dog is a pure dominant, it will transmit a dominant gene of that pair to every gamete it produces. If the dog is a hybrid dominant male, then for a given set of genes it casts the dominant member of the set to half its sperm and the recessive member of the set to the other half. If a bitch, there is an equal chance of which member remains in any ovum. If the dog is recessive for any set of genes, every haploid set of chromosomes will contain one of those recessive genes, although it cannot find expression in the immediate progeny unless it find its gametic mate in the other haploid set of the zygote.

Much time, effort, and labor of love is lost in trifling along with dogs which somehow ought to produce good puppies but equally, somehow, fail to do so. While sometimes such a one will at long last "kick through" with a paragon of excellence, the chances are that if after being given adequate opportunities it fails to give one what one wants, it will be rather consistently a producer of indifferent stock, and it is wise to replace it in the breeding program with another known or believed to produce consistently well.

All of which brings us to the very heart of the mystery—the prepotent individual.

The individual dog or bitch prepotent to produce high excellence in its progeny is the greatest asset the breeder of dogs can possess. From such a prepotent individual the strain can be developed and maintained. If it be a bitch, so much the better, for the services of a dog of recognized prepotency can be obtained to mate with it and it is worth sending to the ends of the earth to find for it the right partner.

A gem of purest ray, such a one! Flora Berkemeyer, the German Shepherd dog bitch, Annie Laurie, the Scottish Terrier, Etfa von der Saalsburg, the Great Dane. What do not their breeds owe to those bitches? Those three are outstandingly famous, but every breed has many of them.

These prepotent bitches can each produce but a limited number of progeny, it is true, whereas a normal male dog can beget literally thousands of puppies if given the opportunity. But one can usually find a good producing male to mate with a good producing bitch, whereas there are not enough of these exceptional bitches to enable a much used male to maintain so high an average of excellence in its progeny.

That these prepotent dogs and bitches exist is generally recognized among breeders and is much discussed, but it is only the astute or the fortunate who take advantage of their existence. They are usually thought to be something of a mystery, to arise without cause, to spring like Athene full-panoplied from the head of Zeus.

They are no such things! They are not mysteries. They are but animals whose gametes are pure dominant or recessive for the various factors which produce the typical characters of their

109

breed. They are purebred animals in the Mendelian sense of the word "purebred." From the breeder's viewpoint, that is the only sense of the word. What does it matter if all of a dog's ancestors have been members of his variety and stud-book-registerites for however many generations if he does not register that variety's characteristics upon his progeny? Even though one of his grandparents were a mongrel, if the genes for such mongrelism did not enter his germ plasm, he is just as much a purebred example of his variety as if all of his ancestors, clear to the dog-Adam, had been of that variety.

It is alleged that there was a white Bull Terrier not very high up in the branches of the family tree of the Airedale Terrier, Elrudge Monarch. If it be true, then breeders of Airedale Terriers will wish that there were more Bull Terrier germ plasm behind some of their other dogs, for Elrudge Monarch was one of the prepotent dogs which made Airedale Terrier history. Any reasonably good bitch bred to him could be expected to have excellent progeny.

This is no plea for mongrelization of our varieties of dogs. On the other hand, it is a plea for purity of race; not merely for stud book purity, but for genetic purity, for the sorting of the genes and the retention of those which determine racial excellence and the elimination of those others which make for degeneration of type.

Stud book purity is desirable, too. But it is desirable only because it helps to establish the Mendelian purity which results in prepotence. Mendelian purity can exist without stud book purity, but it usually does not. Practically, the stud book is of the greatest value to the breeder for it is the conservator and custodian of the race's purity. Elsewhere we have seen how it would be possible, although the phenomenon has never perhaps actually occurred, that a dog could be of no kinship whatever to its own grandsire. The white genes in Elrudge Monarch are further back in the pedigree than grandfather. Furthermore, it is generally recognized that Bull Terrier blood (sic!) was used in the making of the Airedale Terrier breed, for the breeds are

110

in many respects similar. The right Bull Terrier might be expected not to prove harmful to Airedale Terrier type as it appeared a few generations later.

Credit is lent to the allegation of Elrudge Monarch and his Bull Terrier great grandfather by the fact that a son of Monarch out of Monarch's own daughter, Champion Clonmel Rough and Ready, habitually produced puppies with white feet.

How does this Mendelian purity which results in prepotency arise? It comes from a confluence of good germ plasm, from the combination of desirable genes. Usually it springs from parents and grandparents of recognized excellence and prepotency. Some few times it simply crops up from the right combination of ordinarily good type and germ plasm, even from the fortunate mixture of the good genes of parents only hybrid dominant for many of the allelic sets. In such a case, the prepotent individual is a freak, and its litter siblings may be of but mediocre merit and little breeding value. However, it is just as pure and just as potent for all time as if it were of more spectacular lineage and all its brothers were champions.

While such breeding animals may crop out from mediocre ancestry, such freaks are rare, indeed. Even when the pedigree fails to blazon the family excellence, a close analysis will usually reveal the source of the potency. There are very likely to be great, even if obscure, dogs somewhere close behind it in the pedigree.

The great, prepotent dogs and bitches usually derive from a great line of prepotent ancestors. The converse, however, is not true, for a dog may have a spectacular pedigree and never produce a puppy worth the water to bucket him. The explanation lies in the genes.

When a prepotent individual arises in a breed, is it possible to perpetuate that prepotency in a strain? Must the breeder sit idly by and watch this prepotency dissipate itself in a generation or two? The answer is that such prepotency can be conserved and maintained from generation to generation but it seldom is.

It must be noted that a recessive gene must have a recessive

111

allelomorph in the zygote for its expression. Therefore, there can be no such matter as prepotency for recessive characters unless the other party to the mating be recessive or hybrid dominant for such characters. And if that second party be hybrid dominant, the recessive trait can find expression in but approximately half the progeny. However prepotent a dog or bitch may be, its progeny can manifest recessive characters only if the recessive gene be derived from both sides of the house.

That is not true, however, of the genes for the desirable dominant traits. They will manifest themselves in whole or in part if a single parent is pure dominant. The individual prepotent for dominant characters will stamp them upon its progeny regardless of the other parent.

And that is how prepotency is lost. The breeder, seeing an animal's consistency in transmitting excellence, depends upon that animal to such an extent that he grows careless in the choice of mates for him. A dog may stamp the excellence of its germ plasm upon its immediate progeny with great consistency and without very much consideration of the kind of mates it has, but if such progeny has received from only one of its parents the excellence it manifests, it has little prospect of transmitting that excellence to subsequent generations.

And in the mates, it is to be remembered, recessive genes may lurk in hybrid dominance.

If an equally prepotent mate is found for a prepotent dog, his prepotency can be perpetuated and all of the immediate offspring of the mating can be expected to manifest the prepotency. Prepotency is but the purity of dominance or the recessiveness of the various sets of genes. And one gene of each set is derived from each parent.

The breeder's task is to sort and re-sort the genes until he has the desirable genes in pure sets within one organism, and then not to permit their purity to disintegrate. It is simply stated and sounds easy to do but it is a task to try the ingenuity and pertinacity of the most avid breeder.

The Mendelian doctrine simplifies that task. The realization

112

that he is shuffling genes rather than mingling bloods enables the breeder to eliminate many of his false starts from his program before he has made them.

How often we see a breeder of dogs flash like a comet across the prize lists of the dog shows and after only a few years of success to fizzle into mediocrity! Prepotent strains built up either by design or good fortune are permitted to peter out, not because of the breeder's indifference but because he fails to distinguish between the phenotype and the genotype of his dogs. He permits the pure dominance of various sets of genes to become hybrid dominant, and then cannot understand why a given dog fails to produce excellence in his progeny with the consistency its sire exhibited.

The degeneration of good strains is no more a mystery than is the establishment of them and the building up of prepotence. Acquaintance with Mendelism, even the simplified exposition of it contained in this volume, gives one to know how prepotency works, how strains are built up, and how they are usually permitted to lose their individuality.

The adjective "pure" is not a comparative term. A thing is either pure or it is not pure. A dog is purebred for any set of genes if both members of the set are recessive or both dominant. One or the other may be the desired expression in the phenotype. Hybrid dominance, though it may find an expression in the phenotype similar to that of pure dominance, is not purity.

Many breeders of dogs say and believe that the more intensely a trait is bred into an animal the more sure it is to manifest itself in the immediate progeny and through the generations. This is a fallacy. If the genes necessary for the expression of that trait be pure, one from each parent (no matter whether the parents each received one from each of their parents or from only one), they cannot be more intensely carried. And a pure set of genes may be changed to hybrid dominance in one generation, and into allelic purity in two generations. Purity has to be built up. Being reached, it may not be intensified. But having been established, it requires to be maintained.

Mendelism shows us what that purity is, how attained, how perpetuated. It gives a new meaning to purity of blood. "Blood," of course, has nothing at all to do with it. It is purity of gene pairs. If we could bring ourselves to discard the term "blood" from our consideration of heredity and substitute for it "germ plasm," "chromosomes," and "genes," we could shed much of the fuzz from our thinking about the subject and reorient ourselves along the proper genetic lines.

But "blood" has been so long employed that the term is difficult to eliminate. Even when our use of it is awaredly figurative, it is confusing. The term "blood" implies blending. Until Mendelism came into being, blood was a literal term. We thought of heredity as a current of confluent bloods. Now we know that it is rather a current of sands, any white grain of which may be removed and replaced by its black allelomorph.

Excellence in breeding cannot be achieved by the effort to blend two faulty extremes to arrive at the happy mean. If a fault is to be corrected in stock it must be balanced with excellence and not with its antithetic fault. The late Jack Holgate, successful breeder of so many varieties of dogs, whose Southboro prefix was one to conjure with, pointed that out in a discussion of Fox Terrier size some forty years ago. "Don't put a big one to a little one to get the right size, because you will get big ones and little ones, not correct ones. Use the right size for one of the mates," he explained in essence. Whether Holgate knew why or whether his advice was only empiric is impossible to say. But Mendelism furnishes us, as it would have furnished him, with an adequate explanation.

If the good of Mendelism were only in the isolation of attributes which we know and recognize as due to Mendelian unit factors, it would explain little and be of little practical value. Sufficient experiments have not been made, adequate intelligent observation has not been brought into play in our dogs to enable us to recognize a great many of these unit factor traits. In each breed there are traits which the breeder should be able to label definitely as dominant or recessive.

114

Once found, the breeder should surely take advantage of his knowledge, for he can control those traits with absolute certainty. We know that wall eyes are recessive to pigmented eyes, parti-color recessive to self-color, Dudley noses recessive to black noses, congenital deafness recessive to normal hearing, red recessive to black in many breeds, and several other recessives and dominants are recognized. The value of this specific knowledge is great and data should be accumulated.

But it is not in such cut-and-dried facts that the real value of Mendelism lies. There are not yet enough of those facts to make them more than incidentally useful. One should not permit these little sapling trees of unit factors to obscure the vision of the vast forest of Mendelian phenomena.

The great good of Mendelism is in its implication, not in its hard facts. It is a key which unlocks the profound secret of heredity. It explains prepotency and atavism. It reveals why brothers may be unlike and why remote cousins may bear strong resemblance. It offers a fundamental, material basis for all the unexpected traits which crop out in our dogs and which we had hitherto deemed merely fortuitous. It codifies the immutable laws whose workings we had thought but the antics of Puckish Providence.

Practical breeders have been accustomed to scoff at Mendelism—not at the truth of it but at the possibility of its practical application. They have accepted its truth but blinked its implications. Few of them, indeed, understood what Mendelism really is. They have read brief and sketchy expositions of it but have failed to comprehend its workings. "Mendelism" has remained a mere word to them, something having to do with growing garden peas. It has seemed to them to have no more to do with better dogs than has relativity.

They have gone on the old way, their father's way and their grandfather's way, the way which has seemed to them the easy way, but is really the hard way. But the time has come when the breeders who refuse to be guided by Mendelism will be unable to compete with breeders who accept, understand, and use it.

115

The old fashioned breeders will continue to make old fashioned progress with their old fashioned selection, breeding from the apparent best and eliminating the apparent worst. But the progress they make will be in no wise comparable to that of the man who accepts and utilizes the newer knowledge. It is not that one stands still and the other moves ahead, but rather that one moves ahead so much faster than the other and at such increasing momentum that competition is impossible for him who refuses to draw on the seven league boots of modern biologic science.

The late Luther Burbank, even before the more recent work with gene complexes had been accomplished, employed the Mendelian principles and techniques in his breeding of plants. Strangely enough, Burbank did not apparently realize that he was Mendelizing. There are, no doubt, many breeders of dogs who employ the Mendelian knowledge without themselves being aware that they are doing so. It is to be questioned that Jack Holgate had a clear idea of Mendelism when he gave sound Mendelian advice about the breeding of Fox Terriers.

The world is in the debt of Burbank for billions of dollars in the economic worth of the new varieties of plants he produced; and it is not to be gainsaid that Holgate was one of the foremost breeders of fine dogs the world has known. Using the Mendelian principles unconsciously, they made vast progress. Today they would use those principles consciously and persistently, else they would lag in the arts in which they had led.

By means of Mendelism, a virtue which characterizes one strain may be added to a strain which lacks it without sacrifice of virtues already possessed.

In the plant breeding world this is a recognized procedure. Sir Rowland Biffen, using Mendelian principles deliberately, bred the two now most grown varieties of wheat to order. The Dutch government in 1921 undertook to produce a new disease-resistant sugar cane for growing in Java. By 1924 the new variety was ready and now two-thirds of the cane grown in that island is of the improved variety. This, too, was deliberate, conscious Mendelization.

But it will not succeed with dogs? As early as 1828, thirty-eight years before Mendel published his experiments, Good-lake's *Courser's Manual* contained an account of Lord Orford's introduction of Bulldog blood into the Greyhound to improve the courage of that breed, after which he bred the hybrid back and back and back to purebred Greyhounds, retaining the Greyhound type but including Bulldog tenacity. This was a thoroughly Mendelian procedure, even though it anticipated the recognition of the Mendelian laws. *Stonehenge on the Dog,* published in 1859, included illustrations of dogs used in another, similar breeding experiment by one Sergeant-Major Hanley.

It is well recognized that in the nineteenth century Russian Wolfhound infusion was used to refine the skull of the Collie, that the English Foxhound was used to improve the stamina and olfactories of the Pointer, that the long-haired Dachshund was the result of crosses with Cocker Spaniels.

While the breeders who used such drastic means as the crossing of two unlike breeds to obtain a single quality for the improvement of one of them did not possess the label of Mendelism to attach to their technique, yet the genes behaved just as the same genes would have done after the new laws had been discovered. Had those breeders possessed the knowledge we now have, they might have undertaken their work with greater surety and accomplished it in less time and with better results.

It is not here advocated that crosses outside the various breeds of dogs be made for their improvement. Such cross-breeding is not now necessary. These instances are cited merely to show that Mendelian principles can be applied to the breeding of dogs, even to the extent of crossing of varieties and eliminating all of the foreign genes excepting those which produce the expression of traits for which the cross is made.

If breeds may be improved by crossing, so can strains within the breeds and the virtues of one strain annexed to another.

Indeed, every improvement in any breed that has ever been

117

made has been due to the favorable Mendelian behavior of the genes. Every degeneration has been due to unfavorable behavior of the genes. With a sound knowledge of Mendelism, it is possible so to sort the genes that improvement is constant. Much trial and error can be eliminated. The improvement can go always forward.

One objection which may be offered to the extensive employment of Mendelism is that its utilization requires a vast kennel of dogs and many generations to obtain favorable results. Such an objection is not a valid one.

It is true that in the breeding of plants selection can be made from large numbers of experimental organisms. This is essential in the radical out-crosses that are made. In the crossing of breeds of dogs, such as we have here discussed, larger numbers might have hastened the results.

However, in working with purebred stock of a single breed, when desirable qualities have been obtained and fixed in their purity, a single pair of animals only is required for the maintenance of that genetic purity. The extensive breeder can continue the old haphazard breeding, selecting the good stock when it occurs, ignoring the wasters that arise. The small breeder, by utilizing modern knowledge, can eliminate entirely from his breeding stock the producers of merely mediocre progeny, and can, by concentrating his efforts upon stock of tested breeding worth, produce a very high percentage of dogs of great excellence.

There are and have always been many small kennels which turn out excellent puppies with a consistency seldom known in the larger establishments. A conscious application of Mendelism should not destroy that consistency, but rather should increase it. It will enable the small breeder as well as the large breeder to make his matings with an assurance and confidence, with a efiniteness of the end in view, with an absence of guess-work ..nich were hitherto impossible.

It makes possible the formulation of a program of breeding for several generations in advance. Such a program may include

118

the utilization of dogs whose grandparents are yet unborn. It facilitates a planned genetic economy.

To the objection that the employment of the knowledge gained from science changes the breeding of dogs from a creative art to an exact science, the rejoinder is that the more is the pity it does not do such a thing. In that far-off millennium when we shall have a complete map of the genes of the thirty-nine haploid chromosomes of the dog, we many consider dog breeding an exact science.

Meanwhile, it must remain an art to which we may apply what scientific knowledge we may possess or be able to obtain. Is the *Sistine Madonna* a better picture because Raphael did not know enough of chemistry to use pigments which would not alter in four hundred years? Windsor and Newton make better pigments than Raphael used, but we have no Raphael to put them on the canvas with his genius. The chemistry of paint has not removed the artistry from painting. On the other hand, it has facilitated what artistry exists.

And so the knowledge of the genes and chromosomes would no more destroy the breeder's art, as an art, than the knowledge of atoms and molecules would destroy the painter's art.

By the ideals he formulates, and by the approximation of the dogs he produces to those ideals, the breeder of dogs expresses his personality. This self-expression, like any other, is art. The breeding of dogs has not been and cannot be reduced to a formula. The Mendelian laws and the later knowledge based on them do not make for any such formalization of procedure. They but clear the way for the realization of such ideals of their respective varieties toward which the breeder chooses to work.

The implications of Mendelism in dog breeding can only be partially stated. Every breeder who recognizes its value and seeks to comprehend it and to utilize it will read into it implications of his own. It will lift veil after veil, open up horizon after horizon, until the mirage of perfection seems within his grasp.

It is an inescapable law. Used, it will lead to better dogs. Abused, it will wreck any strain.

Spermatogonia

Spermatids

Oögonia

The Chromosomes of the Dog (after Osmaa Minouchi, as published in Japanese Journal of Zoology, Number 1—1927).

Oögonia—76 autosomes plus 2 X Chromosomes.

Spermatogonia—76 autosomes plus one X and one Y Chromosome.

Spermatids—38 plus X; and 38 plus Y.

CHAPTER VIII

The Determination of Sex

Breeders of dogs would like to have a method by which they could so influence the sex of the puppies whelped by their bitches that they should be able to obtain within the litter a preponderance or a totality of the sex preferred. Such a method has not yet been developed. It is entirely within the realm of possibility that at some future date animal breeders will be able to produce only males or only females, as they choose, from any mating. That time is not yet.

Various methods of influencing sex are recommended; none so far developed is of any practical worth. They are in their essence superstitions and old-wives' tales. One or another of them may have within it a germ of truth, which may in time lead to a means of producing puppies of the sex we may want.

Among the methods suggested is the one of breeding the bitch early in the period of heat to produce female progeny, late in her heat to produce male progeny. Such a method is efficient just about fifty percent of the time, which only means that it does not work at all since approximately half the dogs born are of one sex and half of the other, even without any effort to influence their sex. This method, or perhaps its reverse, was recommended by so intelligent an author as Axtell in his *The Boston Terrier*, which appeared about a quarter century ago, along with much other now discredited hocus-pocus.

And yet by forcing a female frog to retain her eggs for three or four days after they are fully ripe, it has been possible to

121

produce from them when fertilized some ninety to one hundred percent of males instead of the usual approximately fifty percent. This might by analogy lead to credence that late breeding tends to produce males.

It may be that very ripe or over-ripe ova are more penetrable by the male producing sperm than are less ripe ones. Out of such a hypothesis might possibly grow a method of influencing sex. Meanwhile, the theory is just a little worse than useless, inasmuch as it tends to complicate the breeding problem and produces no practical results.

Another of the superstitions is that a female well nourished during pregnancy tends to produce a preponderance of females; an ill-nourished female, to produce a preponderance of males. If the theory had any validity at all, the results would be reversed because the male foetus is less viable than the female and would be more likely to succumb to malnutrition. If such a method were efficient at all, it would exercise a selective tendency by destroying the foetuses of the weaker sex, and the resultant preponderance of the stronger sex would be due to fewer (and only the stronger) foetuses reaching their full development. The same result could be more sanely attained by destroying at birth puppies of the unwanted sex.

The sex of the puppy is determined at its conception and cannot be altered thereafter. When the ovum and sperm, each with its haploid set of chromosomes, unite to form the zygote, with its diploid set of chromosomes, the die of sex is cast. Just how and why that is true, we shall set forth here as simply as may be.

Each diploid set of chromosomes contains one pair which are known as the sex chromosomes. As we shall see, this pair is homologous in the female and non-homologous in the male. In the cells of the bitch before reduction division, the two sex chromosomes are alike, the *X-chromosomes*. In the cells of the male dog before reduction division, the sex chromosomes are different one from the other, one of the two being an X-chromosome and the other being a *Y-chromosome,* smaller in size and different in shape from the X-chromosome.

In the reduction of the female germ cell from the diploid to the haploid chromosome count, it will be remembered that one of each pair of chromosomes is retained in the ovum. Therefore, each ovum has one X sex chromosome in its haploid set.

In the first reduction division of the male germ cell (the primary spermatocyte) to form the secondary spermatocytes, which again in turn divide by mitosis to form spermatids, the X sex chromosome goes into the haploid set of one secondary spermatocyte and the Y sex chromosome goes into the haploid set of the other spermatocyte. Thus of the billions of spermatozoa which are produced in the testes of a dog in his lifetime, exactly half of them contain one X sex chromosome to each spermatozoön, and the other half contains one Y sex chromosome to each spermatozoön.

Since the ova all contain one X, and since 50% of the sperm each contain one X, and the other 50% of the sperm each contain one Y, when an ovum is fertilized by a sperm to form the zygote it must contain either two X's or one X and one Y. If it contains one sex chromosome of each kind, an X and a Y, the puppy will be male. If the diploid set of chromosomes in the zygote contains two X sex chromosomes, the resultant puppy will be female.

(The phenomenon of sex determination is here described as it pertains to the dog, although the process is the same in most mammals, including man, and in many other animals, among them our friend *Drosophila.* In many birds and moths, the process is reversed, the sperm all having like chromosomes and the ovum at its reduction keeping one of the alternates of the pair. In some species, the Y chromosome does not exist at all, one haploid set after reduction in the male containing one X chromosome, the other set containing no sex chromosome at all. The results, however, are approximately the same.)

Since the male produces X and Y bearing sperm in equal numbers, the theoretical probability that the ovum will be fertilized by an X-bearing sperm is equal to the probability that it will be fertilized by a Y-bearing sperm.

In man, for whom we have more accurate statistical data than for the other animals, it appears that more ova are fertilized by Y-bearing (male) sperm than by X-bearing (female) sperm. This, despite that the numbers of sperm produced of each kind are exactly equal. It is reasoned that the Y-bearers are perhaps more agile, with less density, and therefore find their way into the oviducts in greater numbers, or that the ova are less resistant to their penetration. At any rate, a few more boys than girls are born.

However, it is also known that more male foetuses die and are aborted than female, that more males die at birth, and that more die in the early part of life. A somewhat greater percentage of males are born alive than females; but, in man, the proportion of sexes is reversed by the larger survival of the females. In fact in man, the number of males dying in the first seventy-two hours of life is twice that of the females for the same period.

All of these facts appear to hold good for most mammals and, except the last fact, for the dog. However, in the dog under domestication, except in the best purebred strains where bitches are considered for their breeding value, the preference for males is so great that better care is given them as a lot and more males reach maturity than females. A census of the domestic canine population would doubtless show a great preponderance of adult males over adult females. This is due, if not to direct female infanticide, to neglect of the young of the troublesome sex.

From the time of conception until late in life the male is less resistant to unfavorable elements in the environment, is, indeed, the weaker sex.

The X-Y combination, while somewhat more frequent, is not so conducive to the stamina of the zygote as is the combination of X-X. The result is that, while slightly more males are born than females, yet the greater resistance of females to unfavorable environment tends to balance the sexes numerically. In the domestic dog, preference for males as pets prompts owners to offer better protection and care to them, and weighs the numerical balance.

For practical purposes, the breeder may well assume that, while his bitches may produce some litters preponderantly or wholly of one sex, in the long run, when the average of a great many litters is taken, it will be found that the sexes are of approximately equal numbers. There is, furthermore, as yet no practical method known by which that ratio may be altered.

The sperm which carries the Y chromosome is smaller than the sperm which carries the X chromosome. This smaller size is sometimes put forward as a possible reason for the greater agility or better ability to penetrate the covering of the ovum, or both, which would result in a greater number of males being conceived. However, it does not seem possible that such is the case, for if the sperm had any such positive advantage we would be forced then to explain how *any* X-bearing sperm preceded any Y-bearing in the fertilization of the ova. Without wishing to labor the point, there is no question that the Y-bearing sperm have a *slight* advantage. However, such a small advantage is more likely to be due to the receptivity of the ovum membrane with respect to X and Y sperm than to any size, agility, or density of the sperm.

The recognition of the difference, minute as it is, in the size and density of the two chromosomes and of the sperm which carry them, has led to a method of separating the Y-bearing sperm from the X-bearing sperm by centrifuging the semen. Unfortunately, the sperm, though separated, are killed in the process. If after such a separation live sperm were available the breeder could use only the sperm to produce whichever sex he might choose in any mating and thus it would be possible for him to produce males or females at will. Such a method would, of course, require artificial insemination, which we already know to be practically possible.

Genetic workers for the Soviet government have brought

125

about the segregation of the two kinds of sperm by use of an electric field but, again, at the cost of killing all of the sperm.

A process to influence sex at conception would be a boon to breeders of all kinds of domestic livestock and would assume great economic importance. It is, of course, to be feared that short-sighted greed might prompt breeders to the production of animals of only the more marketable sex, which would result in a dearth of good breeding animals of the alternate sex. Unless wisely used, it might bring about deterioration rather than improvement of the breeds.

While we are not as yet able to alter the ratio of the sexes, we may calculate that over a long period a group of dogs will turn out approximately the same number of puppies of each sex, with a slight tendency toward a preponderance of males.

We often see a statement that a given male dog sires numerically large litters in which males greatly preponderate. The implication is that the male at least in part determines the number of puppies in the litter and how the litter shall be divided as to sex. We know, and know why, such claims for a dog are specious. We know that the size of the litter is entirely dependent upon the number of ova deposited in the oviducts which are fertilized and develop. (A single ovum may rarely produce identical twins.) And we know that if a male dog deposits enough live and viable sperm to fertilize one ovum, he deposits enough to fertilize a thousand or a million ova. We also know that while the sex of the zygote hinges upon which kind of sperm, X-bearing or Y-bearing, fertilized the egg, the numbers of each kind of sperm are the same, and which kind shall fertilize any given ovum, or the proportions of which kind shall fertilize any set of ova, is a purely fortuitous matter. Therefore, provided that it is producing live and vigorous sperm at all, neither the number of puppies in the litter nor the proportion of the sexes is determined by the sire.

We have said that the sex of the zygote is determined at time of conception by which kind of sex chromosome is carried by the fertilizing spermatozoön. While that is true, it is necessary to

126

say that in the very earliest stages of the embryo, sex does not yet manifest itself. It is, so to speak, on the fence and the sex chromosome in the sperm seems to topple it toward maleness or femaleness.

The early embryo contains the potentialities for either sex, and, indeed, the developed organism, of whichever sex it may be, harbors within itself in vestigial and miniature form the sexual organs of the opposite sex. The early embryo is hermaphroditic and the sex chromosomes determine which sex shall develop.

Thus we see that sex is essentially a Mendelian factor, determined by the sex chromosomes and the genes within them. The female is homozygous for sex, with two X-chromosomes in the zygote. The male is heterozygous for sex, with an X and a Y chromosome in the zygote.

Gynanders, organisms in which one part of the body is of a different sex from the rest of the body, occur among insects but are not known in dogs. Hermaphrodites and intersexes occur in dogs so rarely that no cognizance need be taken of such conditions by the practical breeder. In them the sex chromosomes have gone, somehow, astray. It should be needless to say that if such monstrosities are permitted to survive, they should not be used for breeding, even in such cases as it might be possible to do so.

There are no recognized, specifically sex-limited characteristics in the dog, such as antlers, beards, crests, and manes, which appertain to one sex alone and are known as the secondary sex characters. Of course, the primary sex characters, the genitalia themselves and the developed mammaries of the female, are sex-limited, but they are a part of sex itself.

The so-called sex-limited traits, secondary sex traits, are governed largely or entirely by the hormones secreted by the gonads, which is indicated by the inhibition of their development by early castration.

While there are no specifically sex-limited, secondary sex traits in the dog, there is the matter of sex character, femininity

127

in the female and masculinity in the male, which the breeder must consider. Sex character (to be distinguished from secondary sex traits) is presumed to depend not entirely upon the hormones from the interstitial glands of the gonads, but also upon the hormones secreted by some of the other endocrine glands, particularly the pituitary and the adrenal cortex.

The size and functioning of such glands is a heritable matter and the sex character of breeding stock is, therefore, to be considered.

In no variety of dogs is the disparity of type between the sexes so great as to unfit either sex for the work and service for which the variety was intended or is used. In a few breeds, notably Bulldogs, French Bulldogs, and Chow Chows, the more closely the bitch approaches to the ideal of the male dog in type, outlook, and character, the better she is considered to be. In other breeds, the difference in sex character is small, a degree of daintiness, and added refinement of contour making for femininity in the bitch; an added aggressive outlook, a stallion-like carriage of neck, and a slightly greater size and substance mark the masculinity of the male. This difference is a subtle one and should result in neither weakness of the bitch, on the one hand, nor in coarseness, grossness, or commonness of the male on the other hand.

The slightly doggy bitch is usually and rightly preferred over the bitchy dog. Good judges like neither, and most expert breeders choose to use for reproductive purposes animals which approach in sex character as nearly as possible to the ideals of their sex and breed.

Sex-linked traits are not to be confused with sex-limited traits. (See the glossary if there is any doubt.)

The sex chromosomes carry more genes than merely the ones which determine sex, and it is the other genes in those chromosomes which account for the traits known as sex-linked. A sex-linked trait occurs much more frequently in one sex than in the other, but may occur in either sex. Examples are deafness in albino cats, red-green color blindness, and haemophilia in man, and some color manifestations in chickens.

There are no such sex-linked traits recognized in the dog, although there is little doubt that they exist. This interesting phenomenon of sex-linked inheritance need not concern the breeder of dogs unless he be crossing breeds for the purpose of establishing a new breed. In that case, some traits which are so deeply established in both sexes of our established breeds as not to be recognized as sex-linked may reveal themselves in their true colors.

We are already so well supplied with canine varieties that the hybridization of the established breeds for the purpose of making another breed is not to be encouraged. Therefore, there is little to be gained from any discussion of sex-linkage here, except to warn against confusion of it with sex-limitation. The breeder who desires more information upon the subject can easily find it in any modern text book of genetics. While somewhat intricate in its explanation, the phenomenon is not abstruse or difficult of comprehension.

It is by means of sex that the dog reproduces its species. It is, therefore, the instrument which the breeder of dogs must manipulate to achieve his end. A knowledge of sex and its manifestations will do much to clarify his procedure. However, discussions of details which can have no practical application to the breeding of dogs are omitted here as more likely to confuse than to clarify.

The behavior of the sex chromosomes, as distinct from the other chromosomes, the autosomes, shows us that we are not able as yet to influence the sex of our puppies, and the reason why we are not. The breeder of good dogs has more to concern him than the sex of his puppies. Dogs or bitches, they are equally welcome—if only they are good enough—whichever they may be.

CHAPTER IX

Sterility, Impotence, and Cryptorchidism

Dogs, as a lot, show little variation in their sexual functions, and the breeder's difficulty in inducing them to reproduce is rare. In the event of either sterility or impotence in a dog, the counsel of a competent veterinarian is indicated. Though he may or may not be able to remedy or alleviate the condition, all such are by no means hopeless.

While the veterinarian should be consulted in such cases, the breeder should know at least enough about these phenomena to cause him to recognize them when they occur among the dogs of his kennel.

Sterility and impotence are terms that should not be confused. While both may exist in the same animal at the same time, the conditions are not identical. Sterility is the failure of either sex to produce functional gametes (sperm or ova) which are capable, when properly united with those from the other sex, of developing into living foetuses. Impotence is the inability or disinclination of the male dog to perform the act of copulation. Either state may be permanent or only temporary. With understanding and proper management, either can usually be remedied.

A bitch cannot be, in strict sense, called sterile or barren if she conceives puppies at all, even though her ova are not viable enough to permit of the development of the foetuses and the bearing of her puppies alive. A bitch who habitually aborts her puppies is no more sterile than another who habitually bears live puppies but of so frail constitutions that they die.

It is by no means easy to be sure of sterility in the bitch. What seems like sterility may so easily be something else. A mere failure, even habitual failure, to conceive does not imply sterility. If a bitch has ever been definitely known to be in whelp, barring serious illness or great general debility, she is not likely to become sterile, at least not until age puts an end to her reproductive life.

A good many bitches come regularly and normally into heat, accept the congress with the male, and yet never conceive. A breeder is likely to consider such a bitch sterile and, indeed, she may be. The opening from the vagina into the uterus may be so tightly closed that the sperm get no further than the vagina and fail of their function. The dilation of the *os uteri,* which any veterinarian will perform for one, just before breeding her will frequently enable her to conceive. If indicated, it is a simple and harmless process and is worth the trial.

Over-acidity of the vaginal and uterine tracts will often destroy the sperm before they reach the ova. Dosage of the bitch with bicarbonate of soda for a few days before breeding her, douching with a bicarbonate of soda solution, either or both, will often so overcome the acid condition as to make possible conception. These methods should be used with caution for over-alkalinity is as harmful to sperm as over-acidity.

In the male dog, sterility is a good deal easier to recognize definitely. An examination of his semen under the microscope will reveal whether the spermatozoa are alive and active. If they are, it is to be assumed that sterility does not exist.

However, a dog who fails to prove fertile after being bred to several bitches known consistently to produce, even though the dog has been recognized as previously fertile, should be removed from public stud until the reasons for his failure are established and his fertility is not open to doubt. To accept bitches for breeding to a sterile dog is to rob their owners of more than the money paid for the breeding fee; it is to waste the valuable time of the bitch which might be spent in producing puppies by some other dog.

Permanently sterile male dogs are frequently, although not always, of an erratic and temperamental, sometimes shy, frequently vicious, nature. The converse is, however, not true, and merely a strange disposition does not, without any other reason, imply sterility. A male dog seriously lacking in masculine sex character of type and bearing is also open to suspicion of sterility unless and until his fertility is proven.

Complete castration of the male, the removal of both testes, always results in sterility, as does the spaying of the bitch if both ovaries are removed. A dog may function reproductively with a single testis as may a bitch with a single ovary.

Permanent sterility may be produced in the male by means of a very simple surgical operation in the severance of the sperm duct or the removal of a section of it. This operation is not to be confused with castration. It does not alter the dog's disposition or his amative instinct and it is difficult to detect that it has been done. In a few cases when dogs have proved fertile in one ownership only to prove sterile in another ownership, it has been suspected that dishonest vendors have had such dogs artificially sterilized to prevent the buyer from obtaining stock from the dogs.

Such suspicions are sometimes unjust. A change of environment, food, and management may render a dog sterile; or it may, without understandable cause, restore the fertility of a dog that has been temporarily sterile. In fact, it is to be recommended that a dog who habitually fails to produce with adequate opportunity have his whole environment changed, that his ration be largely of raw, lean beef, and he be exercised to the limit of his enjoyment for activity.

Neither obese nor emaciated dogs of either sex, particularly female, are fit to reproduce their kind, and often fail when it is sought to have them do so. Reduced or built up, as the case may be, to a healthy state of hard flesh, such dogs who have failed to breed satisfactorily may prove excellent breeders.

Prolonged exposure to X-radiation is known in many cases to produce sterility in either sex and a male so exposed should be tested for his fertility before being placed at public stud.

Sterility in an otherwise normal and healthy dog is difficult to understand and to overcome. There is little to be done, when one has made sure that the condition is really sterility, except to experiment in alterations of diet and living conditions.

Impotence of the male dog, while most annoying to his handler, can usually be remedied. The utmost of patience, kindness, and consideration is required in the handling of such a case. Sometimes no other remedy is necessary. If the impotence is not complete or permanent, harsh treatment and loss of temper on the part of the handler may aggravate and prolong it.

Impotence may be due to one or more of several causes and the first procedure in dealing with it is to find and remove the cause, if possible. The cause may be organic, functional, or often, merely psychic.

The sexual organs may be so malformed that copulation is impossible. Such malformation may be congenital or may result from injury. Surgery may or may not be an effective remedy.

Mere *phimosis,* a contraction of the prepuce in such a manner as not to admit of normal erection, can be easily corrected with minor surgery.

Functional impotence may result from glandular imbalance, from general debility, or from obesity, which may itself be of glandular origin. A correct and complete diet, including plenty of raw beef and milk, with systematic exercise to put the dog into the optimum of condition, will often overcome his sexual indifference. Indeed, a reluctant dog may sometimes be induced to breed by having him play violently until well tired and then, after a short rest, taken to the bitch.

It should not be expected of a dog that his sexual instinct should exhibit its strongest manifestation immediately following a heavy meal or when the animal is much fatigued. If he is at all disposed to impotence, such matters should be taken into consideration in handling him.

133

Drugs to whip up a waning or absent sex ardor should be used only with moderation and discretion. Most of the aphrodisiac drugs are deleterious, many of them positive poisons. Tincture of cantharides (Spanish fly), which is perhaps most frequently used for such purpose, is a violent irritant and can do very serious injury to the dog.

Dogs vary in their tolerance of strychnine and the correct dosage for the individual is difficult to determine. As everyone knows, it is a violent heart stimulant and dangerous poison. Caffeine is less hazardous and is sometimes useful.

Fowler's solution of arsenic, used in graduated dosage over a period of time as a systemic tonic, may serve to increase the sexual ardor of a dog. However, once used to it, a dog deprived of his arsenic is liable to deteriorate, and its use should not be begun unless it is intended to continue it.

Perhaps the least harmful of the aphrodisiac drugs and the most efficient is *hydrochlorate of yohimbin.* Why it is not better known and more used is not easy to understand. It is or once was put on the market in veterinary form under the trade name of "Vetol." Excellent results often follow its use. Daily dosage with yohimbin for a few days will sometimes enable a dog to breed who is unwilling or unable to do so without it.

The same drug can be used to induce menstruation in bitches that have skipped their season.

These drugs or any others should be given only with the advice of a competent veterinarian or by a practical dog breeder who is familiar with their dosage and with the results to be expected of them. The benefit to be derived from them may be easily cancelled out by the harm that accrues from their careless or ignorant use.

Many more cases of partial or complete impotence in dogs is of psychic rather than of physical origin. They especially demand the handler's comprehension and consideration. Gentleness in dealing with such an animal, encouragement and sympathy are the soundest treatment.

A psychically impotent dog is likely to be one of a very

134

sensitive disposition. In an early sex experience, such a dog may have been injured, punished, or even shamed to such a degree that he thereafter associated copulation with the unpleasant incident. A dog of more callous temperament would not be deterred from the manifestation of his normal, sexual instinct, but one of a more delicate nature may be rendered impotent.

Such a dog requires to be psychically reconditioned. Especially shall he not be made aware of how great a trial he is to his handler's patience. Only the gentlest treatment and kindest encouragement to breed should be given him, and he should be removed from the bitch and returned to her at frequent intervals. Alternate petting of him and of the bitch to whom it is desired to breed him may stimulate his interest in her.

A judicious use of yohimbin or other aphrodisiac drug may so increase the sexual urge as to overcome the fear which deters the dog. If he can be induced to breed to a few bitches and can so be conditioned to disassociate the sexual act with the unpleasurable experience which brought about his impotence, there is a likelihood that thereafter he will breed without urging.

True impotence seldom exists in the bitch and the word is not often correctly applied to her. Tumors or neoformations in the vagina may make copulation for her impossible or painful. Such conditions require surgical attention.

Some bitches, though organically normal and in full heat, refuse to be bred. They may flirt with the dog and encourage him, but evade coitus. Usually such bitches are virgin and their reluctance is due to fear, although there are some bitches who never recover from such fear and their handlers have difficulty with them each time that they are to be bred.

Such bitches are not impotent. Often patience, encouragement, and sympathy will induce them to accept congress with the dog. If such means do not suffice, it becomes necessary to force such a one, first making sure that there are no obstructions

135

which might cause pain or injury to her. If small, she can usually be held, supported by collar and loin. If of a large breed, it becomes necessary to muzzle her, tie her up on a very short lead, and support her under the belly to prevent her sitting down or breaking away. Care should be exercised to show her no more indignity than necessity warrants. Impatience should be concealed and the bitch should be petted and caressed. The restraint of such a bitch need be of but brief duration, for she will usually stand quietly after copulation has taken place. There is really no more pain for her than for the bitch who welcomes congress with her mate and her refusal is actuated only by unwarranted fear.

The testes are at the birth of the dog in the abdominal cavity and descend into the scrotum at a few months of age. In some dogs one or both of the testes fail to descend and the dog goes through life retaining the gonad in the abdomen. Such a condition is known as *cryptorchidism*.

When both testes are buried in the abdomen, the dog is never consistently fertile. That such animals do sometimes beget puppies is attested by the registration of their progeny in the stud book, although there are breeders who are inclined to look with suspicion on such registrations. To employ such a dog for breeding is at least hazardous and is better avoided if it be possible to obtain from another source the attributes for the sake of which one might make use of him.

When one testis has descended normally into the scrotum, one need not have the same fear of infertility. While dogs with one testicle visible in the scrotum may not exhibit quite the consistency as stock-getters as do dogs showing the normal two, the unlikelihood of their fertility is not such as to deter the breeder who wants in his puppies qualities that such a sire may bring to them.

Worse than the hazard of infertility in such a case is the hazard of introducing cryptorchidism into one's strain. Since cryptorchidism is a recognized genetic recessive factor, once introduced into the strain, there is always the probability that it will pair with another recessive of the same kind and consequently manifest itself in the phenotype.

Cryptorchidism is seen most frequently in a few breeds, notably in Bulldogs and in some of the Toys. It may be considered as a minor unsoundness when single, and as a somewhat more serious unsoundness when double. Judges of dog shows were at one time prone to assume a lenient attitude toward cryptorchidism and attach little if any penalty to it in its single form. The American Kennel Club, however, has now ruled that cryptorchidism and monorchidism are both unsoundnesses of such proportions that dogs manifesting either condition must now be disqualified from competition. Monorchidism may still not prevent a dog from being used for breeding purposes. There are cases on record in which a double cryptorchid dog has been awarded the prize for best dog of any breed in large, all-breed shows.

Sterility, impotence, refusal to breed, and cryptorchidism are comparatively rare among dogs. Such abnormalities need not confuse or deter the breeder. A cognizance of them must sometimes perforce be taken, however, and the practical breeder should be aware of their significance and of the means best employed to overcome them.

CHAPTER X

Inbreeding, Line Breeding, and Outbreeding

Among dog breeders, wherever two or three are gathered together, there is likely to arise a discussion of inbreeding, line breeding, and outbreeding and of their respective merits and dangers. When the interest is so great and the convictions are so dogmatic (no pun intended!), it is surprising that opinions are not based upon sounder information.

Some breeders outcross their dogs (or think they outcross them) through fear of the degeneracy of type that they believe results from all inbreeding. There are others who line breed (or think they do) in an effort to obtain the good results of inbreeding without assuming its alleged, and sometimes real, hazards. These men are like the Irishman who cuts off a puppy's tail a joint each day so that it will not hurt him so much as to cut it off all at once. There are yet others who, having been told that good dogs are produced by inbreeding, accept inbreeding uncritically as a matter of policy. They inbreed (and know that they inbreed) merely for inbreeding's sake. A fourth class inbreed one generation to obtain their type and outcross the two following generations to restore to their stock whatever stamina may have been lost by the inbreeding process. All of these kinds of breeders sometimes produce good dogs, despite that all of the policies and reasons for them are ill founded.

There are, of course, a few breeders who know exactly what they are doing. They inbreed when inbreeding is indicated; they line breed with a purpose; and they outcross to obtain certain characteristics which they desire to annex to their stock.

A sound working knowledge of genetics and of the theory of the genes will enable one to comprehend the reasons why inbreeding, line breeding, and outbreeding should produce their respective results. Without such knowledge, a real insight into inbreeding is impossible. The careful consideration of the various chapters on genetics which appear in the earlier part of this book, is essential to the fullest comprehension of what we say here.

It is necessary to keep in mind that the breeder is not mating dogs but is joining together sets of genes enclosed in their chromosome capsules.

We should know exactly what we mean when we speak of inbreeding, line breeding, and outbreeding. Few breeders have any clear conception of just where one leaves off and the other begins. In fact, it is impossible to make any hard and fast definition of the three terms; first, because writers have been given to differ somewhat in their application of the words, and, secondly, because a given degree of relationship between two dogs might be greater or less than the same given relationship between two other dogs. Remote cousins may be, although they are not usually, more closely related genetically than are full brother and sister, which latter is considered to be the closest possible kinship.

It is this latter fact which has caused the loose definitions of the words. An understanding of the manner in which the genes and chromosomes carry the family traits, or drop them, from generation to generation, and of genetic probabilities, permits one to see why a brother may be so much more closely related to one full sister than to another or why King George V of England was so much more like Czar Nicholas II of Russia, his first cousin, than like Kaiser Wilhelm II of Germany, also his first cousin.

Thus the matings of cousins may be close inbreeding while the mating of full brother and sister may be only line breeding. This, it is to be understood, is not usually true and is cited

139

only to show why it is impossible to declare exactly where line breeding becomes inbreeding.

Outbreeding is, literally speaking, the mating of unrelated animals. As a matter of fact, however, within any purebred variety of dogs, absolute outbreeding is all but impossible. This statement will seem a heresy and will, we hope, be challenged by many breeders. It is none the less true.

If one will examine the complete pedigrees of, let us say, the six generations of ancestors behind any two purebred dogs of any given, recognized breed, it may be asserted with confidence that one will find that the two dogs have at least one ancestor in common somewhere in the pedigrees. It is more likely that there will be several common ancestors in the six generations and that the name of one or more of them appears more than once in one or both pedigrees. An examination of their pedigrees, which included the names of the ancestors only to the great grandparental generation, may not reveal the kinship, and the breeder, in mating the purportedly unrelated dogs together, may believe that he is making an outcross.

A pedigree of twenty generations shows (with duplications) some two million ancestors; a pedigree of thirty generations shows (with duplications) more than two billion ancestors. A clerk working every day, including Sundays, and recording ten thousand names per day, would require more than five hundred years to compile such a pedigree. It is possible to produce a canine generation each year, although the average canine generation is perhaps some two to three years. Since the population of purebred dogs of all breeds of the entire world has never at any one time been a billion or even half that enormous number, it is easy to see that duplications of names would be necessary in such a pedigree. The registrations in the stud book of The American Kennel Club for all breeds of dogs have recently passed the two million mark. It is quite unnecessary to go to the pair of dogs (or was it a pair of each breed?) with which Noah herded the other animals on the Ark, to find common ancestors for any two domestic dogs.

Within every generation of every breed there are fashionable or prepotent sires which are much used and which influence the breed's destiny. Not only is it unnecessary to consider thirty generation pedigrees, each with its two billion names, but a six generation pedigree of any two contemporary dogs of the same breed will reveal the name of one or more dogs as the common ancestor of both.

Genetically, the perfect outcross would be one between two animals of the same breed, one of which was homozygous dominant for all traits and the other homozygous recessive for all traits. This kind of genetic purity does not exist in modern breeds.

It is easy, therefore, to perceive how impossible it is to make what is known as a perfect outcross within a given breed of dogs.

Elsewhere we have shown that kinship is not always genetically what it seems to be, that it is theoretically possible that even full brothers may be actually unrelated. These facts do, indeed, make outcrossing *theoretically* possible from a genetic point of view. However, if the dog breeders who utter their glib opinions and prejudices about the comparative merits of inbreeding and outbreeding have ever accepted or considered those facts, this writer is not aware of it. Outcrossing as generally discussed is the mating together of animals whose pedigrees list no ancestors in common.

Line breeding is the breeding together of animals whose kinship one to another is shown by their pedigrees to be more or less remote. Inbreeding is the breeding together of closely related mates.

Both terms are loosely used and what one breeder may consider to be rather close inbreeding, another breeder may think of only as line breeding. Matings such as brother to full sister or to half sister, parents to progeny, full uncle or aunt to niece or nephew respectively, are almost universally accepted as inbreeding. The mating together of cousins (animals with one or two grandparents in common) and of animals of more

141

remote kinship one to another, is usually considered as line breeding. What shall we say of the matings of an animal to a half-sister or half-brother of a parent, of two animals having all four grandparents in common but neither parent in common (double first cousins), of grandparent and grand-progeny.

A consideration of genetics and the genes leads to the conclusion not only that it is undesirable to draw too sharp a line of demarcation between line breeding and inbreeding, but also that such demarcation is impossible. The same relationship which may amount to mere line breeding between one pair of dogs may be intensive inbreeding between some other pair of dogs.

It is perhaps neither necessary nor desirable to abandon the terms inbreeding and outbreeding; but they do demand to be clarified and if they are to be used at all they should be used with a full awareness of their meaning.

That meaning is much deeper than anything that can be conveyed by a mere statement of the formerly recognized kinships, such as brother and sister, cousins, uncle and niece, half this and half that. In the light of biology, such kinships may mean little or may mean much.

The true relationship between animals is determined by the likeness of their chromosomes and the genes within them. When like alleles from a common ancestor come together from each gamete to form the zygote, inbreeding occurs, although the parents of that zygote may be but tenth cousins. When unlike alleles unite to form the zygote, even if the parents are full brother and sister, outbreeding occurs.

Except in identical twins, which are always of the same sex and cannot be mated together, it is for practical purposes impossible to find two dogs with all genes of identical origin; and even if such a pair were found, the reduction of the basic sex cells would not, in all likelihood, bring together in the zygote the haploid sets of chromosomes to make a diploid set (except as to the sex chromosomes) exactly like that of the parents. Such a mating, if it were possible, would be the most intensive

142

of inbreeding and would result in progeny almost exactly like the parents. Since it is not possible, the breeder who chooses to inbreed his stock intensively can approximate such matings only so far as his perception in choosing mates genetically alike, and his good fortune in the reduction of the basic sex cells will permit.

Line breeding is effective as such only insofar as it brings together in the zygote haploid sets of like genes. Inbreeding tends to bring together such like sets of genes even more than does line breeding. In its very essence, that is what inbreeding is. Line breeding, then, is only modified inbreeding, and when it serves the purpose intended it is indeed inbreeding.

Thus, the distinction between line breeding and inbreeding is a false one. If line breeding succeeds in intensifying and purifying the attributes of the line-bred strain, it is because it functions as inbreeding, and its hazards, if it accomplishes its purpose, are as great as inbreeding. If it does not succeed in intensifying and purifying the strain, and if the hazards of inbreeding are avoided, it not only is not inbreeding but, in a genetic sense, is not even line breeding.

The line breeder is like the urchin who goes to the creek the first sunshiny days of spring and is reluctant to plunge into the cold water. He splashes a foot into the stream tentatively while he stands shivering in goose-flesh on the bank. He knows that he wants to swim, yet is afraid of the coldness of the water. The inbreeder taunts that the last guy in is a sissy, and dives in. He may get cold, but he has had his swim.

In breeding, as in anything else, one cannot make an omelet without breaking some eggs.

A clear comprehension of the behavior of the chromosomes and their genes enables one to realize just how and why the results of inbreeding are what they are. Such realization is impossible without a knowledge of the gene theory. The reader who has mastered that theory can and will make his own deductions from it as to the policy of inbreeding.

Long before the genes were known, before Mendel published

his experiments and made public the laws he had discovered, inbreeding of plants and animals was practiced. Many of the plants are self-fertilized and even in the wild state are inbred from generation to generation. It is also fully recognized that animals in their breeding habits are not constrained by incest "taboos."

It may be argued that in the wild state natural selection eliminates the weak and the unfit, to which replication is to be made that in domestic strains of livestock, artificial selection, the will of the breeder, does or at least should do the same service to the species.

When, as a child, the senior author of this book read in Dr. Mill's *The Dog in Health and Disease* that statement that "he who cannot drown should not breed," it appeared to him as heartless cruelty. Now, the statement to him assumes the humane meaning which its writer intended it to convey, and to it must be added that especially ought not such a one to inbreed.

Every purebred variety of domestic livestock that we have, including all of our breeds of dogs, was produced, maintained, and developed through inbreeding. The earlier breeders who brought those varieties into being employed inbreeding empirically. It worked. They knew not why it worked. Often it failed, and they knew not why it failed.

They could make no progress without inbreeding and yet the sorry results which inbreeding often enough produced for them frightened them. They had not the theory in the light of which to analyze those results, good or bad. Our fears are all of things we do not understand. They were like children afraid of the dark.

Seeking the benefits of inbreeding, while abjuring its injuries, these early breeders invented line breeding. They, of course, did not know that line breeding, insofar as it succeeds in its purpose, is, in fact, inbreeding. They only knew that less degeneracy resulted from it, despite that improvement was likely to be less rapid. They were content to crawl ahead with line breeding rather than run forward with inbreeding, since the

144

danger of stumbling was not so great. They made haste slowly. But they were not avoiding the pitfalls as they believed they were. They were only covering up recessive faults with hybrid-dominance. The faults remained in the stock.

Degeneracy is purgation of the strain. Inbreeding brings it to the surface where it may be skimmed off and got rid of. In the long run, degeneracies are a blessing to the breeder. It is by their expression in the phenotype that they can be eliminated from the stock and its purity fixed.

When absolute outcrosses do succeed in producing typical stock, the explanation lies in the phenomenon of *heterosis*. Heterosis, the hybridization of unrelated strains or varieties, produces great vigor and stamina for a single generation in the burying of undesirable recessive factors in each line under favorable dominants from the other line. The recessives are, however, only buried, not eliminated, and may crop out alive and kicking in subsequent generations. We cannot cheat nature as easily as we think. Mules are useful animals and their stamina is proverbial. It is just as well that they are not fertile, however, because their stamina of hybridism would be lost in their progeny as it is in the progeny of such hybrids as are able to produce offspring.

The crossing of two distinct and unrelated breeds of dogs may produce mongrels of great stamina in the first generation, mongrels whose average size at maturity will be greater than the mean size of the two parents. Such mongrelism will also bury many of the traits of each breed which have been selected and preserved through many generations. In the breeding of such mongrels, either among themselves or to purebred mates of the same breed of either parent, the stamina derived from heterosis is lost and at least some of the attributes of the pure-bred lines will reappear. The stamina is for the hybrid genera-tion only, not for the strain. Any purebred attributes which are recessive are only buried and not lost, although it may re-quire many generations of selective breeding to eliminate from

145

the progeny of such mongrels all of the traits of the outcross parent.

The hybridizing of strains within a breed brings results which are in kind, even if not in degree, analogous to those which derive from the hybridization of breeds. This will be obvious if the reader will consider that a strain is simply a variety within a variety. Dogs are dogs; Foxhounds are Foxhounds, and are more or less distinct from other breeds of dogs; each of the old and long established packs of English Foxhounds constitutes a strain, the attributes of which distinguish its members from the Hounds of every other pack.

Foxhounds are cited as an example to show that strains are breeds within breeds, because the strains of Foxhounds are kept more distinct and pure than are the various strains of most other breeds of dogs. In most breeds there is a frequent crossing of strains, each of which is rendered less distinct by the addition of the germ plasm (we refrain from the temptation to say "blood" instead of "germ plasm") from another strain.

The dogs of the various packs of Foxhounds could be crossed and the progeny would be Foxhounds, but would not be distinct and pure members of the strain of either of the parent packs, would derive some attributes from each, and might, through a combination of dominant factors, manifest traits which neither parent strain was known to possess. Just as Foxhound parents of distinct strains would produce Foxhounds, so Pekingese crossed to Great Danes would produce dogs, but those dogs would be neither Pekingese nor Great Danes.

The breeds have been established through inbreeding and continuous selection toward a definite end, all of the recognized and distinct varieties having been derived from the various wild varieties in combination. So the various strains have been derived from inbreeding within varieties and the continued selection for wanted attributes.

Continued hybridization of varieties tends to bring about reversion to the mean of the race, and persistent intercrossing of distinct and unrelated breeds results in a race which approximates in its type the wild races from which the domestic varieties have been derived. The Dingo, once believed to be a wild dog indigenous to Australia, is now recognized to be a feral domestic dog which has developed a uniformity of type through the crossing and intercrossing of domestic dogs reverted to the wild, and the influence of natural selection.

As the crossing of varieties tends to cause the progeny to revert to the mean of the races, so the crossing of strains tends to produce a reversion to the stock from which the separate strains have developed and to result in mediocrity.

This is not intended to imply that strains should never be crossed. Indeed, it is not intended to imply that breeds should never be crossed. It is only to warn that the re-establishment of true breeding purity after an outcross of either a strain or a breed is a tedious and difficult businesss.

The crossing of breeds should be undertaken only with the end in view of establishing a new breed which will fulfill some purpose or answer some need for which there is no already recognized variety. The developing and fixing of type for such a new breed requires many generations and is not a task to be lightly assumed.

The manufacture of the Airedale Terrier and of the Doberman Pinscher breeds by the crossing, re-crossing, and intercrossing of breeds already recognized and fixed were noteworthy achievements in breed hybridization. So, from the intercrossing of other breeds, was the production of the Irish Wolfhound breed which, it is believed, had become extinct as a breed. If any valuable breeds of dogs we now possess should be wiped out, it would be possible to reproduce its type from the crossing and re-crossing of other breeds; but it would be a long and arduous process. Unless his middle name be Persistence, a breeder is well advised not to make such an effort.

So with the crossing of strains within a breed. Strains may be crossed, re-crossed, and intercrossed to produce another strain which may be better than either of the parent strains. This involves not only the crossing of strains but the deliberate, rig-

147

orous and unremitting selection of type to a definite end.

The more distinct and more nearly unrelated the strains that are crossed, the less the uniformity that is to be expected in the progeny. Outcrosses, if undertaken at all, should be with a definite purpose and it should not be expected to fulfill that purpose in a single generation. Any virtues which may be added to a strain through outcrossing to another strain cannot be looked upon as inherent in the first strain until they have been purified and fixed within that strain through inbreeding. Outcrossing is only to be employed as a means to an end and as a preliminary to the fixation of its good results, if any, through inbreeding.

As a matter of practical fact, the various so-called strains within the various recognized breeds of dogs are seldom distinct and uncorrupted with the germ plasm of other so-called strains. The various strains within a breed are usually all derived from some one or more mutual ancestors who are to be found not very far back in the pedigrees of all of the dogs of the breed. If these common ancestors who occur in the various strains were great dogs (and they would not have been employed as the foundation blood for strains had they not been for their own generation), there is little hazard in the so-called outcross. But the common ancestors preclude its being truly an outcross and it is only because it is not an outcross that it is not hazardous.

Bad results from outcrossing can be eliminated through persistent inbreeding and selection, and the good results so derived may be retained and perpetuated by the same means. Outcrossing is for the breeder who is willing to devote generations to the addition to his strain of a virtue which it lacks. If possible, that virtue should be brought into the strain through an only partial outcross, since outcrossing is quite as likely to destroy virtues already possessed as to add others that are wanting and wanted.

The crossing of strains for the experienced and pertinacious breeder who knows what he wants and undertakes it for a specific end may bring to his strain the added virtues which he

148

asks of it. It is a risky expedient for the breeder who wants immediate, first generation results or for one who does not know exactly what he is about.

If such a one succeeds in getting what he wants in the first generation from what he believes to be an outcross, it is in all likelihood because what appears to him to be an outcross is in very fact not an outcross at all, and the two so-called strains are so closely related that the good results may be attributed to line breeding rather than to outbreeding.

And it is not the experienced and informed breeders who are forever experimenting with outcrossing of strains. It is rather the novice and inexperienced who hope in one fell swoop to garner in one generation all of the virtues of both outcrossed strains and to eliminate their faults.

Inbreeding is accepted, by those who do not know, as synonymous with degeneracy. The fear of it and the ignorant prejudices against it are widespread. Like most folk beliefs, there must be some justification for the attitude of the uninformed public and of a large part of the breeders toward the practice. In fact, there is some such justification.

The perils of inbreeding are, however, much more apparent than real. It is at once the surest means of establishing in our stock the breeding purity of desirable attributes and the means of bringing to light undesirable recessive factors which may lurk in the germ plasm of a strain. If such of those animals as show the defective traits are eliminated from the breeding program and are not permitted to reproduce themselves, generation by generation those undesirable qualities can be cast out of the strain, their appearance being less and less frequent, until the strain is finally purged of them.

Meanwhile, the desirable dominant factors are, through inbreeding, changed from hybrid-dominance to pure dominance, and desirable recessives are captured and retained. Thus is developed the prepotence of the members of the strain. For that, indeed, is what prepotence amounts to—the possession of like

149

genes in the two haploid sets of chromosomes that form the zygote.

An animal's greatness as a breeding force depends upon that prepotence. Formerly prepotence was more or less fortuitous. We knew that a few dogs had it; most dogs lacked it—even most good dogs. Now we know what it is, how it can be built up and how it can be conserved from generation to generation.

Some of the great prepotent dogs have derived from pedigrees which seem to show no close inbreeding; but the inbreeding is there—like genes have met. And when like genes meet in the zygote, inbreeding results.

It is only because closely related mates are prone to be similar in their genetic makeup, and therefore like genes are likely to meet, that inbreeding is effective. It may occur without apparent inbreeding, but it is by deliberate inbreeding of selected individuals that we are able to bring it about with comparative frequency.

It is necessary to divorce our concept of inbreeding as it applies to dogs and as it applies to our own species. In man, under our present state of civilization, inbreeding would doubtless be disastrous, despite that some of the world's finest minds have resulted from cousin marriages.

No animal except man offers any objection to incest, nor, indeed, is believed to recognize it as such. That, even in man, the taboo against it is not instinctive is proved by the frequency with which even now the laws prohibiting it are known to be violated, and by the incestuous marriage-matings which were obligatory among the Ptolemies, the Peruvian Incas, and the ancient Hawaiian royal lines. The early Greeks, a people not notably intellectually or physically deficient, permitted the marriage of half-brother and half-sister.

Of the numerous hypotheses thus far advanced to explain the incest taboo in the human family, by far the most satisfactory is that of Bronislaw Malinowski. In his article, "Culture," in the *Encyclopedia of the Social Sciences,* Malinowski posits that the violent emotions arising from sexual affection, if not limited to the father and mother, would tear apart the family. "A house divided against itself cannot stand; it will become all one thing, or all the other." The incest taboo therefore serves to preserve, not only the basic family unit, but also the intimate kin group as it is defined by the given society.

In any event, there is now no known human society, primitive or civilized, in which the taboo does not function. It was a part of the Mosaic law, and from the Hebrew religion was annexed into the Christian doctrine which has dominated the culture of Western Europe and America.

It is well that it should do so. So long as we harbor and protect the unfit, especially so long as we permit the unfit to reproduce themselves, and so long as monogamy enables the mediocre to reproduce at the same rate as does the fittest of the race, incestuous matings could not be tolerated in the human race. With scientifically supervised human marriages (or at least matings) and a Spartan law which would render possible the destruction of the unfit, the human race could, through judicious inbreeding, mold its own betterment with the same certitude with which it molds the destinies of its domestic animals. It could breed to order savants and scientists, pugilists and pole vaulters. In a few generations of supervised inbreeding, idiocy, various insanities, predispositions to various infectious diseases, color blindness, haemophilia, and a host of ills that human flesh is heir to could be eliminated or at least greatly reduced in the general population.

This is no plea that such a regeneration of the human race should be undertaken. This book is no Huxleyan *Brave New World*. The mention of the possible application of inbreeding to our own *Homo sapiens* is made only to argue that the justified taboo of the practice, as pertains to the human species in a culture like our own, becomes a stupid prejudice when we apply it to our dogs and other domestic animals. In them, we can supervise and determine the matings; we can breed only from the best; we can mate the few superior males to a vast number of females; and we can eliminate the even moderately unfit from our breeding programs. On no count does any objection to inbreeding in mankind apply to inbreeding of dogs.

There can be no doubt that the taboo against human incest has functioned to deter and often prevent breeders from the employment of inbreeding for the improvement of their livestock. It was only because reason prevailed over prejudice that inbreeding was employed for the very establishment of the various breeds and that it has been utilized consciously for their development.

Are there then no hazards in the inbreeding of dogs? Is inbreeding the infallible prescription for the attainment of perfection?

It is by no means so simple. There are hazards involved, but not so great as is sometimes believed. And ill-considered inbreeding is the worst possible policy in any effort to produce fine dogs. Inbreeding is a loaded gun which must be pointed in the right direction to accomplish the purpose for which it exists.

It can perpetuate and intensify the faults of a strain or of an individual dog in the same manner in which it can perpetuate and intensify the desirable attributes. And it can manifest in the phenotype faults which exist in the genotype but which cannot be located there with our present techniques.

It is generally believed that inbreeding produces general constitutional weakness and loss of stamina. The fact is that it intensifies the existing genetic traits. Inbreed to strength, and strength in even greater measure will result; inbreed to weakness, and the result is further degeneracy of type.

Whether one outcross or whether one inbreed, selection is necessary for improvement of the line. Outcrossed stock will so tend to mediocrity and the burying of unwanted recessive factors of one line under dominant factors of the other line that the rigorous selection which is necessary for the preservation of the stamina of inbred stock is impossible in outcrossed stock. But it is to be remembered that such unwanted recessives are only buried; they are not lost. They are liable to recur in subsequent generations. And the virtues which are presumed to be derived from outcrossing are, insofar as the outcross is real and not merely apparent, only the hybrid dominance of certain genes, subject to disappear in another generation.

Inbreeding is not an end in itself but is only a means to an end. It is a method of holding fast to that which is good and of casting out that which is bad. It establishes homozygous dominant purity and brings into manifestation homozygous recessive alleles, good or bad, by the union of like pairs of genes.

Purebred varieties, such as our various races of dogs, have been selected for certain attributes since the origin of the breeds, and in them, animals lacking in those desirable attributes have been cast out of the breed and have not been permitted to reproduce their kind. Through constant selection, such breeds have been purged of the factors which were considered as undesirable, and as a consequence undesirable recessives are less likely to appear in purebred races, when they are inbred, than in such stocks as those of the human race, which have not been inbred and the undesired qualities eliminated.

There is a point beyond which degeneracy cannot go and the organism survive. The continuous elimination of degenerate factors from the various strains of purebred livestock has purged the races of their degenerative recessives until we may now inbreed those races without the fear of degenerative consequences. The longer the races exist, the more intensely they are bred in and in, and the more rigorously selection is maintained, the less the dangers from inbreeding. The breeders who developed the various breeds in the only manner that development was possible, which was by means of intensive inbreeding, were beset much more by the dangers attendant in that process than are the modern breeders with their established races already purged for them of those degeneracies they fear. Once the purgation is complete, and it is now in purebred dogs so nearly complete that the hazards are minimized, no further degeneracy from inbreeding is possible.

The degeneracies, which were buried in the germ plasms and

153

brought to the surface through inbreeding, and with which earlier breeders had to contend, inculcated in them a healthy fear of the practice and they have handed that fear on to us along with purebred and purged races in which the hazards do not for practical purposes exist at all.

The vast number of self-fertilizing plants (that is, inbred in every generation since the origin of the species) have been purged of their degeneracies through natural selection which destroyed the organisms which were unable to cope with their environments. The artificial selection of the breeder prevents from reproduction domestic plants and animals which manifest attributes which fail to please him or serve his ends.

An experiment in the prolonged inbreeding of white rats has been carried on by Miss King, a worker at the Wistar Institute. For twenty generations she bred together full brothers and sisters, which is recognized as the most intensive form of inbreeding, selecting her breeding stock constantly for its vigor and stamina. At the end of the twenty generations of intensive inbreeding, Miss King had a race of rats of greater than average size, greater fecundity, and greater longevity than the stock with which the experiment was begun. Inbreeding plus selection resulted in the improvement of the strain. Without selection, this would, of course, have been impossible.

What, then, are our conclusions about inbreeding, line breeding, and outbreeding as policies for the dog breeder? First, we find that the terms, and therefore the policies, within a purebred variety are not so different as has sometimes been supposed. Outcrosses are not absolute since all typical animals of any breed are more or less closely related. In inbreeding it is only theoretically possible to bring together identical haploid sets of chromosomes, no matter how close the relationship of the mated animals. Line breeding is but a modification of inbreeding, and so far as it achieves its purpose is in very fact inbreeding.

Secondly, outcrosses, as nearly as it is possible to make them, should be made only for the purpose of annexing some desirable attribute or attributes to a strain, and they must be subsequently fixed within that strain through inbreeding.

Thirdly, inbreeding of purebred stock is not so hazardous as has been supposed, and with adequate selection for vigor, stamina, and fertility those qualities can be intensified through persistent inbreeding.

Fourthly, inbreeding and selection make for the genetic purity which results in prepotence, which can be deliberately achieved and preserved in a strain.

Fifth, and most important of all, we find that the inbreeding results in the union of like genes in the zygote. A comprehension of the theory of the chromosomes and genes, as the conveyors of its inheritance to the organism, enables us to understand why inbreeding plus selection should purify the race, produce prepotency, and enable us to produce the kind of dogs we want. All is in the genes and the chromosomes which carry them. Not to understand their behavior is to miss the point of this entire argument.

In subsequent Chapters XV and XVI, entitled respectively, "Choosing a Brood Bitch," and "Choosing a Stud Dog," we shall make further use of the facts of this chapter.

Ch. Chee-Chee of Sprucewood

CHAPTER XI

The Pedigree

The word "pedigree" is derived from the French *pied de gris,* which translated means "crane's foot." Its use is due to the fancied resemblance to the long, spreading toes of the crane of the manner in which the lines of names diverge to record the ancestry of an animal.

The term "family tree" expresses the implied idea even better than does "crane's foot," for the generations of ancestry branch out from the individual as do the branches of a tree from a trunk. The trunk throws off two main limbs, analogous to the parents, each of which divides into two smaller limbs, the grandparents, and each of those limbs divide to form two even smaller limbs, the great grandparents, and those limbs may divide and subdivide *ad infinitum* to show the more and more remote generations of ancestry.

The pedigree of the dog is its family tree, the record of the names of its ancestors and of their relations to one another and to it. The pedigree often includes the name of the breeder of the dog, the date of the dog's birth, its own and its parents' numbers in whatever stud book they may be registered, and other data about the animal. These added data, however informative, are not properly a part of the pedigree.

Pedigrees are now usually published simply as columns of names, which in each successive column from right to left are more widely spaced. This arrangement places the names of the parents in the first left hand column, the names of the parents'

Am. & Can. Ch. Golden Knoll's King Alphonzo

- Ch. Golden Knoll's Shur Shot
  - Ch. Stilrovin Shur Shot
    - Stilrovin Bullet
      - imp. Ch. Rockhaven Rory
        - imp. Ch. Speedwell Pluto
          - Eng. Ch. Michael of Moreton
          - Speedwell Emerald
        - Can. Ch. Rockhaven Amber
          - Ch. Speedwell Pluto
          - Saffron Penelope
      - imp. Patience of Yelme
        - Cecil's Pride
          - Haulstone Robert
          - Uncle Tom's Win
        - Biltonpru
          - Ottershaw Brian
          - Lass of Dartnell
    - Gilnockie Coquette
      - imp. Ch. Bingo of Yelme
        - Beppo of Yelme
          - Mack of Yelme
          - Diana of Ible
        - Alveley Biddy
          - Eng. Ch. Haulstone Marker
          - Babette of Quinton
      - Can. Ch. Rockhaven Russet
        - imp. Ch. Speedwell Pluto
          - Eng. Ch. Michael of Moreton
          - Speedwell Emerald
        - Saffron Chipmonk
          - Eng. Ch. Haulstone Dan
          - Dame Daphne
  - Kingdale's Toast
    - Tonkahof Admiral
      - Gilnockie Beppo
        - imp. Ch. Bingo of Yelme
          - Neppo of Yelme
          - Alvely Biddy
        - Can. Ch. Rockhaven Russet
          - Ch. Speedwell Pluto
          - Saffron Chipmonk
      - Ch. Tonka Belle of Woodend
        - Rockhaven Tuck
          - Ch. Speedwell Pluto
          - Saffron Chipmonk
        - Rockhaven Judy
          - Eng. Ch. Marine of Woolley
          - Ch. Rockhaven Lassie
    - Amber Lass
      - Ch. Beavertail Butch
        - imp. Ch. Rockhaven Rory
          - Ch. Speedwell Pluto
          - Can. Ch. Rockhaven Amber
        - imp. Ch. Rockhaven Glory
          - Can. Ch. Rockhaven Rust
          - Can. Ch. Rockhaven Carole
      - Whitebridge Judy
        - imp. Ch. Bingo of Yelme
          - Beppo of Yelme
          - Alvely Biddy
        - imp. Ch. Speedwell Tango
          - Corney of Rivey
          - Sheena of Ricketts
- Sunnyshine of Sans Souci
  - Sir Gay Roxie
    - Donald of Great Cove
      - Turlough Timothy
        - Donkelve Punch
          - Donkelve Jester
          - Golden Shadow
        - Ottershaw Colette
          - Ottershaw Sunclad
          - Ottershaw Electra
      - imp. Marcie
        - Vycta of Dewstraw
          - Bruyan of Dewstraw
          - Rosye of Dewstraw
        - Sphinx of Dewstraw
          - Speedwell Nimrod
          - Kathryn
    - Ch. Early Autumn Sunshine
      - Wind of Woodend
        - Rockhaven Tuck
          - Ch. Speedwell Pluto
          - Saffron Chipmonk
        - imp. Ch. Sprite of Aldgrove
          - Eng. Ch. Kelso of Aldgrove
          - Rovina of Aldgrove
      - Duchess Diana of Kentford
        - Teddy Wyanti
          - Nap of Woolley
          - Lady Diana
        - Tucker of Sunny Slope
          - Cockle of Gypsy Land
          - Donkelve Mist
  - Sally of San Souci
    - Rick Rooney of Roc-Roix
      - Beavertail Bruno
        - imp. Ch. Rockhaven Rory
          - Ch. Speedwell Pluto
          - Can. Ch. Rockhaven Amber
        - imp. Ch. Rockhaven Glory
          - Can. Ch. Rockhaven Rust
          - Rockhaven Roxy
      - Duchess of Roc-Roix
        - Ch. Goldwood Pluto
          - Ch. Sprite of Aldgrove
          - Speedwell Boine
        - Belinda of Willow Lake
          - Onyx of Emley
          - Donkelve Punch
    - Ch. Princess of Many Trails
      - Donald of Great Cove
        - Turlough Timothy
          - Ottershaw Colette
          - Vycta of Dewstraw
        - imp. Marcie
          - Sphinx of Dewstraw
          - Rockhaven Tuck
      - Ch. Early Autumn Sunshine
        - Wind of Woodend
          - Ch. Sprite of Aldgrove
          - Teddy Wyanti
        - Duchess Diana of Kentford
          - Wind of Woodend
          - Tucker of Sunny Slope

Pedigree chart — **Am. & Can. Ch. Chee Chee of Sprucewood**

Parents
- Highland March Echo
- Tomboy Toby of Sprucewood

Grandparents
- Ch. Highland Royal Flush
- Lanenberg's Princess Pat
- Butch's Buff
- Co-Co of Hillrire

Great-grandparents
- Ch. Tonkahof Bang
- Golden Treasure
- Ch. Beavertail Butch
- Chee-Chee
- Ch. Beavertail Butch
- Kingdale's Sunshine
- Beautywood's Buckshot
- Cheyenne of Vox Pox

2nd great-grandparents
- Ch. Goldwood Pluto
- Buff of Golden Valley
- Bruce of Willow Loch
- Heather of Willow Loch
- imp. Ch. Rockhaven Rory
- imp. Ch. Rockhaven Glory
- Ch. Goldwood Pluto
- Jill of Chateau d'Or
- imp. Ch. Rockhaven Rory
- imp. Ch. Rockhaven Glory
- Tonkahof Admiral
- Honey of Golden Valley
- Peter of Woodend
- Fld. Ch. Shelter Cove Beauty
- Tom of Chateau d'Or
- Mollie of Chateau d'Or

3rd great-grandparents
- imp. Ch. Rockhaven Rory
- imp. Ch. Sprite of Aldgrove
- Nero of Roedare
- Fld. Ch. Patricia of Roedare
- imp. Ch. Rockhaven Rory
- Rusty Heger
- Rockhaven Ben Bolt
- Belle of Willow Lake
- imp. Ch. Speedwell Pluto
- Can. Ch. Rockhaven Amber
- Can. Ch. Rockhaven Rust
- Can. Ch. Rockhaven Carole
- imp. Ch. Rockhaven Rory
- imp. Ch. Sprite of Aldgrove
- Rockhaven Tuck
- Sackcloth of Chateau d'Or
- imp. Ch. Speedwell Pluto
- Can. Ch. Rockhaven Amber
- Can. Ch. Rockhaven Rust
- Can. Ch. Rockhaven Carole
- Glinockie Beppo
- Ch. Tonka Belle of Woodend
- Fld. Ch. Goldwood Tuck
- Fld. Ch. Golden Beauty of Roedare
- Fld. Ch. Rip
- Rockhaven Judy
- Rockhaven Ben Bolt
- Happy of Willow Loch
- Rockhaven Tuck
- Sackcloth of Chateau d'Or
- Gold Dust Rory
- Cinders of Chateau d'Or

4th great-grandparents
- Ch. Speedwell Pluto
- Can. Ch. Rockhaven Amber
- Eng. Ch. Kelso of Aldgrove
- Rovina of Aldgrove
- Sandy of Nutwood
- Rockhaven Queen
- Rockhaven Pluto Boy
- Lady of Roedare
- Ch. Speedwell Pluto
- Can. Ch. Rockhaven Amber
- Speedwell Boine
- Onyx of Emley
- Eng. Ch. Marine of Woolley
- Can. Ch. Rockhaven Lassie
- Stilrovin Terrence
- Rusty Heger
- Eng. Ch. Michael of Moreton
- Speedwell Emerald
- Ch. Speedwell Pluto
- Saffron Penelope
- Ch. Speedwell Pluto
- Chiltington Light
- Ch. Speedwell Pluto
- Wilderness Tangerine
- Ch. Speedwell Pluto
- Can. Ch. Rockhaven Amber
- Rovina of Aldgrove
- Eng. Ch. Kelso of Aldgrove
- Ch. Speedwell Pluto
- Saffron Chipmonk
- Ch. Speedwell Pluto
- Ginockie Lady
- Eng. Ch. Michael of Moreton
- Speedwell Emerald
- Ch. Speedwell Pluto
- Saffron Penelope
- Ch. Speedwell Pluto
- Chiltington Light
- Ch. Speedwell Pluto
- Wilderness Tangerine
- Ch. Beingo of Yelme
- Can. Ch. Rockhaven Russet
- Rockhaven Tuck
- Rockhaven Judy
- Rockhaven Tuck
- Rockhaven Pluto Boy
- Lady of Roedare
- Speedwell Reuben
- Eng. Ch. Speedwell Tango
- Eng. Ch. Marine of Woolley
- Eng. Ch. Rockhaven Lassie
- Eng. Ch. Marine of Woolley
- Eng. Ch. Rockhaven Lassie
- Ch. Toby of Willow Loch
- Belle of Willow Loch
- Ch. Speedwell Pluto
- Saffron Chipmonk
- Ch. Speedwell Pluto
- Ginockie Lady
- Rusty Heger
- Ch. Rockhaven Rory
- Ch. Speedwell Pluto
- Ginockie Lady

parents (the grandparents) in the second column, and so spaced that the name of the progeny appears midway vertically between the names of its parents. The pedigree may include as many generations of ancestors as its maker chooses to record or of which there are available data.

We include on pages 158-159 of this book a seven generation pedigree of an extremely notable litter of Golden Retrievers. Its notability is in the fact that nine of its thirteen members became champions of record. The other four, it is alleged, were all good enough to win their championships, but their owners were not "show-minded" and did not choose to exhibit them. They were bred by Mr. and Mrs. Millard C. Zwang, of Minneapolis, and handled in the shows by Mr. Hollis Wilson, the expert professional handler, through whose courtesy this information about the litter and its pedigree are provided. This litter was whelped March 16, 1954. The names of the members which achieved championships are as follows:

Ch. Sprucewood's Chocki, who in three months of showing was four times best dog of any breed in all-breed shows and won nine Sporting Groups;

Ch. Sprucewood's Chore Boy, who has had two Best in Show wins, including the National Golden Retriever Specialty Show for 1955;

Ch. Sprucewood's Color Girl;

Ch. Sprucewood's Chee King;

Ch. Sprucewood's Coquette;

Canadian and American Ch. Sprucewood's Chinki;

Ch. Sprucewood's Chuck O'Luck;

Ch. Sprucewood's Ching; and

Ch. Sprucewood's Chee Whiz.

There will be less amazement at the winning record of this marvelous litter when it is considered that the immediate parents, much alike, are among the very foremost of their breed, Golden Retrievers. The sire, as shown in the pedigree, is the American and Canadian Champion Golden Knoll's King Alphonzo, who has been twenty-seven times Best in Show in all-breed shows, best in one national specialty show and best in three regional specialty shows, three times winner of the Speedwell Pluto Challenge Cup (1953, 1954, and 1955) for the top winning Golden Retriever of the respective years, the Alexander Spur Trophy for 1954 for the winner of the national specialty show.

The dam of this litter is Champion Chee Chee of Sprucewood and is of equal excellence to the sire. She has been five times best of all breeds in all-breed shows, and has won the national specialty show twice (1952 and 1953), with which wins was included the Alexander Spur Trophy; and she won the Speedwell Pluto Trophy for 1952.

The seven generation pedigree shows us that the line breeding of this litter is not intensive. Yet, if one will pursue the pedigree into its further reaches, one will note that time after time and time again the names of the same dogs appear in it on both sides of the house, notably the name of Speedwell Pluto and his major offspring, the same Speedwell Pluto in whose memory the trophy was established.

Another litter notable for the excellence of its many members is the one of which the pedigree is shown on pages 162-163. It is the Doberman Pinscher litter, bred by Dorothy M. Harding of San Gabriel, California, whelped September 8, 1951, which Miss Harding designates as the "Opera Litter." In it were eight champions, one more that has points toward championship but retired from the shows to be bred, and two never exhibited, eleven in all. The names of the champions are:

> Ch. Harding's Faust, with seven Bests in Show, including two specialty shows, forty firsts in Working Group, 87 times Best of Breed;
> Ch. Harding's Oberon;
> Ch. Harding's Rigoletto;
> Ch. Harding's Mignon;
> Ch. Harding's La Traviata;
> Ch. Harding's Thais;
> Ch. Harding's Tosca; and
> Ch. Harding's La Boheme.

Pedigree chart — **Ch. Rancho Dobe's Primo**

Ch. Rancho Dobe's Primo

- Ch. Alcor v Millsdod
  - Ch. Westphalia's Uranus
    - Periclos of Westphalia
      - Ch.Kurt vd Rheinperle-Rhinegold
        - Aster of Westphalia
          - Helios v Siegestor
          - Sgn.Ch.Illisa of Westphalia
        - Anita zur Immermannhoehe
          - Bodo v Stegerpark
          - Asta v Burghofplatz
      - Princess Latonia of Westphalia
        - Ch.Big Boy of Whitegate
          - Ch. Claus vd Spree
          - Chifrieda vd Koningstad
        - Baladere of High Larches
    - Sgr.Ch.Jessy vd Sonnenhoehe
      - Ital.Ch.Cherloc v Rauhfelsen
        - Helios v Siegestor
          - Stolz v Roeneckenstein
          - Ulla v Siegestor
        - Prinzess v Simmenau
          - Kunz vd Rodeltal
          - Lotte v Roeneckenstein
      - Alice vd Sonnenhoehe
        - Ch.Dewald v Ludwigsburg
          - Stolz v Roeneckenstein
          - Gilly v Rheinadler
        - Asta II vd Sonnenhoehe
          - Curt v Brandenstein
          - Asta I vd Sonnenhoehe
  - Ch. Maida v Coldod
    - Ch.Carlo v Bassewitz
      - Boby v Hohenzollernpark
        - Figaro v Sigalsburg
          - Sgn.Ch.Alto v Sigalsburg
          - Asta v Stolzenberg
        - Corina v Sigalsburg
          - Sgr.Ch.Lux vd Blankenburg
          - Asta v Stolzenberg
      - Fiffi v Heimfeldt
        - Sgn.Ch.Alto v Sigalsburg
        - Fee v Roedeltal
    - Inka v Lindenhof
      - Ch. Luz v Rodeltal
        - Axel v Hardtgeburge
        - Merri v Winterburg
      - Hella v Winterburg
        - Sgr.Ch:Hamlet v Herthasse
          - Sgn.Ch.Alto v Sigalsburg
          - Cortess v Steyerberg
        - Adda v Adelshoehe
          - Baldur v Siegestor
          - Alli v Nevill

- Ch. Rancho Dobe's Kashmir
  - Int.Ch.Roxanna's Emperor v Recmon
    - Ch.Emperor of Marienland
      - Ch.Domossi of Marienland
        - Ch.Blank vd Domstadt
          - Sgr.Ch. Muck v Brunia
          - Cora v Ruppertsburg
        - Ch.Ossi v Stahlhelm
          - Sgr.Ch. Troll v Ehrelsberg
          - Cleopatra v Burgund
      - Ch.Westphalia's Rhemba
        - Ch.Kurt vd Rheinperle-Rhinegold
          - Astor of Westphalia
          - Anita zur Immermannhoehe
        - Sgn.Ch.Jessy vd Sonnenhoehe
          - Ital.Ch.Cherloc v Rauhfelsen
          - Alice vd Sonnenhoehe
    - Ch.Westphalia's Roxanna
      - Ch.Kurt vd Rheinperle-Rhinegold
        - Aster of Westphalia
          - Helios v Siegestor
          - Sgn.Ch.Illisa of Westphalia
        - Anita zur Immermannhoehe
          - Bodo v Stegerpark
          - Asta v Burghofplatz
      - Sgn.Ch.Jessy vd Sonnenhoehe
        - Ital.Ch.Cherloc v Rauhfelsen
          - Helios v Siegestor
          - Prinzess v Simmenau
        - Alice vd Sonnenhoehe
          - Ch.Dewald v Ludwigsburg
          - Asta II vd Sonnenhoehe
  - Rhumba of Rancho Dobe
    - Ch.King Adam of Wagner
      - Ch. Ames v Sidlo
        - Prinz Noah of Pontchartrain
          - Int.Ch.Illisa of Pontchartrain
          - Ch. Hans v Tannenhaus
        - Vnt.Ch. Asta of Oxho
          - Can.Ch.Gilda of Leal's Farm
          - Ch. Luz v Roedeltal
      - Ch.Katrinka v Sidlo
        - Udo v Guesthalia, P.H.
          - Krienhild v Brunia
          - Prinz Noah of Pontchartrain
        - Woska v Tipler
          - Fonda of Middletown
    - Juno of Moorpark, C.D.
      - Sgr.Ch.Ferry v Rauhfelsen of Giralda
        - Sgr.Ch.Troll v Engelsburg
          - Sgr.Ch. Muck v Brunia
          - Adda v Beck
        - Sgr.Ch.Jessy v Sonnenhoehe
          - Ital.Ch.Cherloc of Rauhfelsen
          - Alice vd Sonnenhoehe
      - Casa del Canto's Comanche
        - Kurt v Lindenhof
          - Sgr.Ch. Muck v Brunia
          - Bessi v Rothhousegrund

Ch. Harding's Faust

Ch. Harding's Faust
W-289961
Owners
Patricia & Clair Stille
4506 Saugus Avenue
Sherman Oaks, Calif.

Ch. Beau-Jo's Coda

Tomareck Bolse

Ch. Gretchen v Stolzenfeltz

Ch.Dictator v Glenhugel

Ch.Echo of Marienland

Ch.Dietrich v Koenigsheim

Erika v Stolzenfeltz

Ch.Blank vd Domstadt

Sgn.Ch.Ossi v Stahlhelm

Ch. Domossi of Marienland

Ch.Westphalia's Rembha

Ch. Claus v Bayernstolz

Kaiserin v Koenigsheim

Yan of Pocahontas

Elsa v Trabandt

Ch.Blank vd Domstadt
Cora vd Ruppertsburg
Sgr.Ch.Troll vd Engelsburg
Kleopatra v Burgund
Ch. Blank v Domstadt
Cora vd Ruppertsburg
Sgr.Ch.Ossi v Stahlhelm
Ch.Kurt vd Rheinperle-Rhinegold
Sgn.Ch.Jessy vd Sonnenhoehe
Helios v Siegestor
Int.Ch.Jockel v Burgund
Willi v Bayernstolz
Ch.Hans of Kurtiska
Veldi v Heindall
Yan of Pocahontas
Myra of Pocahontas
Tell v Schlingelhop

Hella vd Winterburg
Sgr.Ch.Hamlet v Herthasse
Cora vd Ruppertsburg
Sgr.Ch.Muck v Brunia
Adda v Heck
Helios v Siegestor
Freya v Burgund
Sgr.Ch.Muck v Brunia
Cora vd Ruppertsburg
Sgr.Ch.Troll v Engelsburg
Cleopatra v Burgund
Astor of Westphalia
Anita zur Immermannhoehe
Ital.Ch.Cherloc v Rauhfelsen
Alice vd Sonnenhoehe
Helios v Siegestor
Sgr. Jessy v Lobenstein
Erka v Graaf Zeppllin
Voska v Bayernperle
Ch. Baron of Silvergate
Wilhelmina v Kurtiska
Ch.Prinz Carlo of Plantation Grove
Chicka of Silvergate
Ch. Big Boy of Whitegate
Yucca of Pocahontas
Pocahontas Jockel
Witzi of Pocahontas
Fritzi from Duffield
Frieda from Duffield
Int.Ch.Kurt v Schwarzwald-perle
Amrie vd Schwarzwaldperle

Terri v Winterburg
Sgn.Ch.Alto v Sigalsburg
Contess v Steyerbery
Baldur v Siegestor
Gilli v Newill
Ch. Luz v Roedeltal
Hella v Winterberg
Sgr. Artus v Thumshoehe
Algunde v Bulow
Stolz v Roeneckenstein
Cilla v Siegestor
Lux v Saumhof
Yessy v Lobenstein
Ch. Luz v Roedeltal
Hella v Winterberg
Sgr.Ch.Hamlet v Herthases
Ada v Adelshoehe
Sgr.Ch.Muck v Brunia
Adda v Heck
Helios v Siegestor
Freya v Burgund
Helios v Siegestor
Freya v Burgund
Sgn.Ch.Illisa of Westphalia
Bodo v Stererpark
Asta v Durchofplatz
Helios v Siegestor
Ch.Dewald v Ludwigsburg
Sta II v Winterberg
Stolz v Roeneckenstein
Cilla v Siegestor
Sgn.Ch.Alto v Sigalsburg
Hedda v Margaretenhof
Ch. Hans v Tannenhaus
Voska v Luisenheim
Stolz v Roeneckenstein
Closilos vd Residenz
Sgr.Ch.Burschel v Falkensee
Ch. Midi of Silvergate
Prinz Noah of Pontchartrain
Gretchen v Tagen
Prinz Noah of Pontchartrain
Vonda of Middletown
Beau Modern of Silvergate
Ch. Midi of Silvergate
Ch. Claus vd Spree
Ch.Prinzessin Elfrieds v Konigstad
Flora of Pocahontas
Ch. Kurt v Rheinperle-Rhinegold
Kiss Flash of Rhinegold
Claus v Rauhfelsen
Mercy of Pocahontas
Dragon v Heridendort
Josephine vd Spree
Artus v Schlingelhop
Melinda v the Roceman
Helios v Siegestor
Adda v Bad-Heidelburg
Felix vd Sternenstrasse
Mosken v Brandthof

The pedigree shows the names of the greatest members of the Doberman Pinscher breed.

The two litters of which the pedigrees are shown here are very unusual in that the members of them showed such excellence throughout, which is an earnest that the parent stock had been almost wholly purged of its undesirable genes. Up until some two decades ago a litter of any breed in which more than a single champion developed was rare indeed. Lightning had struck twice in the same place. It has now come to be well-nigh commonplace for a thoroughly well bred litter to embrace two or three dogs worthy of their championships, and sometimes four or five. Of course, the number of possible champions is limited by the number of puppies in the litter; it is impossible to make more champions than there are dogs. And to make a champion one must exhibit a dog, frequently with a long and arduous campaign. Many bitches, especially of the smaller breeds, produce only a limited number of puppies at a single pregnancy, and a record number of champions in one litter from such bitches is out of the question.

Moreover, championship is not the final test of excellence in a dog. Although the word *"Champion"* before the name of a dog implies that it is one of considerable merit, there are champions and champions, some of such magnificence in their conformation and usually their style and showmanship as to make their names famous forever, and some only good enough to get by in the limited competition in which they have won.

Many fine dogs, even great ones, fail to make championships, either because of their owner's failure to exhibit them or for some other reason such as their being prematurely crippled or their early death. So it is impossible to estimate a litter entirely by the number of champions it contains. But that number of champions is at least an indication of the merits of the litter as a whole. A multiplicity of fine dogs in a single litter is a mark of the excellence of the genes in the parental germ plasm and the consistency of that excellence. A single good dog implies that the correct genes were present in both parents, but two or

164

more good dogs from the same parents are evidence that the parents carry the right genes and transmit them more than as a mere accident. Such parents were formerly (and are yet sometimes) said to "nick." Such a nick was in the past considered merely fortuitous, but we now know why dogs produce fine progeny with such consistency.

The significance of a dog's pedigree is seldom evaluated at its true worth. For many persons, a pedigree means at once too little and too much. How often do we hear an owner vaunt the length of his dog's pedigree, which is declared to be "as long as his arm!" He frequently has never read the document and does not know anything about the data it sets forth. It is, to him, merely his dog's "papers." It contains cryptic lists of meaningless names arranged in more or less widely spaced columns. He knows, vaguely, that it is a catalogue of his dog's ancestors, a sort of warranty of the purity of his dog's lineage. He takes a pride in that purity, much as he may take pride in tracing his own lineage to a Mayflower Puritan or to a Norman invader of England. He values the pedigree for its length, although upon examination it is usually found that only three or four generations of ancestors are recorded in it. He is unaware that if the dog (or both his parents) be registered, the pedigree could in all likelihood be extended to ten or even twenty generations.

Often he counts the names of champions of record in the pedigree, usually without consideration of the nearness or remoteness in the ancestry of those championships, and that by adding one more generation to the record the number of championships could perhaps be doubled. These championships are sometimes rubricated, or at least underlined, to imply a significance which they do not, in fact, possess.

When Earl Haig gave a Sealyham Terrier to Will Rogers he told him that if the tyke knew how great his ancestors were he would not speak to "any of us." An excellent pedigree, however, does not always mean an excellent dog, and the gene theory has deflated pride of ancestry, especially of remote ancestry. It proved that an organism may derive exactly nothing at all from

165

some remote progenitor. Among dogs as among men, there are unworthy sons of worthy sires. Two litter brothers, identical in their pedigrees, may be much alike in their physical type and genetic constitution, one or both; or they may be so different in both respects that one may be a great individual and become a "pillar of the stud book," while the other is a waster both for exhibition and for breeding.

There is a proverbial story of a judge of dogs who, when an exhibitor expostulated with him about the low position of his dog in the prize list of a show and boasted of the animal's fashionable pedigree, replied, "Next time, bring the pedigree and leave the dog at home."

The pedigree does not make the dog. The dog, if he be good enough individually and genetically, does make the pedigree.

The pedigree may be in essence only a statement that all of the dog's progenitors for a certain number of generations are all of a stated variety. In fact, a large part of the pedigrees are little more than that, mazes of names of obscure dogs, here and there perhaps illuminated by the name of some more or less obscure champion. To the uninitiated, a pedigree is a pedigree. But such a pedigree has, in fact, little significance and no value.

No pedigree is of any worth if the dog whose lineage it records is sterile or is not to be bred from. The record of a dog's ancestry is only of service as an earnest of the kind of progeny he is likely (or liable) to beget. One is presumed to evaluate the prospective generations ahead of the dog from the recorded generations behind him.

That this is possible is true only in part. A good pedigree confirms what a dog's type and his proved ability to produce good stock has already proclaimed. The proof of the stud dog is in his puppies. The roll of his ancestors is but an obligato to the tune of his genes.

It is not to be denied that the son or daughter of two parents who are themselves of eminent ancestry and recognized producers of stock of consistent excellence is likely himself, when mated adequately, to produce well.

166

Even in this twentieth century we have yet found no way to gather figs from thistles, nor Kadota figs from Mission fig trees. Dogs yet bring forth, each according to his kind. Blood (sic!) will tell. The pedigree is far from being a scrap of paper.

The knowledge of inheritance as transmitted by means of the genes renders absurd our former attitude toward the pedigree and our former methods of analyzing it.

Francis Galton's was one of the great minds of the nineteenth century and he was among the first of the workers who sought to bring the laws of heredity into some semblance of systematized arrangement. We still accept, although with crossed fingers, his so-called "Law of Filial Regression," which declares, in effect, the tendency of races to revert to mediocrity. It is what dog breeders mean when they use the term "the drag of the race."

Galton reached his conclusions from statistical studies. He found that the adult children of very tall parents tended to be, while taller than the average of the population, not so tall as the mean height of the parents; the children of short parents, shorter than the average but of greater height than the mean height of the parents. His statistics reveal the tendency of exaggerations of type in the parents to grow smaller or to disappear in the progeny.

While Galton, in gathering his statistics and arriving at his conclusions, failed to separate the environmental influence from the influences of heredity, we recognize that those conclusions, as stated in the "Law of Filial Regression," are, on the whole, correct. We recognize, however, in the light of genetics, how much more a mongrelized race, such as our own, is prone to such "filial regression" than is an intensely inbred race like our purebred races of dogs. Genetics reveals how outcrossing and mongrelism, which latter is but the extreme result of the former, bring about the burial of exaggerations of type in hybrid-dominant mediocrity. Galton did not know that these exaggerations of type might well have inscribed upon their tombstones, "they are not dead but sleeping."

167

This "filial regression," as Galton learnedly called it, this "drag of the race," in a dog breeder's vernacular, impresses upon us the imperative need of eternal vigilance and unremitting selection through the generations. The pedigree, intelligently read, indicates whether or not that selection has been exercised among the dog's progenitors.

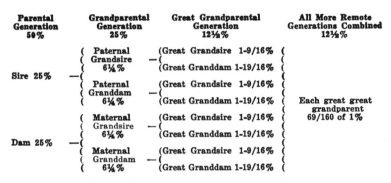

Parental Generation 50%	Grandparental Generation 25%	Great Grandparental Generation 12½%	All More Remote Generations Combined 12½%
Sire 25%	Paternal Grandsire 6¼%	(Great Grandsire 1-9/16% (Great Granddam 1-19/16%	
	Paternal Granddam 6¼%	(Great Grandsire 1-9/16% (Great Granddam 1-19/16%	Each great great grandparent 69/160 of 1%
Dam 25%	Maternal Grandsire 6¼%	(Great Grandsire 1-9/16% (Great Granddam 1-19/16%	
	Maternal Granddam 6¼%	(Great Grandsire 1-9/16% (Great Granddam 1-19/16%	

Galton's Law of Ancestral Inheritance
(Now Discredited)

However, it is Galton's other so-called law, "The Law of Ancestral Inheritance," which has for so long corrupted our interpretation of pedigrees and rendered futile much of our breeding procedure which was predicated upon our application of that "law" to the pedigrees of our dogs.

"The Law of Ancestral Inheritance" declares that the organism derives from its immediate parents fifty percent of its total heritage (twenty-five percent from each parent); from its four grandparents, twenty-five percent of its heritage (six and a quarter percent from each grandparent); and from each succeeding generation in the pedigree, it derives one-half of such fraction as has been left over from the contributions of later generations, and that part is derived equally from the members of that generation.

The part of the heritage derived from each ancestor is thus stated definitely, and the amount diminishes as the ancestor's position in the pedigree grows more remote. It is all so pat and logical. It appeals to our common sense. The ease of its application prompts its employment.

It is in the light of this "Law of Ancestral Inheritance" that we have read and studied our pedigrees, and even yet few of us have learned not to accept it. All that is wrong with the so-called law is that it is not true. Researches in genetics have knocked Galton's "Law of Ancestral Inheritance" into a cocked hat.

While we know that the organism derives fifty percent of its heritage from, or rather through, each parent, we also know, and know why, the contributions from the various members of each of the earlier generations are likely to be very different from each other in their amount and kind. The inheritance from the grandparents is usually unequal and, as we delve further back in the pedigree, we find ancestors who have made no contribution at all to the inheritance. A dog may have descended from certain ancestors without being biologically related to them or without receiving any of their attributes. If one or more of his genes or gene complexes have come from a given ancestor, he is related to it, otherwise he is not.

It is then necessary for us to lay aside any mathematical tables of inheritance when examining a pedigree.

We must recognize that our dog has received his heritage in a more or less lopsided fashion. Some of his ancestors have given him much, some little, some nothing at all. Galton was simply wrong, which, if he were yet alive, he would be the first and readiest to confirm.

This would seem to deprive the pedigree of much of its significance. It does not, in fact, do so, however. It only reveals the true significance. The pedigree is to be accepted as a confirmation even more than as a guide. The pedigree should not wag the dog.

It is not a list of meaningless names. Every name represents a specific dog with known or unknown faults and virtues, which he may or may not have contributed to the makeup of his descendant whose pedigree is under consideration. Each of these dogs in the pedigree has produced progeny, some few and

169

some many, and of various degrees of excellence. To analyze a pedigree, one should know what the various dogs in the pedigree looked like and how well or how ill, how consistently or how sporadically, each has stamped his progeny with the attributes of the breed.

No breeder of dogs, however well informed, can know all about every dog whose name he sees in a pedigree, but a familiarity with the history of the breed will enable him to recognize a large part of the names in the pedigrees he reads. He says that one dog had and produced good coats but that his hindquarters were faulty, another dog was noted for his head and put good heads on his progeny, a third dog was exceedingly good except for a bad mouth.

The pedigree is of significance only in relation to the dog it represents and to the progeny he produces. One cannot read the pedigree and visualize the dog, although one may from the dog make a logical guess at the approximate pedigree.

One may examine the dog and consider what of his attributes he may have derived from what ancestors. One may examine his progeny with a purpose to discover what of his attributes he transmits to them, and what attributes of which of his progenitors.

If the pedigree reveals the repetition of the name of some ancestor, showing that the germ plasm of that ancestor was linebred or inbred to produce the animal whose pedigree it is, it may be assumed that such doubling and possibly redoubling of lineage has resulted in establishing in the germ plasm of the dog under consideration the traits, attributes, and type of the ancestor whose germ plasm is inbred into him. This assumption may be incorrect, but it may reasonably be made, especially if the dog himself exhibits a strong resemblance to the doubled ancestor.

Some breeders, in arranging their matings, consider only the pedigrees of the mates and disregard the individuals entirely. To do so is to assume that the progeny will bear no resemblance to the immediate parents but only to grandparents and more remote progenitors.

Such a procedure is as ill advised as to consider only the individual mates and to disregard the breeding that produced them. Both mates count—the individual mates and their pedigrees. The mates are to be the parents in the pedigree of their progeny; their parents, as shown in their pedigrees, will be the grandparents of the ensuing generation.

Quite as important as the individuals or as their pedigree is the kind of progeny that they may have previously produced. In evaluating that earlier progeny in the consideration of what a dog is likely to produce at any proposed mating, the collaboration he has had from his mate or mates, their excellence, breeding, and suitability for him must be taken into account. That a dog has failed to produce superior progeny from an inferior or unsuitable mate does not condemn him as a breeding animal so much as similar failures when he has been adequately mated.

However, a careful observation of several litters of progeny from a dog or bitch, will usually reveal a consistency in the production of good, bad, or mediocre progeny which is greater than is usually believed. The mates, undeniably, make great difference in the quality of the progeny, but a dog prepotent for good or for evil will exhibit that prepotency, no matter to what purebred consort of his own breed he may be mated.

A numerically large litter which has been adequately reared and which does not exhibit a high average excellence and an approximate uniformity of type has been unfortunately bred. The parents, one or both, have been wrong or the mating of them has been wrong. Either or both might produce better progeny with other mates—or they might not. In consideration of a litter's merits for the purposes of determining the value of one of the parents as a breeding animal, one should not lose sight of the litter's pedigree and should give due weight to whether it shows a confluence of the germ plasm or some great exponent of the breed not many generations removed. If the parents are closely related through their common descent from

171

a great producing ancestor, there is more reason to expect uniformity and excellence in the litter than if the parents are only remotely related or if the common ancestor is a mediocre dog.

Of course, a dog cannot be judged by his progeny until he has produced. Somebody must assume the hazards of breeding an untested young dog or bitch. The assumption of that hazard is only justifiable if the dog seems promising from his excellence as an individual and from the excellence of the germ plasm from which he sprang, as revealed by his pedigree. It is true that some indifferent dogs with indifferent pedigrees have proved to be great producing forces. Such dogs are flukes and have derived from some remote ancestors a fortunate combination of the genes which they hand on to their progeny. For every one such success, there are a thousand such indifferent dogs that are failures as producers of good stock, and the odds are long ones against the breeder who experiments with mediocre dogs of obscure or indifferent ancestry.

Even when such a dog has been tested as a producer and his progeny exhibits a consistent excellence, it is to be remembered that that progeny is liable in its turn to produce progeny which shows reversion to mediocrity.

In making a mating, the parties to it must be looked at as individuals; their past performance as producers, either with the same mate or with other mates, must be taken into account; and their pedigrees are to be analyzed and scrutinized. The breeder who neglects any of these three considerations risks failure.

The pedigree, taken alone, is negligible. A dog may be well bred and yet be a useless mediocrity, but a good dog is very likely to be found to be a well bred one. The pedigree is a guide. It offers a clue as to what traits may be hidden in his germ plasm ready to blight his progeny. It provides the data which enable one to determine what may be a suitable mate for him. It permits one to choose for him a mate with similar "blood lines" leading to some great common ancestor; or to

172

recognize a degree of out-crossing, if one is bent upon such procedure.

But the pedigree must not be considered as an end in itself. No pedigree is better than the dog it represents. If the dog is unworthy, it is a hazardous gamble to experiment with him just because his pedigree is spectacular.

That is not to say that an excellent dog with a single fault may not have that fault corrected in his progeny and that such a one is to be discarded for breeding. A dog may be an excellent producer and yet have some acquired attribute, or even an inherited one, which may render him useless for exhibition. But it is wise to consider of a dog's faults whether they are of such a kind they may be overcome in the progeny, whether they are faults merely of the individual, of the family strain, or of the race, and whether, even if they can be buried in the immediately ensuing generation, they will not be given to reappearance in later generations. The analysis of the pedigree should show whence the fault may have come and enables one to avoid mating the animal to another whose type or ancestry shows a similar fault, thus avoiding the aggravation or perpetuation of it.

We are reminded of the famous *mot* of Mrs. Drew, the grandmother of the Barrymores, who, in discussing her sons as box office attractions, declared that "John Drew and Sydney didn't." So with two dogs who may be litter brothers or litter sisters; one may produce well, the other fail. If they are thoroughly well bred and of prepotent parents, it is likely that many or all of the litter will be valuable producers: even then, some will excel.

It all depends upon the distribution of the chromosomes and of their particular genes. Dogs with none but desirable genes, purebred for every desirable factor, if such dogs exist, can be depended upon for such prepotence that, given a mate carrying the desirable recessive factors, he is certain to produce well. Such dogs are no problem. Mated to equally reliable consorts, their progeny can be depended upon to have and to transmit their own excellence, which need never be lost. It is to a consum-

173

mation in such a strain that all of our energies as breeders of dogs must be directed.

But it is with lesser material that most of us must meanwhile work. We seek to eliminate the bad genes from our strain, to hold fast to the good ones. Our pedigrees indicate to us where those good genes and those bad genes are likely to lurk. As a guide, the pedigree is by no means infallible: it shows from what ancestors a dog has descended but does not show which of those ancestors have contributed to his type or to his germ plasm, nor does it show what or how much the so-called "contributors" have given of themselves. These data the dog must himself provide. The pedigree is only the clue, surprisingly dependable but sometimes false. The breeder who disregards it is lost.

It is better to accept the discredited "Law of Ancestral Inheritance" and treat the pedigree as it has so long been treated than to disregard it altogether. But the wise breeder will look at the pedigrees of his dogs in the light of his knowledge of genetics. He will confirm his pedigrees by correlating them with the dogs whose record they are, and he will observe in his dogs the merits and demerits which the pedigree warns him to look for. He will arrange his matings to avoid the faults and to perpetuate the virtues of the individuals and of their forebears.

Something must be said about the trustworthiness of pedigrees, which is frequently brought into question. No pedigree is better than the word of the man who makes it. There has been, and perhaps is, some faking of pedigrees. It is very little. Few, indeed, are the breeders of any repute who would risk the penalty which would come from having such charges proved against them.

The American Kennel Club, The Canadian Kennel Club, and the Kennel Club (British) do all in their power to maintain the integrity of their respective stud books. The registration of dogs is so hedged about with consideration for the accuracy of the data that there is little likelihood that a dog can be entered in the stud book and given a number on false representation. The disqualification of the person who deliberately corrupts the stud book, and the disqualification of his stock, is so certain to follow its detection that the faking of pedigrees is as foolish as it is dishonest. Very few breeders, even those whose scruples would permit, are willing to risk the sanctions. There is seldom much to be gained from the practice: there is always much to be lost. The pedigrees promulgated by reputable breeders are no more likely to be spurious than the currency you withdraw from the bank.

In purchasing a dog, one should always see to the matter that the dog is registered or that the application for registration is in order, duly signed by the breeder and the owner of the sire. And in mating a bitch to a male dog belonging to another person, one should see to it that the dog is registered. This is not only an earnest of the authenticity of the pedigree, but it saves difficulty which may arise later about the registration of the progeny of the mating.

We have said that no pedigree is better than the word of its maker. While that is true, most breeders of dogs are men of some integrity. Dogs are like any other commodity, however, and it behooves the buyer to deal with a breeder of dogs who is known to be reliable.

Dogs are bought for pets because they are cute puppies and because a woman chooses to gush about them. All puppies, good, bad, and mediocre, are cute so long as they remain puppies. The pedigree with a merely cute puppy for a pet is of little consequence. Unless a dog is to be bred from, the pedigree serves no purpose except to stimulate the vanity of an owner who is not sufficiently familiar with good dogs as to see some cryptic virtue in a list of names on a paper. Those names are of use only as a clue to what the dog's progeny may be like.

It is alleged that litters of puppies of similar ages have been reared together and so mixed up that the breeder has been unable to separate the litters with certitude and that such men are prone to assign the pedigree of one litter to a member of another litter. Such a mistake might be possible, but a breeder careless enough to confuse his litters, one with another, a man

175

who has not sufficient acquaintance with his puppies and their type not to know them apart is not likely to be the kind of breeder who consistently produces good dogs. It requires an eye for small nuances of type to be a breeder of good dogs, and a man with such an eye is not likely to confuse puppies, one with another, which he sees daily.

Occasionally a bitch is accidentally mated to two dogs at one heat. In such case, the progeny is usually best disposed of without pedigrees; however, if both sires are of the same breed as the bitch, and if all three are of such excellence that it can be shown that failure to breed from the resultant progeny would hamper the progress of their breed, registration can sometimes be made with alternate sires. This requires a special dispensation from the governing body which maintains the stud book. It is a complication better avoided when possible.

The pedigrees of the stock to be mated must loom large in the programs of any breeder of dogs. They must not, however, be permitted to overshadow the individual dogs to whom they are attached and the proved efficiency of those individual dogs as breeding material. We breed dogs to produce better dogs and not to establish spectacular pedigrees. The pedigrees are a means to an end, not an end in themselves.

To serve as that means to that end, the pedigree must be considered intelligently and only as a clue. It is necessary to judge what the various ancestors have contributed respectively to the individual and his germ plasm, and to understand that the name of a dog in a pedigree is no assurance of his contribution nor of the size of any contribution he may have made. The heart must not beat fast at the contemplation of a great name in a dog's pedigree unless the dog exhibits in himself the attributes associated with that great name and the ability to transmit those attributes to his progeny.

Pride in a dog's excellence is justifiable, and in his ability to engender excellence in his successors. That excellence has derived from some ancestor or ancestors: it is not some fairy gift from nowhere. The pedigree, analyzed correctly, shows whence

176

it came. From it may be reckoned how that germ plasm may be united to another to preserve and intensify the good we possess and to eliminate or lessen some of the faults.

The pedigree is meaningless when detached from the dog. It must be correlated with him. A given pedigree as applied to one dog may mean one thing and as applied to the dog's full brother may mean something else. One dog may have inherited the major features of his type from one ancestor, the brother from another. A knowledge of genetics and of the manner in which Mendelian factors are carried by the genes enables us to grasp such a concept. That knowledge places the pedigree in its true perspective in the scheme of breeding.

To disregard or dispense with the pedigree is to sail the seas without a chart. To consider pedigrees to the exclusion of individuals is to be so concerned with navigation as to forget our destination, which is the harbor of perfect dogs.

Ch. Golden Knoll's King Alphonzo

CHAPTER XII
Know What You Want

Few people are able to achieve exactly what they want. Anybody can know what he wants, although only a small percentage of the men who breed dogs and call themselves dog breeders really do know what they want or recognize the approximation when they approach to perfection. Even to themselves many breeders will not acknowledge their failure when they fall short of their objective.

To know what one wants is not so easy as it seems. It is not merely wishing. It involves working. To believe that one has made a touchdown when one has only crossed the ten yard line is wishful thinking, which is very human; and to believe that one has bred a great dog when one has bred only a good one is an equally normal fallacy and an equally dangerous one. When the judges give the gate to our *chef d'oeuvre*, it is they who are wrong. Everybody is out of step but Johnnie. That there is anything wrong with the dog is unthinkable.

To acknowledge our failure even to ourselves is a trial to our spirits. But there is no better place to set out to obtain what we really want than the position of acknowledgement that we do not already possess it. The breeder, to be successful, must look his dogs in the face; not only in the face but in the body, front, and running gear. He must not only value the virtues they possess but he must deprecate the faults they embody. If he is off on the wrong foot, he must catch step. If the stock he

179

has is hopeless, he must get new stock or his attempt to breed good dogs is futile.

It is not to be gainsaid that beginning with indifferent stock, a breeder can through careful breeding and selection improve it. But while the breeder with indifferent dogs is improving the stock, the breeder with good dogs with the same acumen and conscientious effort will be improving his already good stock; and while the improvement in the good stock may not be so rapid and so marked as in the indifferent stock, yet the man who has begun with good stock continues to remain just a few jumps ahead of the one who has begun his breeding operations with mediocre dogs. And there is no reason to believe that the breeder acute enough to provide himself with good material for his operations is likely to exhibit less acumen in its manipulation than is he who starts out to make a silk purse out of a sow's ear.

The larger part of us cannot afford to lay out five thousand dollars for a bitch, nor even one thousand dollars, in order that we may begin at the very top. In fact, few men who do begin with such a splurge stick to their guns as breeders of dogs. They may, and sometimes do, continue to buy winning dogs year after year in order to garner a mantelpiece full of silver cups and to feed their cheap vanity with a ration of very expensive dog meat.

Such men are but grist to the true breeder's mill. The breeder catches them coming and going. He sells them the good dogs he has bred and he utilizes, for a small outlay, the great stallion dogs for which they have paid fortunes.

But to acquire good breeding stock does not involve the investment of great sums of money. It does involve the knowledge of what one wants and of the material required to produce it. The production of fine dogs involves the skillful utilization of good stock when one has obtained it.

Anybody with enough money can obtain a good dog. He need not even know a good dog when he sees one. He can accept the consensus of judicial opinion and buy the biggest winners at the biggest shows. The dealers will probably sell him some chaff along with the grain and at grain prices, but they are astute enough to see to it that his yen to win is titillated sufficiently to keep him buying.

But merely to win does not satisfy the breeder. He not only wants to possess good dogs; he wants to breed good dogs. It is a kind of mania. Indeed, it is his means of self-expression, a creative art. As the sculptor manipulates his marble, so the breeder of dogs expresses himself in canine flesh and blood.

And what sculptor would hack and chisel at a block of marble without a conception of the statue he intended to produce? He may fail to realize his concept, he may fall short of his ideal; but it is only the knowledge of what he wants that enables him even so much as to attain its approximation.

So with the breeding of dogs. Only a few of the men who call themselves breeders do know what they want and formulate and establish an ideal toward which to work. It is those few who, year after year, generation after generation, breed the best dogs of the several varieties. They are the real breeders of dogs.

This is not so easy as it may seem. It means the expenditure of effort and of study. It is possible to any but a blind man. And it is necessary, even essential.

It means first that one must learn to know a good dog when one sees one. This is a matter about which the doctors disagree. The judges do not all see alike and what may appear a serious fault to one of them may be only a venial fault to some other. But the efficient breeder will correlate the concepts of the various judges and will take from all of them the elements which impress him as correct. This does not imply that he will accept as right only such attributes as his own dogs embody. It is necessary to look at the breed objectively, to consider its origin and purpose, to comprehend the reasons why various attributes of the variety have been imposed upon it.

Those attributes are not merely fortuitous. Trial and error, logic, and the aesthetic sense have joined to determine the characteristics which differentiate the breeds one from another.

181

The standards of perfection of the various breeds attempt to describe that differentiation and in large measure succeed. The successful breeder must know the official standard of the breed with which he works, not merely have read it or even have learned its words by rote. He must know it, must analyze it and seek to decipher its intents. Many fine nuances of every breed are impossible to put into words. The framers of standards are human and standards must not only be kept within reasonable length but also they must leave room for the play of the human equation of the breeder. If the breeding of dogs is to be and to remain a creative art, then the artist must not be too much hampered in his creative concepts.

If the standards laid down specifications minute enough, if the nonessential attributes of the breed were catalogued and detailed to the n-th power, the members of any given breed would be required to be as much alike as two cakes of Ivory soap or they would fail of their conformation to the standard of the breed. The setting forth of only the essential aspects of the breed in the standard, leaving the breeder the freedom to express his own concepts in the nonessentials, is undoubted wisdom. Such a policy makes possible the varied assortment of excellence and the play of the breeder's fancy while detracting nothing from the fitness of the dogs.

But the breeder's work is done within the somewhat broad frame of the standard. That instrument may leave much unsaid, but the specifications which it does lay down are not to be violated with impunity. In order to know what one wants it is necessary to know the bold general plan of the dog set forth in the official description of the breed.

The breeder who is familiar with the standard of his own breed only, however, is likely to become a narrow specialist. He is prone to become a breeder of Greyhounds, Bulldogs, Fox Terriers, or whatever his specialty may be, before he is a breeder of dogs. A fine member of any breed must be a fine dog first. It makes no difference how many of the arbitrary "points" of his own breed a dog may possess, if he is not a good animal and a good dog, how can he be a good Wolfhound, or Pomeranian, or what not?

The standards of breeds other than his own, especially of breeds kindred to his own, will repay a breeder's study. While it may not be necessary to observe the minutiae of type of the other breeds as closely as he observes those of his own, a sound familiarity with the others cannot but redound to the sounder knowledge of his own variety. The breeder of English Setters will know better what kind of English Setter he wants if he knows the standards of the Irish and Gordon members of the Setter trinity also. Those differences are much deeper than the merely arbitrary differences of color and pattern; they are differences of fundamental structure and have their reasons. It is only by the comprehension of wherein one breed differs from another breed that one can comprehend wherein the members of that breed are alike. And one cannot love English Setters half so well, loves one not Setters in general, field dogs, and the whole galaxy of the dog tribe even more.

These standards offer one a more or less hazy concept of what is wanted—excellent so far as it goes or can go. But in order to know a breed of dogs it is necessary to apply its standard to living dogs, to fit those dogs into the standard.

The place to do this is where the dogs are, the dog shows, the kennels of other breeders, and one's own kennel. The breeder must know his own dogs and all about them before he can undertake to mate them successfully. He must recognize the particulars, if there are any, in which they excel; and the particulars, and of these there are certainly some, in which they fall short of perfection. It is necessary to recognize faults before one can concisely and deliberately set out to correct those faults.

All too many breeders blink the shortcomings of their own dogs. The desire to be believed to excel, the yen to win, is too often greater than the desire actually to possess and to breed excellent dogs. Owners of dogs frequently, in an effort to convince others of the perfection of their dogs, actually convince themselves—usually, only themselves.

The man, or woman, who chooses to dissemble to others his dog's failings only succeeds in convincing them of his lack either of perspicacity or of veracity. If he lies to others, he will do well not to lie to himself. He must know what he has and must acknowledge it to himself to the end of obtaining what he wants. If one knows what one wants, one cannot but recognize how much and wherein what one has, falls short of it.

Concerning oneself only with one's own dogs, one is liable to become astigmatic in looking at them. One may complacently accept one's own as a standard and make no effort at improvement; or, just as likely, the minor faults of one's stock may appear major ones, impossible to correct through any scheme of breeding.

To compare one's dogs with those of other successful breeders is by no means a waste of time. It shows one not only what one has, but also what one wants to obtain.

The best place to do this is at the dog shows. There the best dogs of the community are on public exhibition. There breeders and exhibitors meet and discuss the merits and demerits of their dogs and take counsel in the solution of their problems. It is for them a holiday on which to ride their hobby.

An exhibitor is usually glad of the intelligent interest in his dogs on the part of a spectator and will permit the examination of his exhibit at the bench. The judging is, of course, public, and to sit at the ringside, catalogue of the show in hand, and watch the sorting of a numerous entry is as entertaining as it is enlightening. Judges of dog shows are human and fallible; their awards do not always meet with nor merit the approbation of spectators. At most shows, however, the awards are pretty sound and, in the absence of specific and well formulated reasons why one should not accept the judge's verdict, it is safe to assume that it is correct.

Some of the comment which one will overhear at the ringside about the various dogs in competition is worth listening to; but one will do well to consider how much of it is prejudiced and how much merely ignorant. In the heat of partisanship,

184

words which should never be spoken sometimes escape. One should consider not only which dogs win and which dogs are defeated but the reasons for their triumph or their rejection.

Even when the breeder has no dog with which he may reasonably expect to win, he is often wise to enter the best he has in the show and to exhibit him there. The possession of a dog will give him an entree to breeders' discussions, if he will avail himself of it. The opportunity to listen and ask questions is frequently valuable.

Rivalries of breeders are often bitter, but plans and ideas are seldom secret. The comments on the type and attributes of the dogs by the exhibitors are often illuminating. Many of the exhibitors know their breeds quite as well as does the judge who makes the official awards. To be a successful breeder of dogs, it is necessary that one know the breed one is manipulating well enough to recognize the comparative merits of competing dogs. One may not choose to be a licensed judge of the breed, but one should be sufficiently familiar with the nuances of faults and virtues of that breed to be able to judge it if called upon.

The judge of dogs exercises a critical faculty. The breeder is more than a mere critic—he is a craftsman. If he is a careful craftsman, he will know not only how to make it but also what it is he seeks to make.

The how and the what are equally important. One is of little service without the other. The laws of breeding are the same whether they are to be applied to humming birds or to elephants, to Chihuahuas or to Great Danes. The breeder who can breed successfully one variety can breed another with equal success if only he will formulate with equal vividness the ideal toward which he is going to work. He need not exchange his lathe for another: he has only to change the spindle to execute the new design.

The breeder will not seek to breed pigs from porcupines, nor Mexican Hairless dogs from Old English Sheepdogs. To know what materials to employ, it is necessary to know what the finished product is intended to be like.

All dogs of a given breed are in many ways alike but all are different, one from another, in details. The dogs of any long time breeder are prone to greater resemblance to each other than are the members of the variety in general. This resemblance is due to the reflection of the breeder's ideal in his stock. One breeder lays his emphasis upon the perfection of one feature of the variety, another breeder chooses to emphasize another feature. The attribute which a breeder chooses to emphasize is the expression of his own personality; nay, of his very character.

It is impossible to lay equal stress upon every aspect of a variety. Of course, any wise breeder will seek to produce well-balanced dogs, dogs of much excellence in all their departments and without glaring faults anywhere. But, willy-nilly, one man may be a stickler for correct heads; to another, coat will seem of primary importance; the third will consider the propulsive power of the hindquarters the absolute *sine qua non* for excellence. Each of these men will seek also to obtain as much merit as possible in all parts of the dogs, but the one attribute which is their hobby will mark their stock.

It is impossible to avoid such an over-emphasis upon one virtue. Breeders do not intend to become cranks about a single feature. Their intent is to emphasize the excellence of the whole animal, but to all of us there are primary essentials. Something in our own nature, character, or experience, something we do not recognize has dictated what those primary (for us, at least) essentials are to be. We have no will to permit the tail to wag the dog, nor a good coat to obscure a bad structure, or a classical head to blind one to shortcomings of body.

This over-emphasis upon a single point of excellence would be well enough if it could be made without neglect of other equally important points. It cannot be. When over-emphasis is laid upon one feature, under-emphasis upon another feature must result. Every breeder worthy of the name will make such over-emphasis but the better the breeder, the more he will strive not to entertain a lopsided ideal. He will seek to consider the whole dog, not merely the various parts. He will criticize his ideal from time to time just as he criticizes his stock to ascertain its embodiment of that ideal.

The ideal need not and ought not to be static. Familiarity and experience with a breed will lead to a gradual change of concept. Things which one has thought primary may later appear to be of only secondary moment and one may come to a realization that a feature which one has thought of incidental interest is really an essential aspect of the breed.

But the ideal should be formed with a reason for every aspect of it and should not be changed without an equally good reason. When that good reason presents itself, one should not hesitate to sacrifice one's preconception.

Not only are the ideals of the individual breeder not static, but the breeds are themselves not static. Within the framework of the standard, the ideals of the whole lot of fanciers of that breed may change. What they desired last decade may have been attained and a whole new nebula of minutiae of type may have appeared in their heavens. This change is a slow one and the individual breeder will conform unconsciously, if he is in at all intimate contact with the fancy as a whole.

There are fads that beset breeds. These mere fads are not to be mistaken for the evolutionary trend of the breed. They are merely ephemeral penchants for some spectacular phenomenon and are prone to last a season or two and to disappear.

The drift of the breed toward a finer concept of perfection is to be encouraged and followed. The fads are to be ignored. So to ignore them may prevent one's winning with one's dogs under faddist judges while the fads endure but, in the long run, one will have better dogs and more success with them if one does not run after each showy and reasonless innovation that appears. Fads are liable to sidetrack the major purpose, to breed logically constructed and well balanced dogs.

Most persons who mate two dogs of a breed together to

get some puppies, do merely that. They have no accurately formulated ideal of what they wish to produce. The true breeder has in his mind a blueprint of the perfect dog and he sets out to execute in flesh and blood and bone the plans he has formed. Such a breeder knows what he wants. He is the architect of his strain's destiny.

An intelligently formulated ideal is the effective breeder's first requisite. From that ideal he will choose the stock with which to realize it.

CHAPTER XIII

Heredity and Environment

The rearing of puppies and the care of dogs after their maturity, their feeding, housing, exercising, training, grooming, and exhibition, are all outside the province of this book, which seeks to discuss only the breeding of better dogs as a creative art. It is true that the breeder of dogs usually functions also as their keeper and caretaker but it is only with the breeding aspect of his task that we are here concerned.

The comparative influences of heredity and environment and their respective importance to the organism is a question that has been debated time out of mind. It is, however, a question unworthy of debate. No living organism is without heredity, else it would not be a living organism. It is never without environment at least partly conducive to its survival, else it would die.

Of course, the dog breeder is concerned not that the puppies he produces may merely survive; he desires that they shall flourish. For this, a wholly favorable environment is necessary.

It is as rational to argue whether a man can best survive without a head or without a heart as to dispute whether heredity or environment is the greater influence in the life of a dog or man or amoeba. In the figurative sense, men may be said to live without either head or heart, but in the literal sense, both are essential.

However well or ill a dog is to be reared and cared for, a prerequisite is that he must be bred and born. So bred and born,

189

he has a heredity. This heredity is but the configuration of the genes that form the zygote. That heredity, expressing itself in a favorable environment, determines what the organism will become.

If the complex of genes is the pattern for a Chihuahua, no possible environment can turn it into a Great Dane; if the genes are those of a Greyhound, no food, grooming, or exercise, care or medication, can cause them to produce a Bulldog.

If a dog be genetically patterned for mediocrity or less, no environment can make him excellent. The converse, however, is not true. A dog may have an excellent heredity and be bred and born to be a great dog, only to have his excellence fail of its fruition through neglect, incorrect food, disease, or some other environmental factor. He may be starved or stunted or made rachitic or crippled, deformed or even killed. There is no denying the effect environment may have upon the dog. This is no effort to belittle its influence. The care that is given him, the food he eats, the security of his housing, the very kindness or disdain with which he is treated may make him or mar him, assuming that the potentiality for excellence is in his germ plasm.

But no power on earth can make him better than his genes determine that he shall be. He must be well born before he can be well reared. The breeding comes first. The Dalmatian does not change his spots, nor the Mexican Hairless his hide.

Heredity is in the long run but the genetic environment of the variety. Only as certain genes existed in the ancestors and were transmitted through them to the organism is heredity possible; and the pre-natal environment of the foetus in the dam's uterus is quite as determining of the dog's fate as any similar period of his post-natal life. He may be starved or injured or killed before he is born. Whatever may happen to him after the gametes fuse to form the zygote is chargeable to his environment. The heredity is in the two haploid sets of chromosomes, with their attendant genes, that unite to form the zygote.

190

It is a waste of time and effort to rear and care for dogs so ill bred that even with an optimum environment they have no possibility of development into representative specimens of their variety. It is equally a waste of time and effort to breed fine animals only to have them ruined in the rearing. The work of producing a fine dog is only half done when the right parents are bred together to produce him. The other half is in the rearing and development of what has been well bred. If the breeding has been injudicious, the good care is futile.

The correct rearing of a dog involves very largely the exercise of that rare quality known as common sense. Only ordinary intelligence is required. Well nigh anybody should be able to rear a dog if only he does not neglect or postpone the things which are all but self-evidently needful to be done.

The rearing and care of a dog involves primarily an adequate ration of food suitable to a carnivore and a supply of fresh water. It includes fit shelter and quarters. It involves the freeing of the animal from internal and external parasites, cleaning, grooming, exercise, training, and companionship; all of which are parts of the dog's environment. The prevention of disease and suitable treatment and care of the dog, if and when he is ill, are a part of correct rearing. If available prevention is used, much treatment is seldom necessary. Even that canine scourge, distemper, can now be avoided by proper prophylaxis, which any efficient veterinarian will undertake.

Many books have been written upon the theme of the care, feeding, and management of dogs, although much of the information contained in them should not be accepted too seriously. From them can be gleaned ideas, however, which can and should be utilized as the circumstances warrant. Most of these books are replete with old-wives' tales and mistaken concepts handed from one ignorant generation of dog keepers to another. Care should be exercised to extract the grain of truth from the chaff of superstition contained in them.

191

The correct management of a dog depends somewhat upon the individual dog, his variety, age, temperament, upon the individual owner or keeper, upon the purpose for which the dog is used or intended, and upon the facilities available for his maintenance. The keeping of a Pekingese in a one room apartment is very different from the keeping of a pack of hounds in a kennel, and that in turn is different from the shepherd's keeping of his herding dogs upon the range. The workman's modest kennel in his back yard is perforce different from the elaborate establishment in which the millionaire may house his dogs, although the dogs in the one may be as excellent, as well cared for, and as happy as the dogs in the other.

Dogs are only inferior to men in their adaptability to their environment and are likely to thrive if given an even partial chance to do so. This book does not and does not pretend to treat of the rearing, keeping, and management of dogs, but only of their breeding. This chapter is but a warning to the reader that no amount of devotion will develop an ill-bred puppy into a good dog. And also equally to warn him that no matter how excellently bred his dog may be, that excellence requires adequate rearing, care, and management for its fruition.

The warning here given is not so discouraging as it may seem. Judicious breeding implies only the bringing together of suitable mates with full consideration of their ancestry. A dog seldom fails of adequate rearing when the owner's will is to do the best he knows or can ascertain. A good dog is at once a good deal of trouble and a vast amount of joy. He can endure some neglect, but he does not deserve negligence and there is an ultimate limit to the amount of it he can stand.

CHAPTER XIV

Things That Are Not True

Even until the end of the nineteenth century mothers were wont to suspend around the neck of their offspring cloth bags of stinking asafetida in the mistaken belief that it was a preventive of infection. Indeed, the amulet may have been so malodorous as to keep at a safe distance persons who might otherwise have come into closer contact with its wearer and so may have served its prophylactic purpose. The vile substance in itself certainly had no efficacy in the protection of children from disease. Any other means of rendering the child offensive enough to keep him at sneeze-length from others would have served as well.

The theory was superstition, purely and simply, an old-wives' tale handed down from one generation of ignorant crones to another. There are thousands of such erroneous beliefs which range all the way from the concept that tomatoes are poisonous and that feather beds protect sleepers from lightning, to the idea that frequent bathing of the human body is harmfully enervating.

The breeding and keeping of dogs has been cluttered up with as much superstitious trash as has the breeding and rearing of the human animal. The care of dogs has been left largely to uninformed underlings who have wished much of their empiric nonsense upon their betters. Until a comparatively recent time, indeed, science itself has been at little pains to disprove the erroneous ideas which have persisted since the siege of Troy.

We are loath to surrender our pet superstitions. But the world does move.

It is only such superstitions as affect the breeding of dogs that we have here to do with. Even for those which pertain to the keeping and maintenance of dogs—such as that milk causes worms, that a meat diet makes a dog vicious, or that gunpowder is a remedy for distemper—we have here no room.

The breeder who is actuated in his practices by his superstitious beliefs is deterred by just so much from his observation of helpful truths. The breeder who discards an otherwise useful bitch because she previously has had a litter of puppies by a mongrel dog is permitting an outworn and discredited superstition to disrupt his breeding program.

This particular belief that the heredity of animals is, at least in part, derived from mates to which their dams have produced progeny at some earlier time is known technically as telegony. It is often called "the influence of the previous sire." It is entirely disproved, although it received some credence in biology until recent times.

Indeed, Sir John Millet wrote his *Two Problems of Reproduction* in part to prove the validity of telegony. In that work he sought to show that stripes on the colt of a certain horse mare by a horse stallion were due to her having produced an earlier colt by a quagga stallion. Not only was the experiment inadequately controlled but it has since been recognized that many true horse colts show vestigial stripes in their early life.

Implied in the theory of telegony would be a concept that a human child would partake in its heredity of the attributes of any man by whom the mother had previously borne a child, and that maternal half-brothers are more closely related than that relationship is recognized to be. It would also imply that a bitch which had ever been pregnant to a given dog might forever afterward, to whatever dog she may subsequently be

194

bred, produce progeny which would bear a hereditary relationship to her earlier mate.

So-called common sense, it may be said, should have convinced us that such a phenomenon is not possible. But common sense is not to be trusted in the face of scientific credence. However, our present knowledge of the genes and chromosomes is adequate to controvert the theory of telegony. No geneticist of any claim to scientific attainments now harbors the belief that the heredity of an animal is influenced by any sire to whom its dam had been mated except the immediate one who contributed his haploid set of chromosomes to the zygote from which developed the animal under consideration.

Dog breeders would do well to ignore telegony. Long believed true, it is outmoded and discredited. There are, even now, thousands of practical breeders who yet are unconvinced of its falsity and who believe that they would mongrelize their strain by breeding from a bitch which had had an earlier litter by a dog not of her own variety. Many a good bitch is needlessly eliminated from breeding programs by such ill-founded beliefs, and breeding operations are so hampered.

The discredit of telegony does not imply that a bitch may not produce puppies in one litter some of which may be by one sire and some by another. That she may do so, however, it is necessary that she shall be mated with more than one dog at the single heat.

No individual dog has more than one sire. If a bitch should be mated to two or more dogs at a single heat and produce puppies by more than one of them, no single puppy has more than one sire, and that sire is the one whence came the spermatozoön which fertilized the ovum from which he derived. The other dog or dogs to which the dam was mated contributed no part of the heredity of that particular puppy.

A bitch may be mated to two dogs at a single heat and produce a litter of puppies in which some members are by one sire and some members by the other sire. No puppy is by both sires. If one of her mates should be a purebred member of

195

her own variety and the other mate or mates should be mongrels or members of some other variety, such puppy or puppies as result from the mating to the purebred dog are just as purebred as if the other mating had never taken place.

In such a litter it is not always easy or even possible to determine which sire is responsible for which puppy or puppies. Especially is this true at an early age and it is sometimes wiser to destroy the entire litter than to rear any part of it if there is any doubt of the authenticity of the pedigree of the puppies.

There have been a few cases in which bitches have been mated to two dogs of their own variety at the same heat and have produced litters, the members of which it has been impossible to attribute definitely to either sire. In such a circumstance, one of the dogs may be responsible for the entire litter; or some of the puppies may be by one dog, some by the other. No single puppy, however, derives a part of his heredity from one sire and a part from the other. He has one single sire, although it may be impossible to determine which of his dam's mates that sire may be.

It is sometimes possible to obtain registration for dogs of uncertain paternity, provided that both of the possible alternate sires are purebred and that the dam is of such excellence that the perpetuation of her germ plasm is essential for the furtherance of her variety. Such registration of thoroughbred horses with so-called alternate sires is not unusual. It complicates the records, however, and is to be encouraged only in most exceptional circumstances.

Another of the widely credited but mistaken beliefs is the one about "prenatal impressions." By that term is meant that the heredity of the progeny is influenced by mental or emotional processes of the dam during her pregnancy.

The world is full of people who explain their birthmarks by the fancied resemblance in the shape of such birthmarks to something which is alleged to have caused an emotional trauma to the pregnant mother. She may have craved straw-

196

berries or have seen a mouse, hence the shape of the mark. If the mother had gone to the circus, might the child have been born with riding boots? It is useless to try to convince persons who harbor such beliefs that they are not true. But the breeder of animals should be made soundly aware that the belief in such "prenatal impressions" is rank superstition.

The belief is one of great antiquity and has persisted so long that it is difficult to eradicate. Indeed, it is of Old Testament origin. In Genesis is cited the instance of Jacob, who bargained with his uncle, Laban, to accept as wages for his services as a shepherd such parti-colored lambs as should appear in the flock. Thereupon, the wily Jacob is recorded to have set up striped sticks before the pregnant ewes to induce them to produce striped and spotted lambs. There is a greater likelihood that Jacob had a pied ram in the shed in the back yard which Laban knew nothing about.

The ancient Greeks are known to have set up beautiful statues upon which their pregnant women were to gaze for the purpose of bettering the appearance of the children they carried. The fact is that looking at such statues had no effect whatever upon the progeny. Any reader who had read the chapter on "The Chromosomes and Their Genes" in the earlier part of this book will know that this belief is mere superstition and will know why.

This is not to say that an emotional shock, such as a great fright, to the pregnant dam will not in any way affect the progeny. It is to say that it will not affect the heredity of the foetus. It may so interfere with the metabolism of the mother as to affect adversely the nutrition of the foetus temporarily. It may even produce abortion. But the heredity is locked up in the genes and chromosomes of the gametes which united to form the zygote, and it is inalterable.

This matter of "pre-natal impressions" is another of the incubi of superstition which science lifts from the breeder's shoulders. Let him peel wands or carve statues, as many as he will, his bitches will produce neither better nor worse puppies.

197

The time and effort which he may devote to the establishment of such "pre-natal impressions" is entirely wasted and were much better employed in the making of correct matings and in the providing of nutrition and comfort to his stock, or even in the mere twiddling of his thumbs.

Indeed, the belief in "pre-natal impressions" is of a piece with the exploded belief in the inheritance of acquired characteristics. This belief has died hard even in scientific circles and there are even yet a few biologists, a very few of the old fashioned American and new fashioned Soviet, who continue to maintain the possibility of acquired characteristics being transmitted in heredity. Even they do not assume that such transmission is a common occurrence or that it has any bearing upon the work of the practical breeder.

Lamarck, whose name the theory of such inheritance of acquired characteristics bears, died long before Mendel began his epoch-making experiments with garden peas. The influence of Lamarck was so potent that the theories, however erroneous, which he promulgated tend to survive. That environmental influences do or can affect the reproductive cells seems to modern biologists impossible. There is no reason to believe that they do. However, it is also impossible to prove absolutely that they do not.

The tails of sheep have been docked for hundreds of generations and there is yet no tendency toward the natural shortening of that appendage. There is no evidence that the persistent shaving of the human beard for however many generations it has been practiced has any tendency to produce a race of beardless men. For however many generations the ancestors of a child may have spoken a given language, there is no natural disposition on the part of the child to speak that language rather than some other. He learns and uses the tongue he hears rather than the one his progenitors heard and spoke.

No training or conditioning is believed to be heritable. The instinct to point game is derived by inheritance in Pointers and Setters, as the herding instinct is natural to the Collie.

198

These instincts have been developed through generations of selective breeding and are as much a part of the individual as the color of his hair or the shape of his skull. They can be and are transmitted from one generation to another. The training or conditioning which is superimposed upon the instinct, for the purpose of making useful the animal which possesses it, however, cannot be transmitted. A Pointer does not produce better hunting progeny after he has had his education than before. The trainability which made it possible to train him may be handed on to his progeny; the training which he receives, or any part of it, cannot be.

The fact that a dog is trained proves that he was trainable. And the fact that great field trial winners derive from great field trial ancestry is no earnest that the parents' training was transmitted to their progeny, but rather their trainability. Great working dogs are bred from because they work, which proves that they are workable. Such dogs would transmit to their progeny the same ability to work even if they had never been used for work; but only the actual work they do, proves their ability to work and enables breeders to know that they can work.

The same is true of disease. Immunity to or predisposition for certain diseases may be inherent in the animal and transmissible to his progeny. The fact that he has had a given disease proves that he was not immune to it. His progeny begotten before he had the disease will be just as prone to contract it as the progeny begotten after the parent has had the disease.

The evidence in behalf of the inheritance of acquired characteristics may not all be in, and science maintains an open door for any new findings which may be interpreted as confirmation of the largely discredited theory. Such as have been presented, however, do not stand up under critical scrutiny. We do know that, even if it should be demonstrated that such inheritance were possible, it is possible only in a manner and degree that has no bearing upon the practical breeding of livestock and is of but academic interest to the breeder.

It may be objected that alterations in heredity which result from X-radiation may be considered as an acquired characteristic. Such is not the case for the characteristics so transmitted are not first impressed upon the body, but rather the germ plasm is itself directly affected. The use of X-radiation to alter heredity will hardly be of practical use in the breeding of higher animals, although it may revolutionize the breeding of domestic plants and result in a vast boon to agriculture. Experimentation in such X-radiation of gametes is only in its swaddling clothes and since it does not promise to be useful in the production of better dogs, only brief mention is made of it in this work.

Nor do we intend to say that infectious diseases cannot be contracted by offspring from their dam, even before they are born, but only that such diseases are not heritable, although the predisposition to them may be.

Since it is so well established that acquired characteristics are not inherited, it is, therefore, safe to use for breeding otherwise suitable animals which may have been accidentally injured or maimed. The exhibition career of a dog may be ended by a broken leg which affects the animal's gait, or by the loss of an eye. Such animals, however excellent, are liable to be neglected by breeders. Many a fine dog has been needlessly rejected in the stud because some accident has rendered him unsound or unbeautiful. Inherited unsoundnesses are liable to transmission, as are inherited predispositions to the development of unsoundnesses; but no harm can come of utilizing an otherwise useful animal with an acquired unsoundness.

And since educability only, and not education itself, can be transmitted, the fact that a dog has not been trained for a given use need not deter the breeder from employing him to produce progeny for that use. While the proof of the ability to be trained is in the training, a dog will usually show an aptitude for a certain kind of activity before training is undertaken. That aptitude is transmissible in heredity and should, of course, be taken account of. There is no reason to wait for a dog to be trained before he is bred from.

The matter of the age of breeding stock is one about which there is gross misapprehension. That it is desirable to mate aging bitches to young dogs, or vice versa, is a firmly fixed belief, but without scientific foundation. That they be sexually mature and vigorous is the only consideration necessary to be given to the age of animals to be mated. If both are young or both old (short of senescence), the mating is equally as desirable as if one were young and the other old.

Animals reach sexual maturity somewhat younger than physical maturity. A young male dog physically immature should not be bred from often enough to deplete his stamina, however excellent he may be. Indeed, this is especially true if he is of great excellence. But neither should a mature dog be over-used. However, there is no reason to expect that the offspring from a sexually mature but physically immature male dog will be inferior to the offspring which the same dog may beget later in his life.

Nor, on the other hand, is there any good reason why an aging dog should be discarded from the breeding program so long as he is fertile.

Statistics have been gathered and tables made to show the ages of various great sires at the time of the conception of their various successful progeny. Interesting, such data may be, but they will not bear critical analysis unless they be accompanied with further data to show what opportunities these sires may have had (both as to the number and excellence of the mates bred to them) to produce excellent progeny at other ages.

To breed from a bitch at her first heat if she is physically immature is doubtful wisdom. While maternity may tend to develop her, the nourishing of the foeti and lactation may deplete her stamina. Each such case is to be considered separately and when doubt persists, it is wise to wait for the second heat before breeding. Some breeders, especially breeders of Bulldogs and Boston Terriers, consider that an early litter, before the

pelvis skeleton is thoroughly calcified, conduces to easier whelping of the first and of subsequent litters. There is grave doubt
that the theory is valid.

Very old bitches are certainly questionable breeding material.
Metabolism slows up with advancing age; and, while an old
bitch may contribute to her progeny a heredity similar to that
she gave her earlier offspring, she may not be able so adequately
to nourish the developing foeti nor to provide her young with
milk of pristine quality or quantity.

There is also a prevalent theory that a bitch should not have
two successive litters by the same dog, no matter how satisfactory
the mating or how excellent the results from the first union. To
believe this is to believe nonsense. It is true that if a bitch has
produced a superlative offspring in one litter, the laws of probability are that she will not produce another so excellent in
her subsequent litter. Great puppies are not frequent enough
for that. But if the mate by whom she produced the superlative
puppy is the best and most suitable mate for her at one time,
there is no reason why the mating should be discontinued.
That she has produced a satisfactory litter is proof that she
is a sound brood bitch and is equal proof that her mate was
well chosen. The comprehension of the behavior of the genes,
and the realization that the gametes are separate and individual entities, is ample refutation for this erroneous concept
that mates necessarily should be changed from litter to litter.

As untenable as these other fallacies is that an organism derives certain attributes unvariably from its sire and certain
other attributes from its dam; as, for instance (and this is the
most prevalent version of the idea), that the exterior portions
come from the sire, the viscera and constitution from the
dam. We know that everything heritable is the result of the
pairing of genes, one of each pair deriving from each parent.
The resemblance of any attribute of the organism may be to
either parent, to some ancestor of a parent, or to both parents
and their ancestors. This superstition is so patently untrue to
anybody who will examine it in the light of the gene concept

that further discussion than to declare that it is untrue is unnecessary.

Dogs are advertised at stud as the "sires of large litters" and are touted as the producers of preponderant numbers of male progeny. These circumstances, so far as the male is concerned, are purely fortuitous. We have seen in earlier chapters that the size of the litter is determined by the number of ova deposited by the bitch, and that the male dog produces exactly equal numbers of male producing and female producing sperm. The male deposits enough sperm to fertilize millions of ova and he deserves no credit for the number of puppies in a litter. Whether an ovum is fertilized by a sperm which carries the X-chromosome or by one which carries the Y-chromosome is as much a matter of chance as anything can be in this world.

Nor can the sex of puppies be influenced or determined by any method yet known. This is discussed at considerable length in Chapter VIII and is mentioned here only because the efforts of practical breeders to obtain a preponderance of puppies of one sex or the other are futile and wasted.

Many breeders consider equal the breeding value of two full brothers more closely related than are other full brothers, and genetic relationship of two brothers depends upon the number of like genes they have received from their parents. We have demonstrated elsewhere how it is theoretically possible that full brothers may be genetically unrelated one to the other. This is a remote possibility, indeed, but it tends to show how variable the breeding worth of full siblings may be. One dog may be a consistently excellent sire and his full brother as great a failure.

It is true that identical twins, both developed from a single ovum fertilized by a single sperm, are as genetically alike as they are likely to be physically alike and that their breeding worth is equal. Among dogs, identical twins are rare phenomena, however, and are seldom recognized to be identical. Unless one has positive knowledge that two dogs are identical twins, one cannot accept a dog as a substitute for his full brother just because of the pedigree relationship.

It is, of course, reasonable to expect that brothers who bear close resemblance to each other have received many of the same genes from their parents, and the progeny of one such brother may be expected to bear a closer resemblance to the progeny of the other than if the two sires were not closely related. But this resemblance is not so great that the breeder is justified in complacency of choice between the two brothers as a mate for any particular bitch.

The belief that breeding animals must be in the optimum of coat growth and condition at the time of mating to produce the best coats on their progeny is perhaps not so prevalent among breeders of dogs as among breeders of cats and rabbits. It is, however, widespread among breeders of many of the longer coated varieties of dogs, particularly of the Toy varieties. There is no reason to think that it deserves any credence.

Excellently coated dogs, especially if of excellently coated ancestry, tend to produce excellent coats upon their progeny; but mates, one or both of which are "out of coat," shedding or in old broken coat or clipped coat, are as likely to produce good coated progeny as are the same two mates at another time when their coats are in nicest bloom. It is not the condition of the coats at the time of mating that must be considered, but rather the ability to grow correct coats. The genes in the chromosomes of the parents determine the length, density, texture, and color of the coats of the progeny and these genes are not altered by the temporary condition of the coats of the parents.

"Like begets like" is an old adage, almost an axiom, of the breeder's art. All that is wrong with it as a guide is that it happens not to be true. That like *tends* to beget like, however, is true. But that tendency may be of greater or lesser degree. Do not count upon it that "like begets like." In many instances like begets similar, although it is not always true. What is begotten is tied up within the genes and chromosomes of the

204

zygote. It may be like either parent or like neither. The old confidence that like can be depended upon to produce like is too simple a rule. The art of breeding animals is much more complicated than that.

Modern genetics sheds a bright light upon the "like begets like" fallacy. Indeed, it enables us to comprehend why all these "things that are not true" cannot be true. If it did no more than discredit these mistaken beliefs which have for so many years complicated breeding practices without adding one iota to the results, they would not have been promulgated in vain. The fact is that they have not only served to show why these untruths cannot be true but they have offered us positive truths to take the place of the superstitions that have actuated the breeders of plants and animals.

These superstitions are difficult to exorcise. To many old-fashioned, practical breeders the denial of their cherished ideas will be heresy. Progress in the development of domestic plants and animals has been made despite the lack of enlightenment of so many practitioners of the breeder's art. But that progress has not been made because of the adherence of breeders to faith in outworn, medieval ideas, but has been made despite such adherence.

To give heed to these principles which are discredited and untrue is to neglect the scientific truths which enable one to formulate a breeding program and to put it into effect with an assurance that it will lead steadily, intelligently, and certainly toward the realization of the ideals toward which the breeder strives.

CHAPTER XV

Choosing a Brood Bitch

All the facts of science are of but little use until they can be and are applied to human activity. The sciences have advanced much more rapidly than has the practical utilization of the wonders which they have revealed to us. This is especially true of the breeding of domestic animals. In the breeding of dogs, which for so many of its exponents has been a sport or a pastime rather than a business or vocation, the lag is somewhat more marked than in breeding of other animals which have a recognizedly greater economic value.

Most breeders of dogs have some vague conception that there is such a phenomenon as Mendelism, but it has remained little more than a word to them. There has been a doubt that it had any practical value in the production of better dogs. A simple exposition of it has been difficult to obtain, and expressed even in its simplest terms it requires some mental effort to comprehend. But that comprehension is worth that effort.

If a clear knowledge of the Mendelian phenomena and of the manner in which the genes behave serves no further purpose than to make the breeder cognizant that he is selecting genes rather than mingling bloods, he is bound to be a sounder craftsman than is one without that concept of the medium in which he works. The edifice of which the breeder is the architect is built up of individual stones, the genes, some black

206

and some white. It is not a structure of poured concrete blended partly from one mate and partly from the other.

The practical breeders of other centuries, despite their misapprehension, accomplished much in the development of our handsome and useful races of livestock before Mendelism was ever thought of. Their empiric selection of breeding stock was merely the choice of the best individuals and the rejection of the worst. True, the method worked—in a way. It is still working—in a way. Present methods are but little different from the old.

But those earlier builders unwittingly rejected many a sound stone and included in their temple many a fragile one. They assumed that their stock was exactly what it seemed to be and made little, if any, distinction between what a given animal was and what he could transmit to his progeny—between the phenotype and the genotype. Those readers who have come thus far with us know how mistaken was that assumption.

The exhibition worth and the breeding worth of a dog may be and frequently are equal. The great show dog or bitch is often the most useful for the breeder. But many great show dogs fail miserably when they are set to reproduce their own excellencies; and, equally true, many dogs which could hardly win a ribbon in the show ring have proved invaluable as breeding animals.

Then how shall one go about the selection of breeding stock? How shall one apply all of this wisdom for which Morgan and other workers in the field of genetics have gone to the fruit fly and considered his genes?

The first concern of the dog breeder is the bitch. No kennel is stronger than its bitches. A single producing bitch may be, and has been more often than not, the very cornerstone of a successful strain of any variety of dog.

The reasons why this is true are not far to seek. The first and best of them is that the breeder must be the owner (or at least the lessee, and the best brood bitches are not easy to lease) of his bitches, whereas the best of the male dogs are at public stud and the breeder may employ the service of the best of them at a moderate cost and may continue the use of a dog which proves to be a satisfactory mate for a given bitch, or may change to another from which he anticipates better results without any disruption of his own establishment. He need make no investment in the ownership of males and may veer from one to another as his fancy and policy may please. His bitches are what they are and he must either continue his operations with what he has or scrap them and get others which he thinks are more useful for his purpose. His foundation bitches are a permanent part of his strain. Their germ plasm will continue to influence his dogs from generation to generation. It is unpleasant to part with such as fail as satisfactory breeders, in order to replace them with others, and we are prone to put up with the unfortunate genes we have in our bitches rather than fly to others of which we are by no means certain.

Thus, in acquiring a bitch for breeding purposes, one is casting a die. With her one may try one dog and if he is unsatisfactory may try another. The good brood bitch is a fixture of the strain.

The bitch contributes one of the two haploid sets of chromosomes which determine every zygote, and her influence on the puppies is exactly half. But even more care in choosing her is necessary than in choosing a male with which to mate her. Bitches produce but a limited number of puppies and if one is to judge a bitch by what she has already produced, one has but few of her progeny to be canvassed for the excellencies which one seeks to produce. This is especially true if she be young; and if she has never had puppies, one is forced to judge her ability to produce what one wants not by her progeny but by her appearance and her pedigree.

On the other hand, most dogs at public stud have a record as producers and it is much easier to evaluate their potentialities from the large number of their progeny than to arrive at a conclusion about a bitch from a consideration of a small number of progeny or none. It is, therefore, unwise to stake the fortunes of one's strain upon a bitch without a very thorough canvass of the traits she is likely to pass on to her puppies.

The breeder who has five thousand dollars, or even one thousand, to invest in a fine bitch may or may not be very fortunate. It is undoubtedly easier to obtain the right bitch if one is not to limit oneself as to her cost, but to do so, even then, requires some perspicacity; and the breeder who is not prepared to make so large an investment must make up in astuteness what he lacks in Bradstreet rating. There is, indeed, an added zest in having chosen well and wisely over having accepted the apparently obvious which may or may not turn out to be what one wants.

One wants a fine brood bitch. If one is prepared to pay a long price, the dealers are liable to foist upon one a great winner without regard to her ability to reproduce her own excellencies or those of her breed.

It is certainly true that many of the best brood bitches have been fine show bitches, too. The converse is also true, that many fine show bitches prove to be first rate breeders. But show worth and breeding worth are not by any means identical, some really great show bitches failing to transmit their own fine qualities to their puppies, and some of the great brood bitches being but mediocre specimens of their breed.

It is, of course, true that all other data being equal, it is wiser to choose the best individual to breed from, but that "like begets like" is not to be accepted as axiomatic. A bitch may fail in one particular aspect which with intelligent mating is not likely to appear in her progeny, and yet may herself be damned as an exhibition animal by that particular "out." She may be too large or too small; faulty in color or in coat; defective in ear carriage; or lacking in temperament or style, and yet may become the dam of paragons.

If she is seriously faulty in several aspects of the ideal of her breed, it is certainly hazardous to breed from her, and particularly it is desirable that the skeletal structure and proportions be approximately correct. If she be of too heavy or too light bone

209

formation, and if she has not sprung from an ancestry of similar failing, with an intelligent mating she need not hand on such failings to any large proportion of her descendants. Especially to be avoided are stilty or proppy shoulders, improperly angulated quarters, long and slack backs, coarse, common skulls, and bad feet. These are faults of the skeleton and are very hard to eradicate.

Especially should the novice beware of the bitch with the long loin, recommended as being desirable because there is plenty of room in which to carry her foetuses. There is an utterly mistaken tradition that brood bitches with long loins should be excused that fault. There perhaps never was a bitch who did not have sufficient room for the development of all the puppies that she conceived. We know that the number of puppies in a litter is not dependent upon the length of the mother's loin, but rather upon the number of ova deposited in her Fallopian tubes. And, in any event, the true breeder is not so much concerned with the number of her puppies as with their excellence or lack of it.

The bitch as an individual is worth consideration. Figs from thistles are no more improbable than fine dogs from a malformed, scrawny waster of a dam. But the appearance of the bitch is important only as an earnest and outward manifestation of the genes she carries and is to transmit to her progeny.

The next consideration may well be the kind of progeny she has already produced. This, too, is but corroborative evidence that she harbors desirable genes, else she could not have given them to her sons and daughters. If she is young, her progeny is either none or few. If it is consistently high class, it is more important in the evaluation of what she is likely to produce again than if she should have produced a single paragon of a dog standing out like a sore thumb in a litter of mediocrities or less. That paragon may be a mere lightning stroke of the meeting of the best genes from both sides of the house, and lightning is not likely to strike twice in the same gene combinations.

In looking at her progeny, too, it is well to take into full account what dog was their sire and how much he may have contributed to the excellence or inferiority of the young. If the mating was a foolish one, the bitch is not to be too incontinently rejected because her young are no better than might be expected from such a union. On the other hand, if the sire of the progeny is one recognized as consistently able to stamp his progeny with his own merits and those of the line from which he sprang, the dam is to be given somewhat less credit for the excellence of her young. But if she has produced consistently well to a good sire, there is reason to believe that she may repeat the performance when mated to the same dog or to another of equal excellence as an individual and of equally good germ plasm. In this connection, it is especially to be remembered that to the wrong mate any bitch, no matter how worthy a breeder of fine stock, will fail as a producer.

The third aspect of the brood bitch to be looked at is her pedigree. Without excluding the importance of the animal as an individual or as a known producer of stock of a given degree of merit, the pedigree is perhaps of greater moment than any other single item.

The pedigree standing alone on paper and leaving the individual bitch out of consideration may or may not mean something. We have seen earlier in this book how it is remotely and theoretically possible that full sisters may be entirely unrelated and that an animal may have derived none of his chromosomes from one of his grandparents on either or both sides. This is a very rare circumstance and perhaps has never occurred. But it is practically possible and not rare that two full sisters or two full brothers are very distantly related, neither look alike nor behave alike, and are not reasonably to be expected to produce progeny which are alike.

A perfect pedigree, one showing a sufficiently long line of perfect ancestry, must needs produce a perfect animal, which, mated to another of equal perfection of type and ancestry, must needs produce perfect progeny. But such infinitudes of perfection are not to be found in living organisms and are seldom to be approached.

In the examination of the written pedigree of our prospective brood bitch, we are certain to find the names of animals whose attributes we would choose not to reproduce, and if we delve into the remoter ancestry many such names will appear. We cannot have perfection either of individual or of pedigree. If it should ever be achieved, the uncertainty and hence the satisfaction of breeding dogs would disappear. But a wise choice of breeding stock reduces that uncertainty to the minimum; and, since the satisfaction depends upon progress rather than upon perfection beyond which there can be no progress, good stock intensifies that satisfaction.

By comparing the pedigrees with the individuals, we may choose individual bitches which in their phenotypes manifest the desirable attributes of the ancestry and which abjure the undesirable. This is but an earnest, not an assurance, that the genotype may coincide with the phenotype.

If one possess the acumen and the money to recognize and buy a great brood bitch who has proved her ability in litter after litter to produce first rate progeny by various dogs, one need waste little further effort upon the choice of bitches. The foundation of the kennel has been laid. But such bitches, the very backbones of their respective breeds, are rare and the breeders wise enough to have acquired them are often too wise to part with them before their usefulness is at an end. Seldom are they to be acquired over the bargain counter. Of this kind, the pedigree is immaterial in the acquiring of a bitch: it will take care of itself. The ability to produce consistently good stock is a guarantee that the genes are right. The pedigree, of course, must be taken into account when one sets out to find a mate for her.

If one cannot have a bitch which has already achieved greatness as a breeder, one can usually manage to obtain a daughter of such a one. Even the unproved daughters are not cheap, especially if they are old enough to demonstrate that as show specimens they are worthy of their celebrated dam. But one can obtain a puppy from the nest or even contract for one before it is born. The delay entailed is not long and is justified by the anticipated results.

In any pedigree the chief name to be considered is that of the dam. There are dozens of dogs by excellent sires to every one from a superlative mother. This is true because the excellent sires serve many bitches, of which only a few are of superior quality.

If the dam is a recognized producer of fine stock and is herself of first rate ancestry, it matters not that she is not herself a great show specimen. The word "champion" before a name in a pedigree may mean very little.

A fine bitch, in the hands of an experienced breeder, will hardly have been mated to an inferior or unsuitable male, which is the reason why the distaff side of the pedigree should overbalance the male line.

Of course, the sire of the bitch is not to be neglected but if the dam is an outstanding one and if the breeder of the bitch knew his business, that sire can well nigh be taken for granted. It is well to note how intense is the inbreeding of that most desirable part of the bitch's germ plasm—whether her sire is on paper closely related to her dam. This may not be entirely apparent without a careful analysis of the pedigree, which may show doubling and redoubling of some particular ancestor, which at last focuses upon the individual under scrutiny, and, if the inbreeding is as real as it is apparent, makes her what she is.

It is still a prevalent belief that any purebred bitch is good enough to breed from. A bitch not good enough to exhibit is, in breeders' parlance, "just a brood bitch." This belief is rather gradually disappearing—but much too slowly. The facts are that really first rate producing bitches are quite as rare as are first rate show bitches, and it is very frequently true that the best show animals are the best brood animals. At very least, no bitch can be too excellent an individual to be bred from.

It is equally true that certain minor shortcomings, especially such as are not obvious in her ancestry, need not destroy the worth of the bitch, as a mother of fine dogs. Many such shortcomings are acquired rather than inherited, such as partial blindness from accident, torn ears, scars, accidental cripplings, and do not detract at all from the breeding worth of an otherwise desirable brood bitch.

The whole question resolves itself into a determination of the genes she has and is likely to transmit. If her gene complex were perfect, she would be perfect, and mated to a perfect dog, she would produce perfect progeny. But dogs and bitches are not perfect. What we seek is a bitch with genes as nearly perfect to produce progeny of the ideals of her breed as it is possible to obtain.

The fact that her dam habitually transmitted desirable genes to her offspring and that her sire transmitted desirable genes to his offspring offers us some assurance that the desirable recessive genes of her race will be present and that the desirable dominant genes will be pure dominants and not merely hybrid dominants.

This means simply that the bitch is purebred in fact—purebred in a Mendelian sense as well as in a stud book sense.

It may be argued that great dogs have not always sprung from great dogs; that the various breeds have had a gradual growth in the manifestation of the ideal. And, hence, it may be said that mediocre dogs are quite good enough to breed from, that we can never more than guess about what will result from any mating and that a good dog is a freak of nature.

It is admitted that there has been a gradual growth of the breeds and that our great dogs have sprung from an ancestry of less excellence. But this improvement has been a gradual, more or less haphazard, and all too frequently unconscious, sifting out of the bad genes of the various strains and the retention of the genes that make for what we want.

This sifting of the genes can be a conscious and deliberate practice which will enable the breeder to use his stock with a degree of assurance of what he will produce from it. That assurance cannot be absolute until one knows all about every gene in every chromosome of every animal one breeds from; and that is, of course, impossible.

However, the realization of the medium in which the breeder-artist is working—the fitting together of gene entities rather than the blending of bloods—enables him to go forward in the light much more rapidly than he can work in the dark. The breeder who will choose his breeding stock with an awareness that he is merely making a mosaic of genes will obtain good results better and earlier than will the one who adheres to the old empiricism, breeders' superstitions, and rule-of-thumb methods.

The choosing of the brood bitch may be approached from either of two angles—with or without having previously selected a mate for her. One may choose a male, either one's own or that of another, from whom he wishes to obtain a litter of puppies. In such an event, the bitch should be chosen, both as to her individual type and especially as to her pedigree, to complement the germ plasm of that male. This somewhat complicates the situation in adding another element to the making of that choice. She must be not only of great breeding worth herself but she must be a suitable mate for a particular male dog.

This method may be entirely justifiable since one may have chosen a male who is so consistently efficient as a sire of good stock that to fail to use him would stultify the breeder's program. Or one may own a dog in whose ability to sire fine stock one may have sound confidence, and for the purpose of offering him a chance to prove that ability one may go about selecting a mate for him. In either of such cases, the breeder predicates his operations upon the male of the mating.

The other angle of approach is that of merely a desire to produce fine dogs. This is, other things being equal, the better way. In it one sets out to obtain the most likely brood bitch and to predicate his breeding upon her germ plasm. Having her, he sets about to select for her the best and most suitable mate among all the many dogs available to which she may be bred. Most great strains have been established is such a manner—often fortuitously. And just as fortuitously, many of them strut their brief hour in the dog shows and degenerate to mediocrity through permitting in a few generations those pure dominant genes to pick up recessive complements.

Eternal vigilance is required to retain the purity of the germ plasm from generation to generation. To that end, both mates for every breeding must be as genetically pure as it is possible to have them. Because the bitch has been most frequently neglected, with the emphasis of choice laid upon the male, and because the breeder has a wealth of males from which to choose, it becomes doubly necessary to concentrate attention upon the choice of the bitch. Having the right bitch, the rest is comparatively easy.

CHAPTER XVI

Choosing a Stud Dog

The small breeder who owns a single stud dog, unless it be one of those so-called "pillars of the breed" around which a strain may be built and upon which his whole breeding program may be predicated, is unfortunate. Pride in his own dog and in the dog's potency in stud, together with a fear that possible patrons of his dog will believe that he lacks confidence in his dog's merit as a sire, prompts him to use the dog on all of his own bitches without regard to his suitability for any of them.

Of course, it is possible for the owner of a great dog to assemble a battery of bitches with an eye solely to their suitability to mate to that dog, making him the bright, particular star of the breeding program. Such a procedure is justified only by the certainty that the dog is one of those very rare, genetically purebred, and hence prepotent animals of which there are in the entire world only a few in each generation of each breed. Even then, it is seldom thought desirable to inbreed from such a dog over several generations without any infusion of the germ plasm from other males. If a dog is free enough from faults in himself, in his ancestry, and in what he produces, the objection to so intensive an inbreeding program may not be valid. We only say that few breeders, even those with the greatest dogs, have the confidence to pursue it.

To say that the possession of a lone, great stud dog of the variety in which a breeder is most interested in his misfortune, is not strictly true. Such a dog may be of vast benefit to the breeder who owns him and to the breed in general. But no dog is the ideal mate for every bitch. The breeder who purposes to utilize only a single male and the male progeny he can obtain from him must make certain that the dog is worthy of such singleness of purpose.

Even then, he must subordinate the choice of his bitches to their fitness as mates for the particular dog. Against such a procedure, deliberately and consistently taken, there can be offered little objection.

The very rarity of dogs worthy of such exploitation, however, makes it certain that few breeders will go about the breeding of dogs in that way.

Human nature being what it is and the breeder's pride in his single stud dog as human as it is, there are and will continue to be a host of breeders who center their activities each around his own stud dog without an objective analysis of the dog's merits and demerits as a sire. It is very easy to blink the short-comings of one's own dog. Such men, with confidence in the dog's fitness, are liable to consider all bitches as grist for the dog's mill and to breed him to all of their bitches without consideration of their suitability as mates for the particular dog.

Such breeders must, perforce, compete with other breeders who possess a large group of stud dogs of so varied pedigrees and type that among them a suitable mate can be found for well nigh any bitch, and both of these kinds of breeders must compete with those breeders who utilize whatever dog may be the fittest mate for a particular bitch, without invidious consideration of who owns the dog or where it is quartered.

These latter breeders are striving for better dogs by whatever means they are to be attained. That the dog they choose to use may belong to their fiercest rival or bitterest enemy does not deter them from utilizing the fittest mate for their bitch.

If their bitches are well chosen to be efficient dams of fine dogs and if their mates are intelligently chosen with a dispassionate eye to the best possible results, the programs of such breeders will seldom fail. They look upon their bitches rightly as the foundation of their kennel and mate those bitches at home or abroad, wherever the best and most suitable mates for them are to be found.

Every periodical devoted to dogs (and there are a host of them all the way from *Pure-bred Dogs—The American Kennel Gazette,* which is the official publication of The American Kennel Club, to little pulp-paper sheets of local circulation) contains advertisements of dogs of the various breeds at public stud, the services of which may be obtained for any bitch worthy to breed from for a consideration. The pedigrees and favorable data about such dogs can usually be obtained by mail from their owners and most such dogs may be inspected by prospective breeders at the kennel where they stand at stud.

The statements made by the owners of a dog offered at public stud are usually facts, but many owners are unable to view their dogs objectively and others deliberately tell only the favorable and withhold the unfavorable facts about their dogs in their stud cards or other advertising matter. Some owners of kennels exploit their dogs at stud with an elaborate ballyhoo of specious or meaningless claims for them.

The breeder with a bitch to be mated is justified in exercising all the critical faculty he has in choosing a mate for a bitch that is worthy of being permitted to reproduce her kind at all. The analysis of the data about all the dogs available, within the radius which he is willing to ship the bitch for the purpose of breeding her, entails some knowledge of the great dogs and bitches which have made the history and influenced the development of the breed, the faults and virtues of the important dogs and important strains. There is available at least one book upon almost every breed, not always very informative, not always unprejudiced and impartial, not always strictly true, but usually stimulating to the critical student of the breed in search of the truth about it. Such books enumerate the great outstanding strains of the breeds, usually set forth the virtues if not the faults of these strains, and name the individual dogs upon which the strains were predicated. The breeder should make

219

himself as familiar as possible with his breed, the books and articles about it should be scanned and compared, the great dogs and great strains should be ascertained, together with wherein lies their greatness. But none of the information should be accepted uncritically. The searcher for truth in such matters must continually ask why, why. Neither prejudice nor propaganda should be permitted to come between him and the real "low-down."

Having obtained all the information at his disposal, he must set about the canvass of the stud dogs available for his bitch. Of them, he eliminates, of course, the patently unsuitable.

In the choice of a stud dog, the first consideration is the proved ability to sire first-rate stock. That ability must take precedence over what the dog himself is like and how he is bred. Indeed, if he is a consistent producer of fine stock, he will usually be found to be a representative specimen of his variety. He may, however, possess a single "out" which has precluded his attainment of high exhibition awards—such an "out" as size, color, or markings, which our knowledge of Mendelism convinces us he may not reproduce unless it be aggravated by the genetic composition of his mate.

If he is a sire of consistent excellence, his pedigree, if studied and understood, is sure to show that he is not ill-bred. The pedigree may not be spectacular. The parents and grandparents may not be the great stars of the breed's firmament; they may have been obscurely owned and seldom exhibited but are very likely, indeed, to be found upon examination fundamentally good dogs.

Going further back into the pedigree it will surely be found that the dog traces to the great ones of his breed, and very likely to a single, great producing individual through several lines of his pedigree.

It may be well to ask whether a dog recognized to be a consistently excellent sire is so in fact or only in appearance. Is he responsible for the great progeny that have sprung from his loins? Is his apparent success due to the actual superiority of the

220

genes with which he endows his sons and daughters or is it due to the clever advertising, propaganda, and ballyhoo of a group of mediocre offspring which have been touted and maneuvered and jockeyed to championships?

Even assuming that the progeny he has sired is of great excellence, it is worth taking into account the opportunities he has had—both the number and quality of the bitches to which he nas been mated. Even a dog of but indifferent genetic excellence may produce rather spectacularly if mated to a host of superior bitches. And, conversely, a dog of no matter how excellent germ plasm, if permitted to prove himself upon only a few bitches and those few of but mediocre quality, need surprise nobody if the average merit of the progeny is but little greater than that of the bitches that mothered it.

Consistency may in some things be a doubtful virtue, but in a stud dog it is a great one. A dog which has proved his ability to sire puppies of consistently high quality, but all short of greatness, must be preferred over one which has produced one or two outstanding celebrities among a host of inferior progeny. This is true even for the breeder whose purpose it is to produce a few super excellent dogs and is willing to breed a lot of culls along with them. The chances of being the person who obtains one of those paragons from such a dog is little greater than winning the major prize in a lottery, while the dog which produces consistently well proves that his genes are desirable ones and when they unite with equally excellent genes in the ova, the zygote of the great dog is formed.

Fine dogs are not freaks and are seldom mere accidents. A study of the pedigrees of great dogs of any variety shows that a mating which produces one great progeny produces more than one much more frequently than would be expected and two or more champions in a single litter have often enough occurred. Such matings will seldom produce any offspring of a quality that is inferior, except by comparison with the stars of its produce.

Hence, it is the ability of a dog to produce a high order of general excellence in his progeny that determines his worth as

221

a sire even more than does the few paragons of winners of championships among his get.

It is not to be denied that it is usually the dog that consistently produces good puppies that also produces the great winners. This is especially true of a dog that has been several years in the stud and has had an adequate opportunity to prove his prepotence. A young stud dog, even one which sires good progeny with consistency, may not have had time for the sky-rocket of near perfection to flare from among the general run of his good progeny.

Indeed, in evaluating the worth of a dog for breeding, it is necessary to consider his age. By that statement it is not implied that a dog is, at any given period between his puberty and senescence, more likely to sire good progeny than at some other period within that range of time, or that the age of the dog should be balanced in any way with the age of the bitch with which he is to be mated. However, a dog only two or three years old who has achieved a record for excellence in the stud is to be given greater credit for that record than is another dog five or six years old with no greater a record—assuming that the two dogs have had approximately the same number of matings per year and to bitches of approximately the same breeding worth.

In such a case, it is easy to understand that the older dog not only would have produced a larger number of progeny with which to prove himself, but also that more of his progeny would have had full time in which to develop and go through an exhibition career. Here again we see that it is a dog's consistency as a producer that counts more than the absolute numbers of his outstanding progeny.

All of which brings us back to the chromosomes and their genes upon which we are forced to continue to harp. It is the genes within the gamete which determine the excellence or inferiority of the individual parent's contribution to his offspring.

If the dog is genetically purebred, that is to say, if he is pure recessive or pure dominant for any given pair of genes, then during meiosis one member of that pair of genes would go into each of the secondary spermatocytes, both of which, as pertains to that particular allelic pair, would be exactly alike. There will, therefore, be consistency in that dog's contribution to the heritage of all his progeny so far as pertains to that particular pair of genes.

The ideal stud dog would be one which was genetically pure-bred in this fashion for every pair of genes and which carried the desirable recessive factors as pure recessives and the desirable dominant factors as pure dominants. Such a dog would be consistent in his contribution to every zygote and any variations among his progeny would derive from their dams. Considering that there are many thousands of pairs of genes in the cell of the dog, nobody knows how many thousands, it is impossible to expect to find such an ideal stud dog.* Our breeds of livestock have not yet been long enough in existence as separate breeds nor has selection been exercised long enough or carefully enough to bring us to the realization of such an ideal. However, the longer a given breed survives and the more carefully the selection is exercised by the breeders, the closer will that ideal be approached.

It is the breeder's problem in the choice of his breeding stock to find the animals which approximate that ideal as nearly as is possible and to use them in his breeding program. It is because so many breeders of dogs—most of them by rule of thumb and empiric selection, without the realization that they were

* By an ingenious method of reckoning, the German geneticist, Spühler, has calculated the number of genes in man's chromosomes to be between 20,000 and 42,000. Now, just for the sake of discussion, let us assume that the dog has only 15,000 genes in his chromosomes and that each gene has one alternate allelomorph. The possible variations from this structure would be $2^{15,000}$, a number so large that it is genetically incomprehensible. Obviously, the dog is not this variable, either in the wild or domesticated state. The answer lies in the fact that the great bulk of the genes is devoted to basic structure: one head, two eyes, two ears, four legs, etc. However, if two given dogs were variable in only ten genes, the number of possible variations for those traits is just over one thousand. Genetic purity in the sense of complete homozygosity for desirable dominant or recessive traits is never found, nor is it to be expected, though it must remain theoretically possible.

223

dealing with genes at all—have chosen so well that our dogs in recent years have grown more uniform and excellent within their respective breeds and are reproducing themselves with more consistent uniformity than hitherto.

For every individual pair of genes, every dog is recessive, pure dominant, incompletely dominant, or hybrid dominant. If he is recessive for any pair of genes, each gamete he produces will contain a recessive gene of that pair. If he is pure dominant, each gamete will contain a dominant gene of the pair. If he is incompletely dominant then the two genes may produce a blended effect *in the phenotype*. (Remember those F_1 pink flowers?) If he is a hybrid dominant, half of his gametes will contain a dominant gene of that pair, the other half a recessive gene of the pair. There is no possibility that any gamete will possess a blended, neutral, or middle-of-the-road content as pertains to any pair of genes. Also, there is no possibility that there will be any blending in the genotype. *The genes themselves do not blend.*

It is to be remembered that the manifestation of any attribute in the phenotype may depend upon not a single gene or a pair of genes, but upon a complex of genes, which will present a mixed pattern of dominant and recessive genes. This, of course, complicates our choice. Herein the pedigree becomes of value.

If a given trait is present in a dog and has been present in all of his ancestors for five or six generations, it is reasonable to assume that the trait has acquired genetic stability. Even so, there is always the possibility that an unwanted recessive may be lurking in the woodpile that was his family tree and is present as a hybrid dominant in the dog under consideration. From such a dog, half the spermatozoa will carry that recessive trait and, if it encounters another like it in the zygote, the resultant organism will be pure recessive as to that pair of genes. Or it may be hidden by its dominant mate in the zygote, in which case there may be no evidence of it in the offspring, which will carry a hybrid dominant pair of genes.

There must be a first time in every breed and every strain

224

when any given pair of genes appear in their pure form, and it is always possible that any dog may have received like genes of any pair, one from each of his parents, both of which were only hybrid dominant.

It has long been recognized that certain dogs were prepotent for attributes which appeared in their progeny with consistency. Few of the breeders who talk of prepotency know how and why a dog manifests it. The secret is out. Both genes of every pair of genes which produces that trait are alike. Further, they are homozygous dominants rather than homozygous recessives. So long as the genes for that trait are kept pure, that trait and the prepotency to produce it will persist from generation to generation. So are great and prepotent strains built up.

Here, then, is the breeder's task—to attain and maintain the purity of the gene pairs that determine desirable attributes in the breed.

The consistency with which a dog transmits a given attribute to his offspring is a mark of the purity of his genes which determine it. This prepotency for the desirable traits of the breed is the very essence of what we must try to find in a stud dog. Having found it and mated to the dog a bitch equally prepotent for the desirable traits, the results can never be in doubt.

In no dog of any breed have we found absolute perfection of genotype or phenotype, nor are we likely to find it. Meanwhile, the desirable must be balanced against the undesirable, the good against the bad. The compromise must be made and the essentials emphasized. In this compromise, this choice of what he chooses to emphasize as essential, the breeder expresses himself as a creative artist. In his dogs is the personality of the breeder reflected. Whether he choose fundamental soundness, exaggeration of breed type, or merely arbitrary, fancy points as his first consideration for emphasis in his strain is a straw which shows which way blows the wind of his character.

Each man chooses what he wants and a prepotency for that choice is what he must look for in his breeding stock.

In the case of a young dog whose progeny, if any, is not numerous enough or old enough to be an earnest of this prepotency—this purity of the gene pairs—it becomes necessary to base a decision in regard to him upon his appearance as an individual and upon his pedigree. In this, there is greater hazard than in choosing him for his proved ability to transmit consistently to his progeny certain wanted attributes. But there are dogs which are good enough as individuals and whose breeding is good enough to justify that hazard. If he is an excellent specimen and his parents were both very superior dogs and consistently good producers, the chance one takes in using him is not a long one.

It is well, however, not to trust all one's eggs to such a basket until one has made certain of its soundness. One is quite justified in taking a flier by breeding one or two bitches to such an unproved dog, but until his merits as a sire are proved in his progeny—and one or two litters from good bitches will prove or disprove them—it is wiser to wait before entrusting all one's best bitches to the fond embraces of such a dog.

Of course, a dog cannot be a great stud dog until some breeder has the courage to use his services and to prove him. If he is one's own dog and if the pride of possession does not blind one to his faults, one is justified in making a more elaborate and extensive test of his powers than if he belong to another breeder. This is true not because by using one's own dog one saves a stud service fee, which is a stupid and false economy, but because one wishes to prove the merits, if he have them, of what may be a valuable, even an invaluable part of one's breeding scheme. If one has acquired the dog by purchase for stud, one must have had definite and well formulated reasons for doing so. If one has bred the dog, one is familiar with his ancestors and a large part of his collateral kin and has retained him for a purpose. It is worth while to prove his prepotence and retain him or prove that he has it not and get rid of him.

But it is not justified to use a dog merely on a hunch and

226

because he happens to be one's own property. More bad dogs are bred because doting owners of mediocre males want to prove that the family pet is a great stud dog than for any other one reason.

It is true that in almost every breed there have been great breeding animals that have not betrayed that fact in their appearance. Such animals are about as rare as valuable pearls found in oysters on the half shell in metropolitan restaurants. When they do crop up, they are usually not as bad individuals as they are reputed to be, but usually have a single "out" which precludes their being of exhibition quality.

That single "out" may result from a recessive gene that is covered up in hybrid dominance in the progeny. But it is all too liable to reappearance in the second or subsequent generations unless caution is used to keep it out of sight in the phenotypes. Here lies the danger of using breeding animals which, however excellent one may suspect their genotype to be, are inferior in phenotype. Their faults as individuals are liable to rise up to blast the breeder.

There are, doubtless, many potentially great stud dogs which, for want of the opportunity to prove their prepotence for good, go to their graves unhonored and unsung. This is not so great a calamity as it appears to be. There are recognizedly efficient stud dogs aplenty in every breed—if only they were used to the full extent of their powers to benefit their breeds. The experimentation to prove the breeding worth of a host of males which as individuals are of indifferent merits, in the hopes of finding one that is prepotent to produce the good attributes of his breed, is like searching for two grains of wheat in two bushels of chaff. The breeder is much better off who seeks to prove the breeding worth only of the promising among the unproved, and, for the most part, to utilize dogs which have been thoroughly proved and found efficient.

High breeding fees deter many breeders from using the best stud dogs. This is due to short-sightedness on the part both of the breeders and of the owners of such males. The breeder were wiser to use the best dogs, whatever, within reason, the cost may be, and if necessary breed fewer litters. The owner of a stud dog would find it more profitable to have his dog kept busy at a low fee than to have him idle three-quarters of the time because of the prohibitive charge he makes for the services of his dog.

Most owners of stud dogs who demand high breeding fees do so not so much as a source of revenue but because they believe that it enhances the prestige of the dog. This is not true. A great dog is a great dog, a thing of beauty and a joy as long as he lives, whether he be maintained in maiden meditation at a high stud fee or whether he be permitted to run the streets and breed to every proud mongrel bitch that comes his way.

Artificial insemination has been recognized as possible in dogs for some two hundred years. With horses it has been in practical use for a long while. By employing it in dogs, it would be possible to divide the semen from a single orgasm of a great dog among several bitches and so would enable the best of the males to participate in several times as many matings as are now possible. By such a process it might be possible to bring about a reduction of stud fees also.

Modern rapid transportation makes feasible the shipment of semen. Without leaving their own kennel and without the nervousness resultant from a long journey among strangers, bitches could so be impregnated with the semen of a distant dog.

This process is not as yet in general use. Whenever the dog breeders arrive at a full realization of the worth to their breeds of a single, great prepotent male dog, such a method of utilizing his germ plasm will be undertaken; and even more than in the past, the best producing dogs will sire a preponderance of the puppies of their respective breeds.

This is not a mere visionary idea but is a practical process which in the economy of dog breeding, a sport and not a business, has been overlooked and neglected.

The breeder who recognizes that an occasional litter by a

great and suitable dog will carry him further than a vast crop of puppies by a mediocre dog is already on his way to success.

By watching the show reports it is not difficult to spot the dogs who are producing the winners. The winners themselves may in their turn produce as well as their sires, but until the younger dogs have demonstrated their prepotency for excellence, the safer measure is to utilize the proved sire.

Breeding animals from a great and successful strain are prone to prove more valuable than those which are mere lone wolves of excellence. By a strain is not meant merely the inmates of a kennel. Many of the largest and finest kennels, especially in America, have been assembled from whatever sources and strains struck the owner's fancy, and there is no close unity of origin among the dogs. The fact that the whole strain or family has a given desirable attribute and has had it for generations is an earnest of the purity in it of the genes which determine that attribute. To be certain to retain that attribute in the progeny, it is best that both parties to a mating shall possess it and shall belong to the same strain.

It is entirely justifiable to cross strains for the purpose of uniting two or more virtues of which each strain manifests but one. However, the immediate progeny from such an outcross will probably disappoint the breeder and it is even likely that both virtues will be lost in their phenotype. But by breeding together the members of the F_1 generation, or by crossing them back into one of the parental strains, the virtues of both strains may, with persistence and good fortune, be united in one animal, eventually obtained in a genetically pure form. Thus is a new and superior strain developed. This is the work of years and in these years many animals inferior to the parent stock may appear. Only the breeder who knows exactly what he wants and why he wants it should undertake such a project.

A knowledge of the behavior of the chromosomes and genes will enable him to understand how the apparent loss of the type of both strains may not be a loss at all, how and why the reappearance of the hidden virtues may be brought about.

229

Such a knowledge of the chromosomes and genes causes one to understand why outcrosses produce such disorder of type, why inbreeding and linebreeding within the strain retain, intensify, and purify in genotype and phenotype.

It also explains the hazards of attempting to balance, one against the other, two faults of mates. Assuming that one has an undershot bitch of a breed which should have an even mouth, she should be mated to a dog of even mouth and of even mouthed ancestry and not to an overshot dog in the expectation of one fault overcoming the other. A bitch too low on the leg should be mated to one of correct station, not to one too high; a sway backed bitch to a level backed dog and not to a camel backed one. One member of the union should be excellent in those features in which the other is faulty. Animals of grossly faulty structure should, of course, not be bred from at all.

The stud dog should be chosen in the light of an objective analysis of the bitch to which it is proposed to mate him and with full consideration of the ancestors behind her. For the realization of fine progeny in the first filial generation, he should be more rather than less closely related to her, with the common ancestor which determines their consanguinity, one of the great common denominators of the breed.

The wise breeder does not fly off on experimental tangents unless he knows exactly what he is seeking to attain and the hazards he is assuming in the quest of it. He knows that the striving for a new virtue for his strain through an outcross is much more likely to result in the loss of what he has than in the addition of something better. He is willing to make haste slowly. Even most of the wise breeders know these things only empirically and from observation. The ones who understand something of the mechanisms of heredity have a small candle to light them through the uncertainty. While great strains cannot be built up in a single generation, the application of this scientifically accepted knowledge will enable the breeder to go ahead at a greater pace and with an added surety.

The breeder who obtains bad results from the use of a dog,

for which he may have paid a large breeding service fee, is all too prone to place the blame for his failure upon the dog. He should ask himself how much of the failure was due to the bitch, her general mediocrity as an individual and as a producer, how much due to his own bad judgment as to the fitness of the mates, one for the other. Was the mating a direct outcross? Did both the mates manifest similar failings?

Assuming that the dog has been a consistent sire of fine progeny, a single failure to a single bitch does not discredit him. The breeder should send to him another bitch, one chosen particularly to breed to him and a member of his own strain.

Breeding arrangements between the owner of the bitch and the owner of the male should be definitely stated. The owner of the male usually upon his stud cards sets forth his refusal to assume responsibility for the injury or death of bitches sent to be bred to his dog or for their escape or misalliance. By accepting such bitches for his dog, he tacitly undertakes to exercise reasonable care that they do not come to harm but the bitch's owner has but uncertain recourse if something goes amiss.

There should be an exact understanding of the amount of the stud fee, how and when it is to be paid. Such payment is usually made in advance of the breeding but some owners of dogs will accept breeding fees on the installment plan.

In the event that a bitch fails to prove in whelp after mating to a dog for use of which a stud fee is paid, it is the customary policy for the owner of the dog to breed the bitch again without charge at her next ensuing heat, provided the dog is yet alive and in his possession. Such a policy is one of mere courtesy. The dog has served the bitch for a given stipend. Assuming that he is not sterile, the fault is not his if she fail to conceive. The obligation for the "return service" exists only if it be specified in the original contract or is stated on the stud cards. Even then, it is not generally considered as of effect unless the owner of the male be informed of the bitch's failure to conceive before the date on which she is due to whelp that he may, if he doubts her failure to conceive, satisfy himself that she is not in whelp.

The second "return service," if the bitch fail twice to conceive, is seldom demanded or given. To ask it is not customary.

A few owners of dogs return the money paid for stud services if the mating proved infertile. This may be a good business policy, although it implies falsely that the failure was on the part of the dog. Unless this arrangement is advertised as the policy of the male's owner, or unless a special arrangement of the kind is made before the mating, it is unreasonable on the part of the owner of the bitch to seek to invoke it.

Frequently, by special arrangement, owners of stud dogs agree to accept one or more members of the resultant litter in lieu of a cash payment for stud service. This is, in most cases, one puppy, the choice of the litter. Sometimes it is the choice of puppies of a specified sex. Sometimes it is even half the litter.

Such arrangements all too frequently result in dissatisfaction to one or both parties to the contract and are even the cause sometimes of subsequent animosity or enmity between them. Unforeseen eventualities arise which are not provided for in the agreement and the final settlement is not always amicable.

This can be obviated by definite terms to the contract, which should be noted in writing, best in duplicate, and signed or initialed by the parties to it. Most dog breeders are not dishonest or deliberately unreasonable, but all are human. There is little need of legal "whereas-es" and "know all men by these presents," and "parties of the first part"; mere notations of what each may expect from the other set forth in work-a-d y words is ample to clarify the deal and to avert controversy.

It is not proposed here to set down what are fair or equitable terms in such contracts but only to suggest that the terms be clearly stated in writing, that as many uncertainties as possible be provided for, and that misunderstanding be so avoided. What is fair in one case might not be equally fair in any other; and what appears fair to both contractual parties need not concern others. A puppy from one litter may be worth his weight in gilt edged bonds, whereas a puppy from another litter or even an inferior puppy from the same litter may not be worth his weight in old newspapers.

Among the conditions that should be specifically agreed upon in such a deal is the age at which choice of the puppy or the puppies is to be made, who is to make it, the age at which the puppy payment is to be made and accepted. In the event that the sex of the chosen puppy is specified, is the owner of the male to accept or be given a puppy of the other sex if the litter should contain none of the sex agreed upon? If the agreement is for half the litter, what is to become of the odd puppy if the litter number is not even? If but a single puppy in the litter survive to the age at which delivery is to be made, shall the owner of the male claim it?

If the owner of the male choose a puppy with which the breeder is loath to part, may the latter pay a cash stud fee and retain the puppy?

The owner of the male, in the event of such a disagreement, stands in a somewhat favorable position since he can withhold his signature from application for registration of the litter in the stud book until a settlement satisfactory to him is made. This right to hold up registration until settlement is made secures the owner of the male in his accepting of the stud fee in installments. However, the breeder should be frankly told that he will not be permitted to register his puppies or to permit their buyers to register them until payment in full for the stud service is made.

The male dog to which a bitch is to be bred should be selected before she is due in heat and arrangements with the owner of the dog for his use should be made. To delay until she is ready to breed may result in finding the dog unavailable, in which case it is necessary to make a hasty second choice of mate for her. Even the second choice may be unavailable.

If it is possible, the owner of the bitch or somebody with whom she is familiar should accompany her on her visit to the dog. If that is impossible and she must be shipped, it is best

233

to send her early in her heat that she may become used to the surroundings in which she is to be bred and to the person who is to superintend her breeding.

If shipped, she should have a roomy and comfortable crate with a basin for water, food in a cloth bag attached to the crate, and a note to express-handlers asking them to see to it that she has such exercise as not to make it necessary to defile her crate. Such a note should reassure such handlers of her temperament if she is friendly, or should warn them if she is untrustworthy. Insurance over and above the liability the forwarding agency assumes on all dogs shipped is desirable, not for its own sake and the indemnity to be obtained for the bitch's loss or death, but for the added care and attention she will be vouchsafed en route.

The owner of the dog should, of course, be notified of when she is to be sent and his reply that he is ready to receive her should be awaited. To have one's good bitch lying in an express office while the consignee is away from home at a dog show or elsewhere is not a pleasant prospect and should be avoided.

There is a belief that bitches shipped to be bred are not always mated to the dog agreed upon or at all. Such dishonesty on the part of owners of dogs or carelessness on the part of kennel employees may occur but it is indeed rare. Photographs of the pair in coitus do not prove that the bitch has not been bred also to another dog. The signed statements of most owners of dogs that the breeding has occurred are usually to be trusted. However, if the breeder is suspicious of the good faith of the dog's owner, the bitch should be shipped not to that owner but to a trustworthy agent with instructions to take her to the dog, have her bred, and take her away again.

One normal breeding service, if the bitch is fully in heat, is usually ample and 'perhaps better than two or more. There is an old custom of breeding twice with some forty-eight hours intervening between services. If a dog is much in use, a policy on the part of his owner of permitting but one service to each bitch will conserve the dog's germ plasm and will give in the long run better results than the double service. Even if it is customary for any given dog to permit him to serve each bitch twice, there is no additional benefit from the double service for any bitch. Of course, if the mates fail to hang together or if for any reason there is doubt of the normality of one service, a second is indicated.

The breeding of a bitch the property of one person to a male the property of another is the mere purchase of the semen of that dog delivered into the vagina of the bitch. The contract of such purchase is a mere matter of business and is in no wise esoteric or involved. Indeed, its very simplicity leads to negligence of the specific definition of its terms and from that negligence come difficulties which could easily be avoided. While there are generally observed customs and practices among breeders of dogs, they are not Medean and Persian laws and may be set aside for terms more agreeable to the contracting parties without violation of any mores of the breeder's cult.

The breeder's true problem is the selection of mates, the bringing together of genes in pairs favorable to the determination of desired attributes in the resultant generation. If the bitch is carefully chosen, little sleep need be lost about the male dog. If she is in herself prepotent for the things we ask her to produce, she may confidently be mated to well nigh any male of her variety who has with some degree of consistency reproduced the virtues of his kind.

If through good judgment or good fortune such a bitch is given the benefit of the fittest mate for her particular type and ancestry—if her sound genes be complemented by another set of equally sound ones—the resultant litter, given a favorable environment, will manifest not only excellence but also supremacy.

It is with the purpose to eliminate, as far as it is possible to do, that element of mere good fortune in the breeding of dogs that this book has been written and to substitute for it as much good judgment as may be predicated on genetic principles.

CHAPTER XVII

A Summary of Color Breeding, Heritable Diseases and Defects, and a Final Word on Theory and Practice

We will attempt in this chapter to summarize the latest findings from genetic researches on the subjects of color breeding and heritable diseases and defects. After that, we will close with a few words of caution for the novice breeder who wishes to use genetic principles in his efforts to improve the breed or strain of his choice.

A. *Color Breeding.*

The genetics of the transmission of coat color is, except for a few colors, extremely complex and, consequently, little understood. This field of knowledge is not one being investigated by scores of researchers; there is no agreement among either breeders or exhibitors as to a specific terminology of the multitude of obtainable colors, and there is a marked unwillingness, though understandable, on the part of breeders to crossbreed in order to ascertain specific color transmissions. In fact, the very idea of crossbreeding may cause a "pedigree purist" to fall into a state of shock.

There is little doubt that the simplest and easiest coat color to breed is one which depends upon a single recessive gene, *e.g.,* chocolate or blue. The colors which are apparently dominant but which prove to be heterozygous mixtures are the ones which cause the greatest confusion. Black or sable, resulting from incomplete dominants or from gene interaction, are much more difficult to establish as true breeding strains.

Even though the possible combinations of coat color factors are astronomical, most breeds are homozygous for a number of factors and usually have only two or three alleles of the others. Genetic prediction is, therefore, vastly simplified.

Blue to blue will yield a clear majority of blue. However, you can get any other color, except black or merle.

Sable to sable gives a majority of sable with a fair number of black-and-tans.

Liver to liver produces a full majority of liver though it is possible for any other color to show, except blue, merle, or black.

Black to black will throw a majority of black, but any other color, except merle, may appear.

Yellow to yellow usually yields only yellows or yellow and white. Certain breeds of yellow may produce recessive cream whites.

Yellow to sable will get all black puppies unless one of the parents is heterozygous sable and yellow. (From a purely theoretical viewpoint, liver, blue, or parti-color could sometimes occur.)

Merle to merle yields 50% of the progeny merle, 25% black, and 25% white. The whites will be both deaf and blind.

Brindle to brindle gets mostly brindles with a minority of fawns.

Agouti to agouti will show mostly agouti, though sable and bicolor may also be thrown, but never plain black.

Liver to yellow will produce a majority of black, though you may get some yellows with liver or black noses, or even a few livers.

Blue to liver yields overwhelmingly black, though if either

parent has the blue or liver in pure recessive, "apricot" may result.

Black to agouti will show mainly black, though any other color of the agouti series may appear.

It should be noted that any of the above colors may also yield an occasional white or parti-white. Within a given breed white bred to white ordinarily gives only white. (Between breeds white to white may yield parti-colors.)

In closing this summary, we are in agreement with Marca Burns (1952) who writes, ". . . breeders could help scientists (and themselves!) by adopting a uniform terminology for describing coat colours. It would be most valuable if an atlas of coat colours could be published, using colour photographs and naming the colour in a manner agreed on by interested bodies. . . . Breeders could then refer to this atlas for the correct colour-description when registering their dogs."

B. *Heritable diseases and defects.*

In considering heritable diseases and defects, the statements which follow should not be regarded as absolute and final. Research in this area has been scanty and all too frequently the conclusions reached are tentative. The data, however, represent the best efforts to date and, with a note of caution, may be accepted at genetic face value.

A Partial List of Heritable Defects and Diseases

Abnormal larynx	Recessive in Skye Terriers.
Anterior pituitary dysfunction	Incompletely dominant to normal.
Asthma	Not known.
Cataract	Mendelian dominant in Alsatians; associated with retinal atrophy in Irish Setters.
Cryptorchidism	Irregular; common in dwarf and short-headed breeds.

238

Deafness	Recessive. (At one time common in white Bull Terriers and was traced to a widely used stud dog that passed on a recessive gene to his numerous progeny.) White Collies from the merle-merle cross are nearly always deaf, and partially or totally blind. The same condition also occurs in Harlequin Great Danes. Albinotic Pekingese also show a high frequency of deafness.
Distemper susceptibility	Not known definitely, though appears to be partially recessive in Bloodhounds, Basset Hounds and Bull Terriers.
Eczema proneness	Seemingly a periodic dominant in Pointers.
Epilepsy	Not known.
Haemophilia	Sex-linked recessive.
Hairlessness	A dominant that seems to be lethal in homozygotes.
Hernia, umbilical	Multiple recessive genes.
Hydrocephalus	Several recessive genes are involved.
Kidney stones, predisposition to	Recessive in Dalmatians.
Microphthalmia	Appears in homozygous merles and harlequins.
Oestrual weakness	Partially dominant.
Overshot jaw	A Mendelian recessive in Dachshunds.
Retinal atrophy	Mendelian recessive gene.
Shyness, extreme	Dominant or partially dominant.
Spinal inflammations	Toy Spaniel and Bull types especially susceptible, though the transmission is not clear.
Tail, absent or short	Irregular; in some instances dominant or lethal in homozygotes.
Tetany	Irregular, may be due to a recessive gene in Scottish Terriers.
Trembling	Irregular in Airedales with the precise transmission not clear.

239

C. *Theory and Practice*

For the following paragraphs we are much indebted to Marca Burns whose informative monograph, *The Genetics of the Dog,* yielded these highly desirable conclusions.

"If at any time it was possible to assess the merits of every living individual in a breed, giving a score number to each dog or bitch according to its quality, it would be found that there was a range from bad to excellent, and if the scores were plotted as a graph, the result would probably approximate to a 'normal curve.' (See page 241.) The merit of animals produced by any dog breeder could be plotted similarly, and the aim should be to produce a strain whose merit-curve lies above (further to the right, page 241) the curve for the breed as a whole. However, if success in competition is the aim, the curve to be considered for comparison is not that of the breed as a whole, but that of other competitors, and it is this level of merit which the successful strain must exceed. If the merits of two breeding animals place them both near one extreme of the curve—whether both are exceptionally good or exceptionally bad—their progeny will tend to be nearer to the average of the breed than the parents are, although the range of the litter will be towards the parents' end of the curve. If one parent is exceptionally good and the other bad, the tendency is for the range of merit of the litter to be similar to that of the breed or strain as a whole. A very mediocre bitch thus tends to produce some puppies better than herself even if her mate is equally mediocre, and if she is mated to a champion stud dog, not all the credit for the improved merit of the litter as compared to their dam is really due to the dog. Similarly, when two champions are mated together, they cannot be expected to produce a litter of puppies all as good as themselves, although the range of the litter should be at the top end of the merit curve, and the best pup as good as, or better than, the parents.

"There is always a danger in talking in terms of tendencies and averages, that these will be taken as rigid and absolute. Part of the art of breeding lies in the selection of mates which will 'nick' with each other and produce offspring which revert little or not at all towards the average of the breed. Once the tendency or 'drag of the race' is recog-

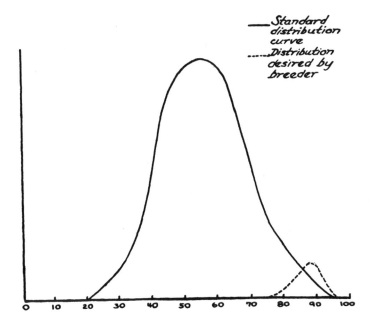

Standard
distribution
curve
Distribution
desired by
breeder

241

nised, the breeder judges his success by the range of merit in his puppies rather than by the production of a few brilliant individuals amongst a lot of duds. The importance of the *worst* puppy of each generation then becomes apparent; if the worst pups produced in the fourth generation of your strain are just as bad and just as numerous as the worst in your first generation you have made no real progress, even though you may have bred a champion. It is a good plan for the breeder of show dogs to give the worst pup in each litter to some neighbour as a pet, and to ask him to bring it to visit the kennels occasionally. Thus the breeder will not be allowed to forget its faults, and will have plenty of opportunity to compare it with the worst of later generations.

". . . Another difficulty in ordinary breeding operations is to establish a criterion of success. . . . The ordinary breeder cannot give equal opportunities to his dogs, and this is particularly true when the objective of the breeder is to produce dogs which will win prizes in the show ring. Wins depend so much on such things as the quality of the other competitors, the whim of the judges, the skill in preparing and handling the exhibit; every breed has had inferior specimens which have become champions through luck or influence, and brilliant specimens which never attained great fame. These elements, which we may call 'luck,' enter into every success which depends upon competition, but competitions for working ability have one great advantage over 'beauty' competitions: a really bad worker will never win consistently in working tests, even if his owner can 'pull strings.' The breeder of show specimens must therefore rely primarily on his own judgment of each animal, whilst the breeder of working dogs can safely rely on competitive success as a criterion of the quality of a dog, even if he has never himself seen the animal at work.

"Although the establishment of an above-average strain should be the objective of each breeder, commercial aspects of breeding exhibition dogs do not entirely encourage such a serious attitude. It is much more profitable to produce and sell one champion than half-a-dozen excellent dogs which just miss championship class. A good dog spoilt for show by one minor fault will sell for little more on the pet market than will a complete dud. Therefore, the common practice of purchasing a third-rate foundation bitch

242

and sending her to the most popular champion stud dog of the moment is often justified commercially though not genetically: if one brilliant puppy results, the reputation of the breeder and even of his brood bitch will be established, even though all the other puppies were hopeless specimens. This is the fault of commercialism in dog breeding and will continue as long as dogs are bought and sold for shows. The serious breeder will only benefit financially if he can afford . . . (to) wait some years until he begins to reap the benefit of the high average quality of his stock. It is also difficult or impossible to establish and maintain a strain if the breeder is unable to keep a large number of dogs. Probably six adults and a varying number of young stock is about the minimum, and even then it would be very desirable to put a few additional bitches out on breeding terms as a reserve in case of heavy losses at home. The great majority of those who make a hobby of dog showing cannot keep sufficient numbers to establish a strain of their own. There is great opportunity for co-operation among small breeders, or between them and a larger kennel with an established strain. An agreed breeding plan and recording system can be adopted, experiences shared and mutual assistance given, each owner taking pride in assisting to develop a high average merit in the strain as a whole. Through such co-operation the smaller breeders could gain the greater numbers of dogs and increased capital which give the big kennel so many advantages; and at the same time their dogs, being distributed in twos and threes among co-operators, would get the personal attention and companionship which is inevitably to some extent denied to the kennel dog . . . .

"The foregoing recommendation on breeding methods . . . can now be briefly summarised in the form of a breeding plan for the foundation of a strain:

"(1) Decide on a few traits which are regarded as essential and on any faults considered intolerable. Whatever the breed, disease resistance, fertility, and absence of deformities, must be included as essentials, and certain character failings, such as viciousness, extreme nervousness, and hysterical or epileptic tendencies, must be condemned.

"(2) Develop a scoring system in which the selected virtues and faults receive marks in accordance with (a) their importance to your purpose or breeding aim, (b) their rarity or otherwise in the breed (or show population of a breed) as a whole. Virtues which are well-established in the breed and present in every individual used or bred need not be scored. As certain traits, rare at first, become established in the strain, their scoring may be reduced in order that greater weight and attention may be given to some other trait. Or the scoring system may remain the same, attention in matings being concentrated on scores for individual traits which require improvement.

"(3) Line breed consistently to the best individual produced until a better one occurs, then line breed to that. The blood of an outstanding dog or bitch can only be conserved by inbreeding to whilst the animal is living, but close inbreeding should only be resorted to when an animal of very exceptional qualities and with no outstanding faults is available. If inbreeding results in unsatisfactory litters this does not condemn the favoured animal, but merely indicates that a less close mating should be made. Wide outcrosses should not be resorted to after the establishment of a strain, but some outside blood should be introduced, e.g., by the use of a dog sired by one of the strain from an unrelated bitch. In the foundation animals relationship need not be close, in fact wide outcrosses will give more variation and therefore greater possibility for selection of desirable combination of traits. Every animal to be used in the breeding programme must pass rigid assessments for individual excellence as well as average excellence of its relatives including progeny when known."

For the dog breeder who wishes to improve a given strain of a given breed of dogs, the science of genetics has placed at his disposal the means whereby it can be done. A knowledge of the fundamentals of genetics, combined with patience and perseverance, will ultimately provide the discriminating breeder with that which he so ardently desires—dogs that are not only a delight to the eyes but that are genetically sound and that will consistently produce their own kind.

CHAPTER XVIII

Conclusion

The art of breeding fine dogs, like the other arts, is long. It requires a never-failing interest, a devotion to the ideal toward which one works, and a persistent study of the methods by which that ideal may be approximated.

A single book is only a stone cast into the still pond of the subject to set up an ever widening wave of inquiry which it may require a whole library to satisfy. This book is intended to be that stone. Included hereafter is a bibliography of a few of the books and articles which have seemed to the authors germane to the subject in hand and from which many of the data contained in these pages have been gleaned. It is hoped that the simple statements of the scientific facts herein set forth may stimulate the reader to a further exploration of the realm of genetics and to the practical application of that science to the improvement of the domestic dog. That quest of truth should not, in fact, end short of infinity. In the breeding of dogs there are always more worlds to conquer.

There are, no doubt, readers of this book who would prefer simply to be assured that their bitch Queenie or Lady is an ideal brood bitch of her variety and that if only Queenie should be bred to John Doe's dog Duke, a litter of champions would be certain to result. To offer such assurance, even if it were possible to do so, would deprive the breeder of the creative joy of

245

his art and would make the breeding of his dogs simply another chore.

We have chosen, on the other hand, to seek to show how the breeder may himself consider the fitness of his stock and how he may himself mate that stock for its betterment.

That is not intended as an implication that the advice of experienced and successful breeders of dogs should be ignored in the making of specific matings, but that advice when asked and given should be critically considered in the light of scientific truth. The breeder who uncritically carries out the breeding scheme of another is not a creative artist at all. He is merely a chore boy who does the bidding of a more creative mind.

Even successful breeders may be the slaves of some or all of the superstitions which it is sought to explode in Chapter XIV, but they are successful despite that slavery rather than because of it. Men have bred fine dogs without ever having heard of a chromosome or a gene and in the belief that Mendelism is some kind of esoteric religious cult. These same men might have bred more fine dogs and better ones if they had had the scientific facts which genetics has supplied. The element of luck in the breeding of dogs has turned the scales sometimes toward excellence, more often away from it. The scientific breeder seeks to eliminate that element as far as may be and to substitute for it a sureness of procedure and a certainty of reward for his efforts.

This, the new science enables him in great part to do. The word "blood" to designate the vehicle of heredity is so firmly fixed in our vocabularies that it is difficult to discard in favor of the gene concept. The breeder who succeeds in substituting genes for blood in his deeper consciousness, who thinks of matching genes rather than of blending blood, has gone far in the resolution of his breeding problems. The knowledge that the picture he seeks to make is to be a mosaic of genes rather than a daubing of blood revolutionizes his breeding practice as well as his thought processes.

The science of genetics is only in its swaddling clothes and its practical application to plant and animal husbandry has hardly yet begun. The workers in its vineyards are pure scientists who have but little concern for the practical use of the truths they reveal. Since Aristotle, and before, men have speculated about heredity, what it was and how it behaved. Except for the revelations of Mendel, however (and those revelations lay dormant and unregarded for a third of a century), only in our time has any progress been made in the resolution of the mystery.

Painter at the University of Texas and Bridges, an associate of Morgan's at the California Institute of Technology, have seen fine bands on the chromosomes of the large cells of the salivary glands of *Drosophila*. These workers believe that these minute bands may actually be the hitherto unbeheld genes.

At the University of Indiana the sex of chickens is influenced by the piercing of the air chamber of the eggs from which they are hatched. This at first glance seems to nullify the theory of the X and Y chromosomes as the determiners of sex. It does not, in fact, do so for the sex chromosomes only predispose the zygote toward one sex or the other, but not irrevocably.

As we have previously noted, Soviet workers have succeeded in separating the Y-carrying sperm from the X-carrying sperm by centrifuging the semen.

The end is not yet. Data continue to pile up. The work gathers momentum. The ensuing years may bring us undreamed of knowledge and may enable us to accomplish more in the realm of practical breeding than now seems possible.

Much of the new knowledge appears not possible of practical application but each new fact leads forward to other facts and the work goes on with even greater acceleration. The wise breeder is interested in these new facts for their own sake and will not go ignorant of the developments of genetic science.

In 1934, Dr. G. G. Pincus, working at Harvard University, was able to produce rabbits by shaking together ova and sperm in a test tube and placing the fertilized ova in the Fallopian tubes of another rabbit for gestation. Later, Dr. Pincus was able to bring about the fertilization of the ova of rabbits by

247

the use of heat and by soaking them in brine, subsequently transplanting them into the Fallopian tubes of an unrelated female, where pregnancy ensued. Except for the deities of some religions, this is the first recorded parthenogenesis of a mammal. Early in this century, Jacques Loeb had succeeded in activating the eggs of sea urchins with brine and the eggs of frogs by needle puncture, but Pincus' is the first success of the kind in the higher animals. The implications of such an achievement for the animal breeder and for the human race are so stupendous as to be well nigh imponderable.

The separation of the X-carrying from the Y-carrying sperm is not yet available to the practical breeder. We are not yet ready to breed Pomeranians by soaking Pomeranian ova in salt water and implanting a hundred of them in St. Bernard oviducts to produce vast, sireless litters. But what the future may bring forth is not unworthy of our speculation.

With the knowledge already at hand, we may so unite the chromosomes and the genes within them as to produce dogs more nearly to our hearts' desire.

Glossary

This glossary is not, and is not intended to be, a dictionary of biological terms. The words and phrases here defined are only such as are used in the text of this book and such as may not be familiar to many readers. At the first use of a term in this text its meaning is explained. The glossary is intended for readers who have not perused the whole text or who have forgotten the definition of a term in their first encounter with it.

Acquired characters. Attributes developed in the body that are of environmental or functional origin, as opposed to those which have their cause in the germ plasm.

Albinism. The absence of any pigmentation.

Albino. An organism which does not have normal pigmentation. In dogs, animals with bluish eyes, flesh colored nose, and white coat.

Alleles or Allelomorphs. Alternative forms of the same gene which influence the same developmental process or processes, but in different ways.

Amnion. The inner membrane in which the embryo of the higher animals develops.

Amniotic fluid. The liquid in which the developing embryo is bathed.

Artificial insemination. The artificial introduction of semen into the genitalia of the female without copulation.

Autosomes. Any chromosomes other than sex chromosomes.

Back-cross. The offspring of the cross of an F_1 hybrid to either of the parental types.

Biology. The science which treats of life and living organisms.

Breed. *n.* A group of domestic animals controlled by man to prevent mixture with dissimilar groups and consequent loss of distinctive traits. In dogs, a breed is the largest group and is composed of more than one variety.

Caesarian section. The surgical delivery of young by section of the abdominal walls and uterus, used when normal birth is apparently impossible.

Castration. The surgical removal of the gonads, particularly of the testicles; not to be confused with other methods of sterilization.

Cell. The unit of protoplasmic structure in living organisms; a small mass of cytoplasm with its nucleus.

Centrosome or centriole. A small body within the cell which divides in mitosis or meiosis and around the divisions of which the split chromosomes group themselves.

Character. A distinguishing attribute or property of an organism. See also *trait*.

Chorion. The outer membrane which encloses the embryo.

Chromatin. A substance within the nucleus of the cell from which the chromosomes develop, so-called from its ability to take a stain.

Chromosomes. Dark-staining bodies which appear during cell division and which carry the heritable factors, the genes. They occur in pairs, one derived from the mother, the other from the father. Members of a pair carry the same allelic genes in identical arrangement.

Cleavage. The division of the fertilized ovum into many cells.

Clitoris. An erectile organ of the female at the anterior part of the vulva; the homologue of the penis.

Coitus. The act of copulation.

Complementary factors. Two or more dissimilar factors which unite to produce a trait.

Congenital. Present at birth, to be distinguished from hereditary.

Corpus cavernosum. Erectile tissue in the posterior part of the dog's penis which is grasped by the vaginal sphincter of the bitch to make possible the characteristic, prolonged coitus of the canine species.

Corpus luteum. (pl. *corpora lutea*) A yellowish mass formed in the ovary by the degeneration of the Graafian follicle after the discharge of the ovum and functioning as an endocrine gland.

Cowper's glands. Small glands in the male near the base of the bladder, not present in the dog.

Criss-cross inheritance. A mode of transmission in which characters of one parent are passed to progeny of the opposite sex.

Crossing over. The exchange of corresponding parts between the members of a pair of chromosomes during synapsis.

Cryptorchidism or Cryptorchism. A developmental defect in which the testicles remain in the abdominal cavity instead of descending into the scrotum.

Cytology. The science which treats of cells.

Dihybrids. The progeny from parents which differed in two Mendelian traits.

Diploid. The double number of chromosomes in all cells except the functional spermatozoa and ova.

Dominant. Said of one of a pair of alleles whose effects are expressed to the exclusion of the effects of the other allele. See also homozygous and heterozygous (*q.v.*).

Drag of the race. The tendency within purebred varieties, when artificial selection is not employed, to revert to the norm of the species.

Drosophila melanogaster. A species of fruit fly which, because of its rapidity of maturity and reproduction and because of the small number of its chromosomes, has lent itself to genetic experimentation.

Ductless gland. See *endocrine glands.*

Duplicate factors. Genes of different pairs which determine the same characters.

Embryo. The unborn organism, especially in the earlier stages of its development; the foetus.

Embryology. The science which treats of the prenatal development of the organism.

Endocrine glands. The ductless glands which produce hormones and discharge them directly into the blood stream. They include the pituitary, thyroid, thymus, parathyroid, adrenal, pineal, and other glands, besides the interstitial glands of the gonads.

Epididymis. An oblong body composed of the efferent duct of the testis, at the posterior part of that organ.

F_1. The first generation offspring of a given mating. The F_2 (2nd generation) is produced by intercrossing the F_1.

Factor. The term originally used for what is now called gene.

Fallopian tubes. The passages by which the ova are conveyed from the ovaries to the uterus and in which conception normally occurs; oviducts.

251

Foetus. The unborn organism, especially in the later stages of its development; the embryo.

Fraternal twins. Two members of the same litter developed from different ova and spermatozoa but with the same parents, distinguished from identical twins (*q.v.*). Litter siblings.

Gene. The basic unit of heredity, believed to be the fundamental factor of inherited characteristics.

Genetics. The branch of biology which deals with heredity, variation, sex determination, and related phenomena.

Genotype. The hereditary makeup of an individual as distinguished from the expression or manifestation of the genes. See *phenotype*.

Germ cell. A cell with a potential to form a zygote, *i.e.*, a functional spermatozoön or ovum.

Gonad. An organ in either male or female in which reproductive cells are proliferated and developed; a testicle or an ovary.

Graafian follicle. The small sac in which the ovum is developed in the ovary and which, after the discharge of the ovum, becomes the *corpus luteum* (*q.v.*).

Gynander. An organism (usually insect) which is part male and part female, the most common type having the male and female areas delineated along the median line of the body, rarely if ever found in the dog.

Haploid. The number of chromosomes in spermatozoa and ova after meiosis; one-half of the diploid number.

Heredity. The tendency of an organism to reproduce itself.

Hermaphrodite. An organism that has the reproductive organs of both sexes.

Heterosis. The superiority over either or both parents of the progeny resulting from the crossing of strains, varieties, breeds or species. Known also as *hybrid vigor*.

Heterozygous. Not pure or true breeding for a given factor. Containing two different alleles of the same gene. A heterozygote produces two kinds of germ cells with respect to the gene in question.

Homozygous. Pure or true breeding for a given character. Having the gene for the character in duplicate, a homozygote produces only one kind of germ cell with respect to that gene.

Hormone. A secretion from any one of the ductless or endocrine glands.

Hybrid. (1) The offspring of two parents of unlike genetic makeup. (2) A heterozygote for one or more genes.

Hymen. The thin membrane which partially closes the vagina in virgins, not present in the virgin bitch; the maidenhead.

Identical twins. Litter brothers or sisters (always of the same sex) which develop from the same ovum and spermatozoön, as distinguished from fraternal twins.

Impotence. The inability to perform the sexual act; not to be confused with sterility.

Inbreeding. The mating together of closely related animals.

Incomplete dominance. In an organism which is heterozygous in respect to any allelic pair, there is a failure of either gene to obscure the potential of the other; also called partial dominance.

Influence of previous sire. See *telegony*.

Interstitial gland. The endocrine gland of the gonad, the hormones of which affect the development of secondary sex characters.

In whelp. Pregnant (said of the bitch).

Lamarckism. The theory, now largely discredited, that acquired characters may be transmitted through heredity; from Lamarck who promulgated that belief.

Lethal. The name given to a gene which, when present in the homozygous condition, causes the death of the embryo. When the inherited condition is one which leads to premature death after birth, it is more correctly called sub- or semi-lethal.

Line breeding. The mating together of animals somewhat related, but less closely related than in inbreeding.

Linkage. The tendency for two or more characters to be transmitted together, because the genes are located in the same chromosome.

Mammal. An animal of a species which suckles its young; a member of the biological Order *Mammalia*.

Maturation. The development of the germ cells, including the reduction division in which the number of chromosomes is halved from the diploid to the haploid number, and the further mitotic division of the cells.

Mendelism. The theory embodied in the First and Second Laws of Mendel which establishes that characters are inherited as entities and independently one of another due to segregation and the independent assortment of the genes.

Menstruation. The periodic discharge of blood or bloody fluid from the uterus of any female mammal, occurring in connection with or in preparation for ovulation.

Metabolism. The process by which living cells in plants and animals are continually worn out by use and build themselves up again by means of food.

Meiosis. The process of cell division occurring in the germ cells that reduces the chromosome count by one-half; reduction division.

Mitosis. The process of cell division in which the chromosomes split lengthwise that the resultant daughter cells may each possess the full diploid number of chromosomes.

Modifiers. Genes which by themselves have no noticeable effects, but influence the effects of other genes present in the same organism.

Monohybrid. The progeny from two parents which differed genetically in respect to a single allelic pair.

Monorchidism or Monorchism. A condition in which one of the testes has failed to descend into the scrotum.

Mutation. Heritable germinal variation of abrupt origin that is passed on to the progeny; may be only a minor variation or may result in a trait much dissimilar from ancestral stocks. So-called sport.

Natural Selection, The Theory of. The organisms likely to have more descendants are those whose genetic variations are most advantageous as adaptations to their way of life and to their particular environment.

Non-disjunction. The failure of the members of any pair of chromosomes to separate in the reduction division of maturation which results in both members of the pair going to one of the daughter cells.

Nucleolus (pl. *nucleoli*). Small bodies formed in the nucleus of the cell.

Nucleus. The central body within the cell containing the chromosomes.

Oestrus. Heat; breeding "season."

Oögenesis. The growth and development of the sex cell of the female into an ovum.

Oögonia. The cells which are proliferated from the primordial germ cells of the female organism which after reduction and mitosis develop into ova.

Orgasm. The climax of the sexual act.

Os uteri. The mouth of the uterus; the opening between the vagina and the uterus. ·

Outbreeding. The mating together of unrelated animals.

Ovary. The organ of the female in which the ova develop.

Oviducts. The passages by which the ova are conveyed from the ovaries to the uterus; Fallopian tubes.

Ovum (pl. *ova*). The functional reproductive cell produced by the female; an egg.

P₁. The parent generation; P₂ grandparent generation, etc.

Parthenogenesis. Reproduction from the ovum without its union with a sperm.

Parturition. The act of bringing forth young; whelping.

Pedigree. A record of the ancestry or line of descent.

Penis. The male organ of copulation.

Period of gestation. The duration of normal pregnancy; in the dog about sixty-three days.

Phenotype. The appearance and/or performance of an individual, *i.e.*, the outcome of the interaction between its genotype and its environment.

Pisum. The genus which includes the common garden pea, such as was used experimentally by Mendel in the discovery of his laws.

Pituitary gland. A tiny endocrine gland in two lobes (anterior and posterior) attached to the base of the brain of all vertebrates, the various hormones from which affect growth and reproduction.

Placenta. The organ in the higher mammals by which the foetus is attached to the wall of the uterus and through which it is nourished and waste products are removed from it. The main part of the afterbirth.

Placental mammalia. Those mammals whose young develop in the uterus and are there nourished through a placenta; the biological Sub-Order of *Eutheria*.

Polar body. A small, nonfunctional cell cast off by the ovum after reduction division.

Polyhybrid. The progeny from parents which differed in several or many Mendelian characters.

Prenatal impression. The alleged influence upon the foetus of the experiences and sensations of the mother in the course of her pregnancy.

Prepotent. Said of an animal with an unusually strong tendency to pass its characteristics on to its offspring. Probably due to the presence of many dominant alleles in the prepotent parent.

Primary Oöcyte. The germ cell of the female immediately prior to its reduction division.

Primitive streak. A scar-like line along the midline of the back of the early embryo.

Pronucleus. The nucleus of a gamete either male or female.

255

Protoplasm. The vital substance of all plant or animal life.

Pure dominant. See homozygous.

Recessive (*gene or character*). A character which is undeveloped or buried when the gene for it develops from only one parent and is associated in the zygote with its dominant allelomorph.

Reduction division. See *meiosis*.

Reproductive cells. Cells set aside in the development of the organism, the function of which is to reproduce it; the cells of the germ plasm in contradistinction to the somatoplasm.

Reversion. The reappearance of ancestral traits not found in the more immediate several generations of ancestors; "throwing back"; atavism.

Scrotum. The pouch in which the testes are suspended.

Secondary sexual characters. Attributes which are normally limited to a single sex, but which have no primary part in reproduction. Examples, beard of the human male, the ornate tail of the peacock.

Secondary spermatocyte. The male germ cell immediately after its reduction division, which divides by mitosis to form spermatids.

Segregation. Manifested in the F_2 (and later hybrid generations) as a separation and distribution to different individuals of the Mendelian characters in which the parents of the F_1 hybrid differed.

Semen. Fluid containing innumerable spermatozoa which is produced by the generative organs of the male and by which impregnation is effected.

Sex chromosomes. The X and Y chromosomes which carry the determiners for sex.

Sex-limited trait. A trait (usually a secondary sex trait) which manifests itself in one sex and is either absent or greatly reduced in the other. Sex-limited genes are in the autosomes, not in the sex chromosomes.

Sex-linked trait. A trait for which the determiner is on the sex chromosomes; specifically, a trait carried by a gene or genes in the non-homologous portion of the X chromosome. Traits carried in the homologous portions of the X and Y chromosomes are said to be *incompletely sex-linked*.

Siblings. Two or more progeny of the same parents irrespective of sex or time of birth.

Somatic. Of or pertaining to the body cells in contradistinction to the reproductive cells.

Species. A group of animals or plants, usually making up a subdivision next smaller than a genus, having certain characteristics which distinguish it from any other group and which are usually inherited. The common criterion for a species is that its members are interfertile.

Spermatozoön. (pl. spermatozoa). The male gamete; a single sperm.

Spermatid. A germ cell of the male resultant from the splitting of the secondary spermatocyte; the stage of spermatogenesis immediately prior to the spermatozoön.

Spermatogenesis. The development of spermatozoa from the primary sex cells.

Spermatogonia. The cells which are proliferated from the primordial germ cells of the male organism and which, after reduction and mitosis, develop into spermatozoa.

Sphincter cunni. Muscles of the vagina of the bitch which grasp the *corpus cavernosum* of the dog, the penis, in coitus and render impossible the withdrawal of that organ until erection subsides.

Spindle. A formation within the cell at one stage of mitosis.

Sterility. The inability or failure to produce live gametes; barrenness; not to be confused with impotence.

Strain. A more or less numerous family of the same breed, the members of which are more or less interrelated one to another and which exhibit a uniformity of type which distinguishes them from members of other strains. See also *breed* and *variety*.

Synapsis. The pairing of the chromosomes prior to the reduction division of the sex cell.

Telegony. The alleged influence of a previous sire on the progeny produced by a subsequent sire from the same mother.

Testicle. See *testis*.

Testis (pl. *testes*). The male sex gland in which the spermatozoa develop; testicle.

Trait. See *character*.

Trihybrid. A hybrid of which the parents differed in respect to three characters.

Umbilical cord. The cord which connects the foetus with its mother and through which it receives nutriment and oxygen; the navel cord.

Unisexual. Of one sex; of or pertaining to plants or animals having organs of but one sex.

Unit character. A character which is heritable independently of other characters.

Urethra. The duct by which urine is discharged from the bladder.

Uterus. The organ of a female animal in which the foetuses are protected and developed before birth; the womb.

Vagina. The passage in the female from the uterus to the exterior orifice.

Variety. A group of animals, usually domesticated, with distinguishing traits as opposed to other varieties; larger than a strain but smaller than a breed.

Vas deferens. The duct by which the semen is conveyed from the epididymis.

Vulva. The exterior opening of the genital organs of the female.

Whelp. (1) To give birth to young (applied to the bitch); (2) a puppy or young dog.

Womb. See *uterus*.

X-Chromosome. One of the two kinds of the sex chromosomes of which, in the higher animals, the female cell possesses two, the male cell but one, plus a Y-Chromosome. *See Y-Chromosome.*

Y-Chromosome. The sex chromosome which is found only in the male cells of the higher animals and determines maleness in the zygote of which it is a part. See also *X-Chromosome.*

Zoology. The branch of biology which deals of animals.

Zygote. The cell and the resultant organism which results from the union of the ovum and spermatozoön.

Bibliography

Ackerman, Irving C. *The Complete Fox Terrier.* New York. 1938.
———. *The Wire-Haired Foxterrier.* New York. 1927.
Ackerman, Irving C. and Kyle Onstott. *Your Dog as a Hobby.* New York. 1940.
Advances in Genetics. New York. Vol. 1-7. 1947-1956.
Ahmed, I. A. "Cytological analysis of chromosome behaviour in three breeds of dogs." *Proc. Roy. Soc. Edinburgh.* Series B., Vol. 61. 107-118. 1941.
American Kennel Club. *The Complete Dog Book.* rev. ed. Garden City. 1961.
———. *Pure-bred Dogs.* New York. 1929.
American Spaniel Club. *The American Spaniel Club Year Book.* New York. 1946.
Asdell, S. A. "Physiology of mammalian germ cells." *Science.* Vol. 116. No. 7, 1952. p. 498.
Ash, Edward C. *Dogs: their History and Development.* 2 vols. London. 1927.
———. *The New Book of the Dog.* London. 1938.
———. *The Practical Dog Book.* London. 1931.
Babcock, E. B. and R. E. Clausen. *Genetics in Relation to Agriculture.* 2d ed. New York. 1927.
Barrington, A., A. Lee, and K. Pearson. "On inheritance of coat-colour in the Greyhound." *Biometrika.* 1904. 3:245-98.
Barrows, W. M. and J. M. Phillips. "Color in Cocker Spaniels." *Journal of Heredity.* 1915. 6:387-397.
Bradley, O. Charnock. *Topographical Anatomy of the Dog.* 5th ed. Rev. by Tom Grahame. New York. 1948.
Bridges, C. B. *See* Morgan, T. H.
Briggs, L. C. and N. Kaliss. "Coat color inheritance in Bull Terriers." *Journal of Heredity.* 1942. 33:222-228.

Brinkhous, K. M. and J. B. Graham. "Hemophilia in the Female Dog." *Science.* 1950. 111:723-724.

Burns, Marca. *The Genetics of the Dog.* Farnham Royal: Commonwealth Agricultural Bureaux. 1952.

———. "Hair pigmentation and the genetics of colour in Greyhounds." *Animal Breeding Abstracts.* 1943. 11:251.

Buzzati-Traverso, A. "The State of Genetics." *Scientific American.* Oct. 1951. 185:22-25.

Castle, W. E. *Genetics and Eugenics.* 4th rev. ed. Cambridge, Massachusetts. 1930.

Charles, M. S. *See* Scott, J. P.

Clausen, R. E. *See* Babcock, E. B.

Conklin, Edward Grant. *Heredity and Environment.* 6th ed. Princeton. 1930.

Coombs, R. D. "Bull-Terrier Breeding." *Journal of Heredity.* 1917. 8:314-318.

Crew, F. A. E. *Animal Genetics: an Introduction to the Science of Animal Breeding.* Edinburgh. 1925.

Darlington, C. D. and K. Mather. *The Elements of Genetics.* New York. 1950.

Darwin, Charles. *The Origin of Species by Means of Natural Selection.* New York: (Modern Library). 1938.

Dobzhansky, T. G. *Genetics and the Origin of Species.* 3rd ed. rev. New York. 1951.

———. "Genetics, 1900-1950." *Scientific American.* Sept. 1950. 183:55-58.

———. *See* Sinnott, Edmund W.

Dodson, E. O. *Genetics, the modern science of heredity.* Philadelphia. 1956.

Druckseis, H. *Geschlechtsverhältniz und Wurfgrösse beim Hund* (Sex ratio and litter size in the dog). Munich. 1935.

Duke, K. L. "Monozygotic twins in the dog." *Anat. Record.* 1946. 94:33-41.

Dunn, L. C., ed. *Genetics in the 20th Century: Essays on the Progress of Genetics During its First 50 Years.* New York. 1951.

———. *See* Sinnott, Edmund W.

East, Edward M., ed. *Biology in Human Affairs.* New York. 1931.

Emerson, Sterling. "The genetic nature of De Vries' mutations in Oenothera Lamarckiana." Repr. from *The American Naturalist.* 1935.

Farris, Edmund J. "Male fertility." *Scientific American.* May, 1950. 182:16-19.

Fisher, R. A. *Theory of Inbreeding.* New York. 1949.

Frankling, E. *Practical Guide to Dog Breeding. New York.* 1954.

Geddes, Patrick. *See* Thomson, J. Arthur.

Glass, Alexander. *See* Muller, George.

Goldschmidt, R. B. *Theoretical Genetics.* Berkeley. 1955.

Graham, J. B. *See* Brinkous, K. M.

Graham, R. Portman. *The Mating and Whelping of the Dog.* London. 1954.

Grahame, Tom. *See* Bradley, O. Charnock.

Haldane, J. B. S. *New Paths in Genetics.* New York. 1942.

Hancock, J. L. and I. W. Rowlands. "The physiology of reproduction in the dog." *Veterinary Record.* 1949. 61:771-776.

Heape, W. "Notes on the proportions of the sexes in dogs." *Proc. Cambridge Phil. Soc.* 1908. 14:121-151.

Hogarth, T. W. "The seven sources of color in Bull Terriers." *Our Dogs.* 1933. 93:1011-1012.

Hogben, Lancelot. *Science for the Citizen.* New York. 1943.

Horowitz, Norman H. "The gene." *Scientific American.* Oct. 1956. 195:78-92.

Hubbard, C. *The Complete Dog Breeders' Manual.* London. 1954.

Huettner, Alfred F. *Fundamentals of Comparative Embryology of the Vertebrates.* New York. 1941.

Humphrey, E. S. and L. Warner. *Working Dogs: an Attempt to Produce a Strain of German Shepherds Which Combines Working Ability and Beauty of Conformation.* Baltimore. 1934.

Hurst, C. C. *The Mechanics of Creative Evolution.* Cambridge. 1932.

Hutt, Frederick Bruce. *Genetics of the Fowl.* New York. 1949.

Huxley, Julian. *Evolution: the Modern Synthesis.* New York. 1942.

———. *See* Wells, H. G.

Iljin, N. A. "Wolf-dog genetics." *Journal of Genetics.* 1942. 42:359-414.

Iltis, Hugo. *Life of Mendel.* Translated by Eden and Cedar Paul. New York. 1932.

Jaffe, Bernard. *Outposts of Science.* New York. 1935.

Jesse, George R. *Researches into the History of the British Dog.* 2 vols. London. 1866.

Jones, D. F. *See* East, Edward.

Jones, Donald Forsha. *Genetics in Plant and Animal Improvement.* New York. 1925.

Kaliss, N. *See* Briggs, L. C.

Kakino, S. *See* Ogama, K.

261

Keeler, C. E. and H. C. Trimble. "The inheritance of dew claws in the dog." *Journal of Heredity.* 1938. 29:145-148.

Kelley, R. B. *Principles and Methods of Animal Breeding.* New York. 1946.

———. *Sheep Dogs. Their Breeding, Maintenance and Training.* 2d ed. Sydney. 1947.

Knight, E. D. *See* Phillips, J. M.

Lea, A. J. "The inheritance of coat and nose colour in long-haired Dachshunds." *Journal of Heredity.* 1943. 45:197-205.

Lee, A. *See* Barrington, A.

Leighton, Robert. *The Complete Book of the Dog.* London. 1922.

Little, C. C. "Genetics in Cocker Spaniels. Observations on heredity and on physiology of reproduction in American Cocker Spaniels." *Journal of Heredity.* 1948. 39:181-185.

Lush, J. L. *Animal Breeding Plans.* 3rd ed. Ames, Iowa. 1945.

McEwen, Robert S. *Vertebrate Embryology.* 3rd ed. New York. 1949.

Mather, K. *See* Darlington, C. D.

Mazia, Daniel. "Cell division." *Scientific American.* Aug. 1953. 189: 53-63.

Mirsky, A. E. "The chemistry of heredity." *Scientific American.* Feb. 1953. 188:47-57.

Mitchell, A. L. "Dominant dilution and other color factors in Collie dogs." *Journal of Heredity.* 1935. 26:424-430.

Mivart, St. George. *A Monograph of the Canidae.* London. 1890.

Moffit, Ella B. *The Cocker Spaniel,* rev. ed. New York. 1937.

Moog, Florence. "Up from the embryo." *Scientific American.* Feb. 1950. 182:52-55.

Morgan, Thomas Hunt. *The Theory of the Gene.* New Haven. 1926.

Morgan, Thomas Hunt, C. B. Bridges, and A. H. Sturtevant. *The Genetics of Drosophila.* Washington, D. C. 1919.

Muller, George., and Alexander Glass. *Diseases of the Dog and Their Treatment.* 4th ed. Chicago. 1916.

Nicholas, R. E. *The Principles and Practice of Scientific Dog-Breeding.* 10th ed. Southampton. 1934.

Ogama, K. and S. Kakino. "A revised check list of the chromosome number in *vertebrata.*" *Journal of Genetics.* 1932.

Onstott, Kyle. *See* Ackerman, Irving C.

Paramoure, Anne F. *Breeding and Genetics.* Middleburg, Va. 1959.

Pardoe, J. H. *Fox Terriers.* London. 1949.

Pearson, K. *See* Barrington, A.

Phillips, J. M. "Sable coat colour in Cockers." *Journal of Heredity.* 1938. 29:67-69.

———. *See* Barrows, W.

Phillips, J. M., and E. D. Knight. "Merle or Calico Foxhounds." *Journal of Heredity*. 1938. 29:365-367.

Pickett, F. N. *The Book of the Alsatian Dog*. London. 1950.

Pincher, C. "Transplanting mammals' eggs; new techniques that may revolutionise animal breeding." *Discovery*. Feb. 1948. 9:50-51.

Pincus, G. "Fertilization in mammals." *Scientific American*. Mar. 1951. 184:44-47.

Prentice, E. Parmalee. *American Dairy Cattle, Their Past and Future*. New York. 1942.

———. *Breeding Profitable Dairy Cattle*. Boston. 1935.

Reynolds, Samuel R. M. "The umbilical cord." *Scientific American*. July 1952. 187:70-76.

Rowlands, I. W. *See* Hancock, J. L.

Scheinfeld, Amram. *New You and Heredity*. Philadelphia. 1950.

Scott, J. P., and M. S. Charles. "Some problems of heredity and social behavior (in the dog)." *Journal of Genetic Psychology*. Apr. 1953. 48:209-230.

Sinnott, Edmund W., L. C. Dunn, and Th. Dobzhansky. *Principles of Genetics*. 4th ed. New York. 1950.

Skinner, A. J. *The Popular Fox Terrier*. London. N. D.

Smith, A. Croxton. "Crossbred dogs." *Field*. 1939. 174:939.

Sonnenborn, T. M. "Partner of the genes." *Scientific American*. Dec. 1950. 183:46-49.

Stockard, C. R., *et al. The Genetic and Endocrinic Basis for Differences in Form and Behavior as Elucidated by Studies of Contrasted Pure-line Dog Breeds and Their Hybrids*. Philadelphia. 1941.

Stone, Abraham. "The control of fertility." *Scientific American*. Apr. 1954. 190:31-33.

Sturtevant, A. H. *See* Morgan, Thomas Hunt.

Thomson, J. Arthur. *The New Natural History*. 3 vols. New York. 1926.

———. *The System of Animate Nature*. New York. 1920.

———. *Life: Outlines of General Biology*. 2 vols. London. 1931.

Thorne, F. C. "The inheritance of shyness in dogs." *Journal of Genetic Psychology*. 1944. 65:275-279.

Trimble, H. C. *See* Keeler, C. E.

United States Department of Agriculture. *Yearbook of Agriculture for 1937*. Washington, D. C. 1938.

Vesey-Fitzgerald, Brian, ed. *The Book of the Dog.* Los Angeles. 1948.

Von Stephanitz. *The German Shepherd in Word and Picture.* American ed. revised from the original German by J. Schwabacher. Jena. 1923.

Waddington, C. H. "Experiments in acquired characteristic." *Scientific American.* Dec. 1953. 189:92-98.

———. "How do cells differentiate?" *Scientific American.* Sept. 1953. 189:108-117.

Warner, L. *See* Humphrey, E. S.

Watson, James. *The Dog Book.* New York. 1905.

Weisman, August. *Germ Plasm, a Theory of Heredity.* London. 1893.

Wells, G. P. *See* Wells, H. G.

Wells, H. G., Julian S. Huxley, and G. P. Wells. *The Science of Life.* 2 vols. New York. 1929.

Whitney, L. F. *How to Breed Dogs.* rev. ed. New York. 1948.

Winge, O. *Inheritance in Dogs with Special Reference to Hunting Breeds.* Translated by C. Roberts. New York. 1950.

Winters, L. M. *Animal Breeding.* 5th ed. New York. 1954.